OH YEAH

YELLO
40

BORIS BLANK
DIETER MEIER

Motorräder waren eine frühe Passion von Boris Blank. Hier sitzt er auf seiner Honda CB750 Four, ca. 1975.

Motorbikes were an early passion for Boris Blank. Here he is in around 1975 with his Honda CB750 Four.

Vorwort: Boris Blank

Hätte damals jemand zu mir gesagt: Boris, im Jahr 2021 werdet Ihr ein Buch machen über 40 Jahre Yello, ich hätte ihn ausgelacht. Aber jetzt ist es da, dieses Buch, und es erfüllt mich mit – ja, mit was eigentlich?

Stolz ist nicht der richtige Ausdruck. Staunen kommt der Sache schon etwas näher. Staunen, dass es mir gelungen ist, den damals sehnlichen Wunsch in Erfüllung zu bringen, Musiker zu werden und davon leben zu können. Das, und ein Leben wie eine Wundertüte, habe ich Yello zu verdanken. Und natürlich dem Moment, als ich Dieter kennenlernte. Nicht zuletzt er ist schuld daran, dass diese Musik unter die Leute gekommen ist. Er hat mich angetrieben und meine Zweifel zerstreut, wenn sie mir wieder einmal in die Quere kamen. Ebenso war es ein Riesenglück, dass ich fast zur gleichen Zeit Patrizia kennenlernte, die Frau, die mich seither durchs Leben begleitet. Sie ist eine Macherin wie ich. Wenn wir zusammen sind, haben wir immer etwas zu erzählen. Und sie ist jeweils der erste Mensch, der meine Musik zu hören bekommt.

Der Anstoss für dieses Buch kam von einem Freund von uns, dem Art Director Aaron Fabian. Er wusste von meinem Archiv und war fasziniert davon. Boris, das muss ein Buch werden, sagte er und bot sich sogleich auch an, die Bildauswahl zu treffen. Dieter und ich fanden die Idee interessant. Wir waren gespannt, welche Aspekte aus dem Leben von Yello jemand, der an unserem Schaffensprozess nicht beteiligt war, auswählen würde.

Im Keller habe ich ein Riesenarchiv. Nicht nur Fotos, Zeitungsausschnitte und Platten, auch Requisiten von den Videos, Masken, Perücken, Kostüme, einfach alles. Erst vor ein paar Tagen habe ich eine Kassette mit Aufnahmen von meiner allerersten Band gefunden, sie hiess Astrodom. Wenn ich so ein Bild sehe oder einen Gegenstand in die Hand nehme, werde ich sogleich in die Stimmung von damals zurückversetzt, ganz ähnlich wie wenn ich ein altes Stück Musik höre, das ich mit einer bestimmten Situation in Verbindung bringe.

Ich bin ein Jäger und Sammler nach dem Motto: «Was ich schon habe, muss ich nicht mehr jagen.» Angefangen hat es nicht mit den Fotos, sondern mit der Musik. Schon als 14-, 15-Jähriger habe ich Klänge und Geräusche gesammelt und mit meinem Revox A77 daraus Musik gemacht. Klang-Collagen, das war meine Welt. Die Engländer haben einen Ausdruck, der mir sehr gefällt: «tickled pink». Das heisst so viel wie «sich freuen wie ein Schneekönig». Ich fühle mich «tickled pink», dass ich meiner Sammlernatur jetzt nicht nur all die viele Yello-Musik zu verdanken habe, sondern auch noch ein richtig schönes Buch. Oh Yeah!

Zürich, im Frühling 2021

Preface: Boris Blank

If someone had said to me back in the day, 'Boris, in 2021 there will be a book about forty years of Yello', I would have laughed in his face – 'He must be out of his mind, completely mad.' But now here it is, this book, and it fills me with – well, actually, with what?

Pride is not the word. Astonishment describes it a little better. Astonishment, that I have succeeded in fulfilling my greatest wish at the time, to become a musician and to be able to make a living from it. For that, and for a life full of surprises and great experiences, I have Yello to thank. Yello and, of course, the moment I met Dieter. It was he who was largely responsible for our music getting out there and reaching an audience. He encouraged me and dispelled any doubts that might have thrown themselves into my path. Another great stroke of luck was meeting Patrizia at almost the same time. She is the woman I have shared my life with ever since. She is a doer, like me. When we are together, we always have something to talk about. And she is always the first person to hear my music.

The idea for this book came from a friend of ours, the art director Aaron Fabian. He knew about my archive and was fascinated by it. 'Boris, there has to be a book about this,' he said, and immediately offered to sit down and select the pictures. Dieter and I found the concept intriguing. We were curious to see which aspects of Yello's life someone who was not involved in our creative process might feel drawn to.

Over the years, I have assembled a huge Yello archive in our basement. It contains not only photos, newspaper clippings and records, but also props from music videos, masks, wigs, costumes – everything. Only a few days ago I came across a cassette of recordings of my very first band, Astrodom. When I see an old picture or pick up one of these objects, I am immediately transported back into the mood of that moment, much like when I hear a record I associate with a certain memory.

I am a hunter-gatherer who lives according to the motto, 'What I already have, I don't have to hunt for anymore.' My quest did not start with photos, but with music. I began to collect sounds and noises in my early teens, and turned them into music with my Revox A77 tape recorder. Sound collages, that was my world. There is an English expression I like very much: 'tickled pink'. I'm 'tickled pink' that my hunter-gatherer nature has not only helped to create all our music, but now also a book I am well and truly pleased with. Oh Yeah!

Zürich, spring 2021

Dieter Meier.

Vorwort: Dieter Meier

Die Sounds von Blank flogen mir zu, wie intergalaktische Sphären. Jede Klangwolke entwickelte sich als dialektischer Prozess von These und Antithese. Blanks «Stücke» entstanden aus einer Eigendynamik, die den Komponisten so weit überraschte, dass aus der Absicht, eine Blume herbeizuzaubern, schlussendlich ein Kamel wurde, das in der Wüste an der Oase das wohlverdiente Wasser saufen konnte.

Yello sind die perfekte Symbiose zwischen dem beflügelten Klangforscher Blank, der täglich in seinem musikalischen Kosmos verschwindet, und dem Darsteller Meier, dem immer wieder unterschiedlichste Charaktere überraschend zufallen. Wenn ich, was selten genug vorkam, die Studiotür leise öffnete, um die neuen Sounds zu hören, erschrak Boris ob meiner Anwesenheit, wie ein Kind, das man aus seiner eigenen Welt herausholt.

So konnte Yello nur entstehen, wenn Blank wie ein Derwisch seinen einsamen Kult pflegte, was mich keineswegs störte, auch wenn ich jahrelang sein Universum nicht betreten durfte. Erst wenn er angekommen war und seine Welten vorführte, war ich zugelassen und ergötzte mich an seinen Klangbildern, getrieben vom wunderbaren Nichts des Daseins. Die Songs flogen mir zu, dadaistisch und minimalistisch.

Wenn wir unser einhundertjähriges Jubiläum feiern, wird es mir, da bin ich mir sicher, noch immer genauso viel Freude bereiten, in Blanks musikalische Szenerie zu springen und als unsichtbarer Darsteller in einem magischen Film wieder aufzutauchen. Ohne Blank und seine wunderbar spielerischen, zum Teil kindlichen Bilder wäre ich nie zum musikalischen Dilettanten geworden. Oder hätte sehr wahrscheinlich nie Musik gemacht. In die Welt von Blank konnte ich reinhechten, und wie ein Wunder flogen mir die Szenen zu.

Bis auf das eine Mal, als ich mit einem Instrumental nichts anfangen konnte und Boris mir die Szene, die er zum Klingen gebracht hatte, beschrieb: «Dieter», schwärmte Boris, «stell dir vor, du bist am Strand in Tonga, eine rote Sonne taucht ins Meer, es kommt eine leichte Brise auf und der Barmann serviert den ersehnten Caipirinha, den du bei leisem Nicken des erhobenen Hauptes kundig in dich hineinschlürfst.» Für den kürzesten Popsong aller Zeiten segelte bedingungsloses Glück um meinen Kopf:

«The sun beautiful, the moon even more beautiful, tschick, tschik ga tschikaah, oh yeah!!!»

So warte ich denn bis auf Weiteres wie ein kleiner Junge auf den Weihnachtsmann Boris Blank, der mich in seiner musikalischen Wundertüte verschwinden lässt.

Zürich, im Frühling 2021

Preface: Dieter Meier

Blank's sounds flew at me like intergalactic spheres. Each sound-cloud evolved through a dialectical process of thesis and antithesis. Blank's 'pieces' emerged from an internal momentum that surprised even the composer himself, to such an extent that the original intention – to cast a spell on a flower – brought forth a camel in the desert, guzzling a well-deserved pint of water at the oasis.

Blank and Meier are the perfect symbiosis: the winged sound-searcher – Blank – who disappears daily into his very own musical cosmos, and the performer, Meier, to whom the most diverse characters appear in a continuous parade of surprises. When, as happened rarely enough, I quietly opened the studio door to hear the new sounds, Boris was startled by my presence, like a child taken out of his own world.

Yello could only come into existence when Blank was left alone to tend, like a dervish, to his solitary cult. This did not bother me in the slightest, even though it meant I wasn't admitted into his universe for years. Only when he had returned again and was ready to present his new worlds was I allowed in to revel in these sound-images, driven by the wonderful nothingness of existence. The songs came to me, Dadaist and minimalist.

I am certain that when we celebrate our centenary it will still be a great joy for me to dive into Blank's musical scenery and reappear like an invisible actor in a magical movie. Without Blank and his wonderfully playful and partly childlike images, I would never have become the musical dilettante that I am today. Very probably I would never even have made music. I could dive into Blank's world, and miraculously all these scenes and scenarios would come to me.

Only once did the magic fail me when I listened to one of his instrumental tracks. Boris tried to help me out by describing the scene he had envisaged when he recorded the track. 'Dieter,' he enthused, 'imagine you're on a beach in Tonga, the red sun is about to dip into the sea, a light breeze is getting up, and the barman brings you the longed-for caipirinha, which you savour with an appreciative and barely perceptible nodding of your raised head.' I felt an unconditional happiness sailing around my head, carrying with it the shortest pop song of all time.

'The moon . . . beautiful – The sun . . . even more beautiful – Tschick, tschik ga tschikaah – oh yeah!!!'

In this way, I continue like a little boy to await the arrival of Father Christmas Boris Blank to allow me to disappear once again into his musical lucky bag.

Zürich, spring 2021

Dieter stemmt den Himmel in die Höhe.

Dieter pushing the sky away.

Mit der ersten Maxi-Single im Yello-Studio in der Roten Fabrik, Zürich. Von links nach rechts: Ernst Arnold, Boris Blank, Carlos Peron und Freundin Heidi.

Showing off the first Yello 12-inch single at the Yello Studio at the Rote Fabrik, Zürich. Clockwise from top left: Ernst Arnold, Boris Blank, Carlos Peron and a friend, Heidi.

Boris und Carlos hatten beschlossen, zusammen in den Urlaub zu fahren. Perons Wunschziel, Abidjan an der Elfenbeinküste, reizte Blank wenig. Stattdessen schlug er eine Reise nach Kalifornien vor. Blank und Peron waren grosse Fans vom geheimnisvollen Plattenlabel Ralph und der damit verbundenen Band The Residents. Man könnte doch das Angenehme mit dem Nützlichen verbinden und den Ralph-Leuten in San Francisco einen kleinen Besuch abstatten! Nachdem Blank und Peron in Los Angeles auf die Teppichetage von RCA und Capitol Records vorgedrungen waren, wo man ihnen schmunzelnd zugehört und eine freundliche Absage erteilt hatte, kamen sie an einem Sonntag in bester Laune in San Francisco an. Tatsächlich nahm bei Ralph Records jemand das Telefon ab. «Just drop by», hiess es, und wenig später sassen die beiden im schummrigen Studio der Residents und legten die Kassette ein, die sie mitgebracht hatten. «Wow, this is seriously outstanding», erklärte der Mann von Ralph und revanchierte sich mit den neuesten Aufnahmen der Residents. «In unserer Naivität hatten wir nicht einen Moment lang das Gefühl, es sei irgendwie frech, was wir da taten», erinnert sich Blank. «Menschen wie du und ich, dachten wir, toll, man trifft sich auf Augenhöhe, alles ganz natürlich. Man war damals ja auch noch nicht celebrity-traumatisiert.» Als Boris und Carlos wieder in Zürich eintrafen, wartete bereits «Special Delivery»-Post aus San Francisco auf sie. Ralph Records wollte Yello unter Vertrag nehmen.

Boris and Carlos had decided to take a holiday together. Peron's preferred destination, Abidjan in Côte d'Ivoire, held little appeal for Blank. Instead, he suggested a trip to California. He and Peron were both big fans of Ralph Records, a label shrouded in nearly as much mystery as the band associated with it, The Residents. How about combining pleasure with professional curiosity and paying a little visit to the Ralph crew in San Francisco? On the way there, they stopped off in Los Angeles and made it to the top floors of both RCA and Capitol Records. They were listened to with friendly forbearance and sent on their way with best wishes and a polite 'Thanks, but no thanks'. It was a Sunday when they arrived in San Francisco, and they were in excellent spirits. Sure enough, someone answered the phone at Ralph Records. 'Just drop by,' they said, and a little later Boris and Carlos were sitting in the dimly lit Residents studio, playing the cassette they had brought with them from Zürich. 'Wow, this is seriously outstanding,' declared their host, and in turn played The Residents' latest recordings. 'In our naivety, we didn't feel for a moment that what we were doing was in any way cheeky,' Blank recalls. 'They're people like you and me – we thought, great, you meet at eye level, everything's totally natural. In those days no one was suffering from celebrity trauma.' When Blank and Peron arrived back in Zürich, a Special Delivery letter from San Francisco was waiting for them. Ralph Records wanted to sign Yello.

Boris am Steuer des AMC Pacer
auf der Fahrt nach San Francisco.

*Boris at the wheel of an AMC Pacer
on the way to San Francisco.*

7/19/79

Boris & Carlos!!!

Great to hear from you! We love your record!

We've been sending you stuff in the mail through the months. Maybe we've had the wrong address?

Yes, we are very definately interested in licensing your product. We would like to make you an offer for the whole world. Is the whole world available? If not, how much?

We are also interested in your film. Please send details.

This fall, we will release 4 LPs and 2 singles. We couldn't release any of your stuff until the Spring.

We are about to sign 2 new groups, the first LPs by each to be out in spring. We'd love for yours to be the third. Maybe the fourth, counting the new Residents LP.

Regarding your film, we are now working on a video-disc. There are possibilities for the future...

Please send us all the information, in detail, that you can.

We want to work with you in the future.

"Not Available" in route. Anything else?

Regards,

Jay Clem & Hardy Fox
Ralph Records

THE CRYPTIC CORPORATION 444 GROVE STREET SAN FRANCISCO, CALIFORNIA 94102 PHONE 415 431-7480

Post aus Kalifornien.

Special Delivery from California.

Blank und Peron feiern
das positive Feedback von Ralph Records.

*Blank and Peron celebrating
the positive feedback from Ralph Records.*

Yellos erster Auftritt am 20. September 1978 im Kino Forum, Zürich, anlässlich einer Multimediashow des Modeunternehmens Thema Selection. Erster Track: «Dead Cat».

Yello's first live show on 20 September 1978, during the multimedia fashion show for the label Thema Selection at the Forum Cinema in Zürich. The set began with the track 'Dead Cat'.

Bei Ralph Records hatte man den Gästen aus der Schweiz angeraten, ihre rein instrumentale Musik da und dort mit einer Stimme zu schmücken. Damit würden sich die kommerziellen Chancen deutlich verbessern, «zumindest in den USA». Ähnlich sah es Paul Vajsabel, ein Zürcher Plattenladenbesitzer, der ebenfalls gern mit Yello ins Geschäft gekommen wäre. Er machte einen Vorschlag. Kurz zuvor hatte er die Single «Cry For Fame» von einem gewissen Dieter Meier veröffentlicht. Dieser Meier, man solle es doch mal versuchen mit ihm. Obwohl er wenig von der Single hielt, liess sich Blank überreden, seine Küche für eine Probe herzugeben. Meier, der in der Punkszene zu Hause war, kam, brüllte, heulte und knurrte die subtilen Vignetten, die ihm Blank vorlegte, in Grund und Boden. Blank war beileibe kein Punk-Fan, musste sich aber eingestehen, dass ihn dieser Meier doch irgendwie faszinierte. Meier seinerseits war überwältigt. «Boris' Klangwelten waren eine Sensation für mich», erinnert er sich. «So etwas hatte ich noch nie gehört.» Als Blank wegen des Radaus aus der Wohnung geworfen wurde, quartierte ihn Meier in seinem Atelier in der Roten Fabrik ein, einem chaotischen Künstlerzentrum am Zürichsee. Gleichzeitig informierte er die Organisatoren einer multimedialen Modenschau im Kino Forum, die ihn für einen Solo-Auftritt gebucht hatten, dass er neu mit Yello aufzutreten gedenke. Blank hasste die Vorstellung, auf einer Bühne zu stehen. Er machte nur unter der Bedingung mit, dass er sich mit seinen Maschinen im Orchestergraben verstecken durfte. Entgegen seinen Erwartungen bewarf ihn das Publikum nicht mit faulem Gemüse. Im Gegenteil, es zeigte sich begeistert.
Da begann sich Blank langsam aufzurichten. Zuerst lugte sein Haar aus dem Graben, dann die Stirn, und schliesslich auch noch das Gesicht.

Ralph Records had advised their guests from Switzerland that by adding some vocals to their purely instrumental music they might significantly improve their commercial potential, 'at least in the USA'. Paul Vajsabel, the owner of a record shop in Zürich, who was also keen on doing business with Yello, took a similar view. He also had an idea. A short while before, he had released a single, 'Cry for Fame', by a certain Dieter Meier. Why not give this guy Meier a go? Blank didn't think much of the record. Sheer pragmatism led him to agree to a try-out in his kitchen. Meier, very much part of the local punk scene, duly arrived to howl, growl, and scream all over Blank's carefully crafted vignettes. Blank, by no means a punk fan, nevertheless had to admit to himself that the sheer presence of this man somehow fascinated him. Meier, for his part, was bowled over by the experience. 'Boris's sound-worlds were a sensation for me,' he remembers. 'I had never heard anything like it.' When Blank, as a direct result of the racket they had produced in his kitchen, was thrown out of his flat, Meier put him up in his studio at the Rote Fabrik, a beautifully ramshackle artists' centre on Lake Zürich. Booked to perform solo at a multimedia fashion show at the Forum Cinema, he immediately changed the arrangement to include Yello. Blank hated the idea of appearing on a stage. He agreed to take part only if he was allowed to hide himself and his machines in the orchestra pit. As it became clear that the audience weren't going to throw rotten fruit at him, but, on the contrary, expressed their approval with unexpected abandon, Boris Blank very slowly became visible, hair first, then forehead, and then, at last, face.

Music Market
NEU

Der legendäre Paul Vajsabel in seinem Plattenladen Music Market. Paul hatte Dieter Meier, Carlos Peron und Boris Blank zusammengebracht. Später war er es auch, der Louis Spillmann verriet, wie er mit Yello in Kontakt treten konnte. Foto: Alberto Venzago.

The legendary Paul Vajsabel in his Zürich record store, Music Market. It was he who introduced Dieter Meier to Carlos Peron and Boris Blank. Later on, it was also he who passed Yello's telephone number to Louis Spillmann. Photo: Alberto Venzago.

22–25

Aufnahme-Session für «I.T. Splash» und «Glue Head» im Studio Sunrise, Kirchberg, St. Gallen, 1978.

Recording session for 'I.T. Splash' and 'Glue Head', Sunrise Studio, Kirchberg, St Gallen, 1978.

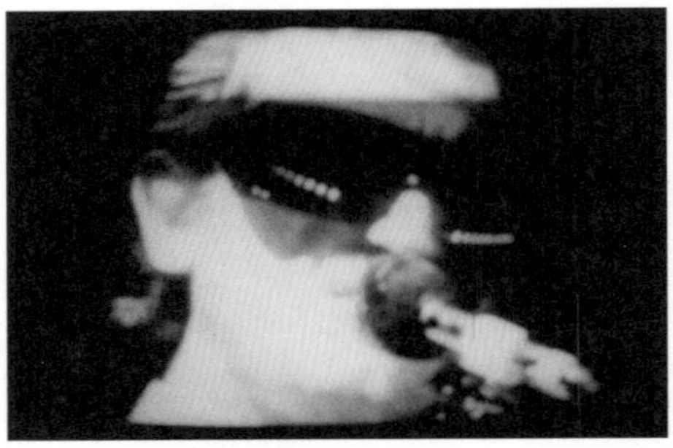

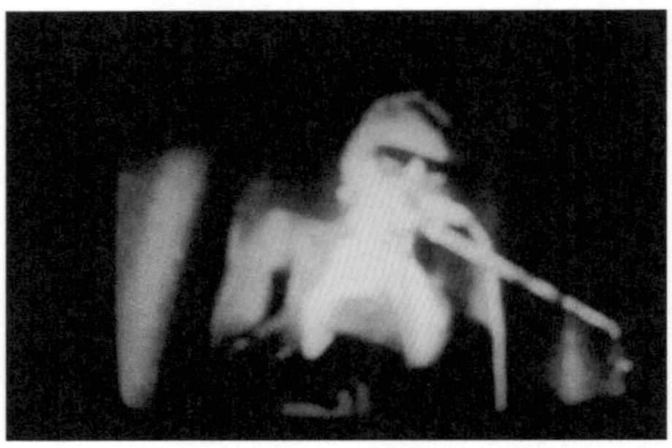
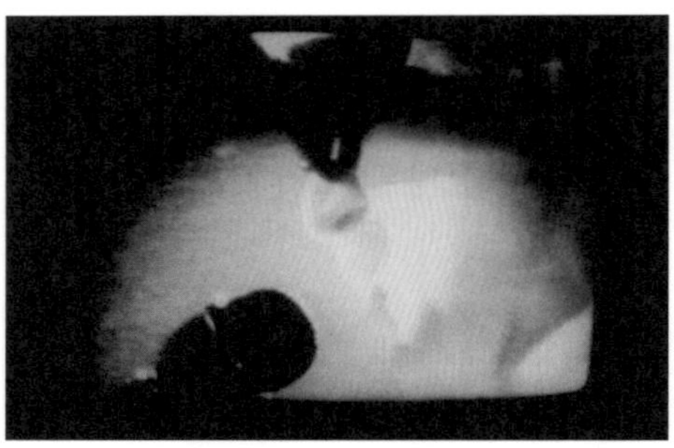
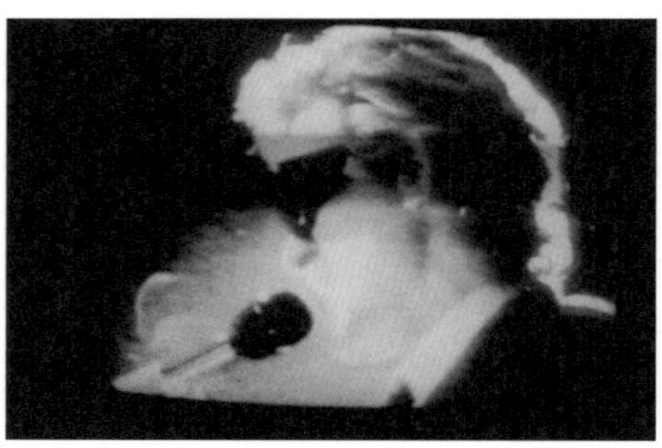
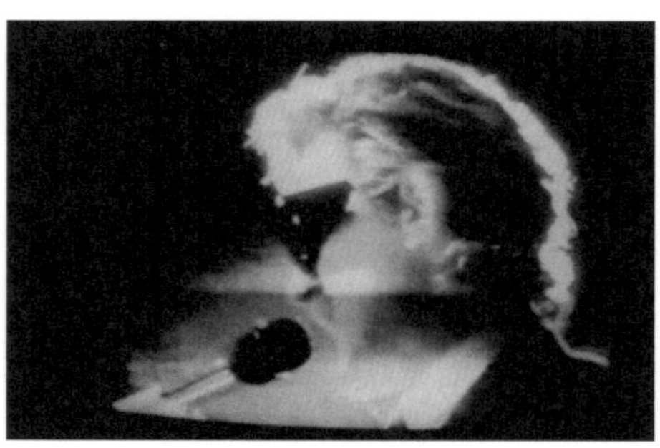

Dieter im Kino Forum.

Dieter at the Forum Cinema.

Nicht verwendeter Cover-Entwurf von
Dieter Meier zum ersten Album *Solid Pleasure*.

*Dieter Meier's unused cover design
for Yello's debut album,* Solid Pleasure.

Druckvorlage von Boris Blank für das Poster
zur ersten Maxi-Single, «I.T. Splash» / «Glue Head».

Boris Blank's print template for the poster advertising the release of Yello's first 12-inch single, 'I.T. Splash' / 'Glue Head'.

YELLO

ANSWERS DISCO

....PUT HER IN THE MOOD, WITH OUR NEW BLACK VINYL MAXI SINGLE........................

I.T. SPLASH/GLUE HEAD

PERIPHERY PERFUME RECORDS
Bäckerstrasse 58, CH-8004 Zurich, Switzerland, phone 2421312

KEYBOARDS

- FARFISA "SYNTORCHESTRA"
- WERSI STRING ORCHESTRA
- ARP ODYSSEY + 16 STEP SEQUENCER
- ARP QUADRA
- ARP 2600
- EMS SYNTHI AKS
- ROLAND SH-09 SYNTH
- ROLAND VOCODER PLUS VP300
- ROLAND CR-78
- ROLAND 808
- OSCAR 1 JPG
- SEQUENTIAL CIRQUITS PROPHET 5
- SEQUENTIAL CIRQUITS PRO ONE

RECORDING

- REVOX A77
- TEAC 4 CHANNEL REEL TO REEL
- OTARI 8 CHANNEL

EFFECTS

- ROLAND SPACE ECHO
- ELECTRO HARMONIX BIG MUFF
- CRY BABY WHA VOX
- MU-TRON FLANGER
- MU-TRON BIPHASE
- MU-TRON III
- BOSS CE 1 CHORUS ENSEMBLE
- ELECTROHARMONIX OCTAVE MULTIPLEXER
- ELECTRO-HARMONIX ELECTRIC MISTRESS

Frühe Equipment-Liste.

Early equipment list.

30–31, 33

Das Yello-Studio in der Roten Fabrik, Zürich, 1980.

The Yello Studio at the Rote Fabrik, Zürich, 1980.

Eines der ersten Pressebilder von Yello, 1980.

One of the very first Yello publicity shots, 1980.

Dieter Meier, unterwegs mit Manager Peter Vitzthum.

Dieter Meier, on the road with manager Peter Vitzthum.

Boris Blank als römischer Kaiser.

Boris Blank as a Roman emperor.

YEL
Claro Que Si

Erstes Poster von Ralph Records.

First Ralph Records poster.

DOWNTOWNER

P.O. BOX 4227 PORTLAND, OREGON 97208

YELLO

by Attilio

Yello-SOLID PLEASURE-Ralph Records

If there were justice in the world, SOLID PLEASURE by San Francisco's Yello would become as popular as Pink Floyd's DARK SIDE OF THE MOON. In fact, Yello is a kind of Pink Floyd 2000. These guys will be one of the best things your stereo has tasted in a long time.

Boris Blank (electronics), Dieter Meier (vocals) and Carlos Peron (effects and tapes) are the three-man nucleus of Ralph Records' newest signing. Although their names and list of quasi-instruments do not give an accurate insight into what it is that they do, Yello's SOLID PLEASURE is more an event than a group of compositions, an experience more than a concept album.

Album-Besprechung im *Downtowner*, Portland, Oregon, USA.

Album review in Downtowner, *Portland, Oregon, USA.*

Der Künstler als lächelnder Body-Builder.
Fotocollage von Boris Blank.

The artist as smiling bodybuilder.
Photo-collage by Boris Blank.

Yello vor der Roten Fabrik, mit Schlagzeuger Felix Haug.
Foto: Bernie Sigg.

Yello outside the Rote Fabrik, with drummer Felix Haug.
Photo: Bernie Sigg.

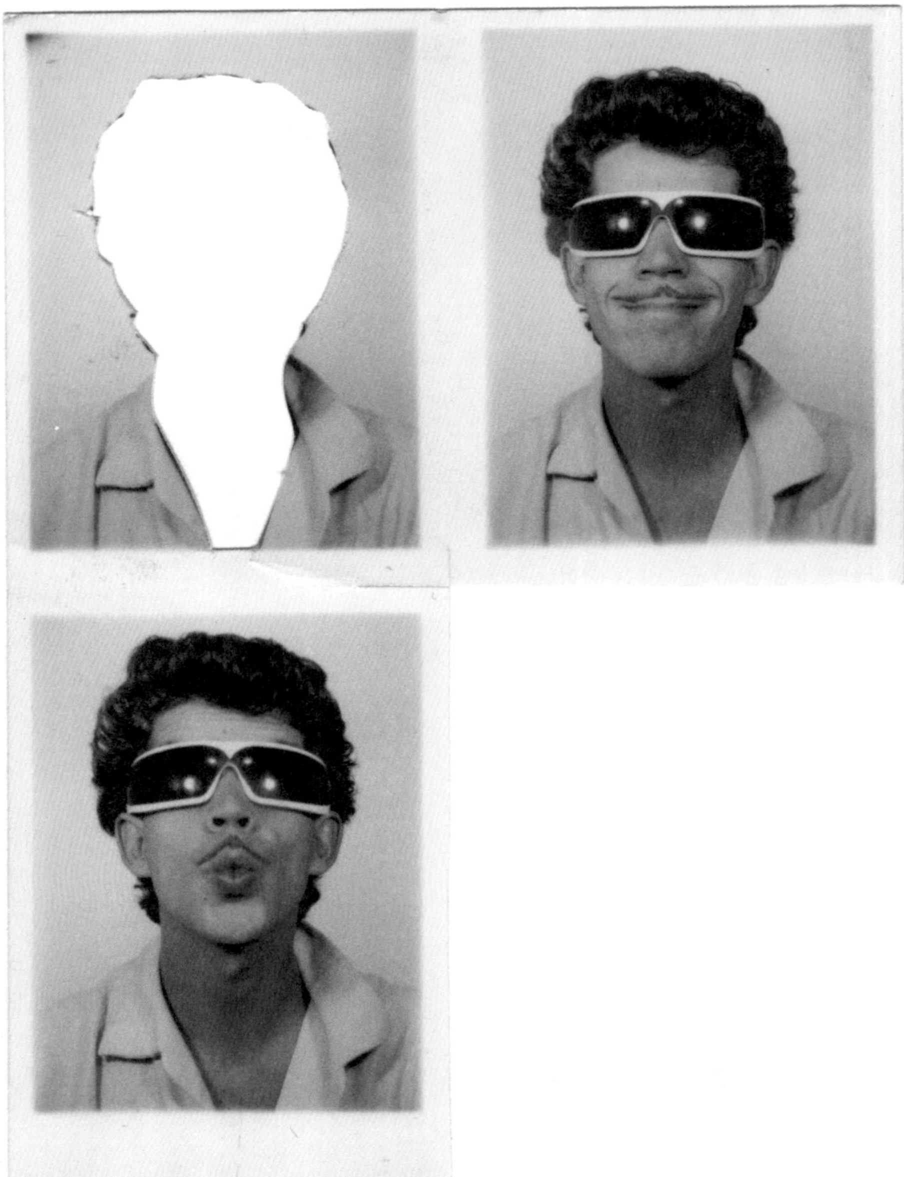

Fotocollage im *züritip* als Beitrag von Yello.

Photo-collage assembled by Yello for the local paper, züritip.

sounds

November 8, 1980

YELLO
'Solid Pleasure'
(Ralph Records
YL8059)****

IT MUST say something about the stiff upper brain cells of the British that, Human League apart, we're basically incapable of producing electronic music that doesn't sound as though it's about to make a grab for the nearest bottle of valium.

While our grim young 'Futurists' (sic) solidify and grow stalactites, bands like this swift trio are proving you *can* sound dangerous and exciting without threatening to top yourself in front of an audience. Yello's anti-freeze travels a similar road to their Residential beneficiaries, but is topped up with a sometimes cynical, sometimes reverential sense of the ludicrous.

They open with an absolutely cuckoo ska-beat forced to mate with a tinkling Yellow-Magic Orch ditty on the dotty 'Bimbo', and quickly establish their roots/targets with 'Night Flanger', loping bass, twirling synth, sudden melodic swells, and sultry vocals, all built up on a steal from The Doors. Morrison would be proud of their update.

'Rock Stop' and 'Eternal Legs' (in the Amon Duul title stakes, close but no cigar) also see them lining up certain targets. The former throws a wobbly somewhere between Madness, Cluster, and the Shadows. The latter is a kooky but respectable lampoon of the Jefferson Airplane school of acid rock vocals, supported by a mekanik synth beat.

'Reverse Lion' (still no cigar) and 'Magneto' are the traditional electronic pieces on the album. The first gears into a tricky beat, sequences throbbing against the time like early Kraftwerk, and the second treads dangerously near the Tangs with its random swarms, clusters, tones and choirs.

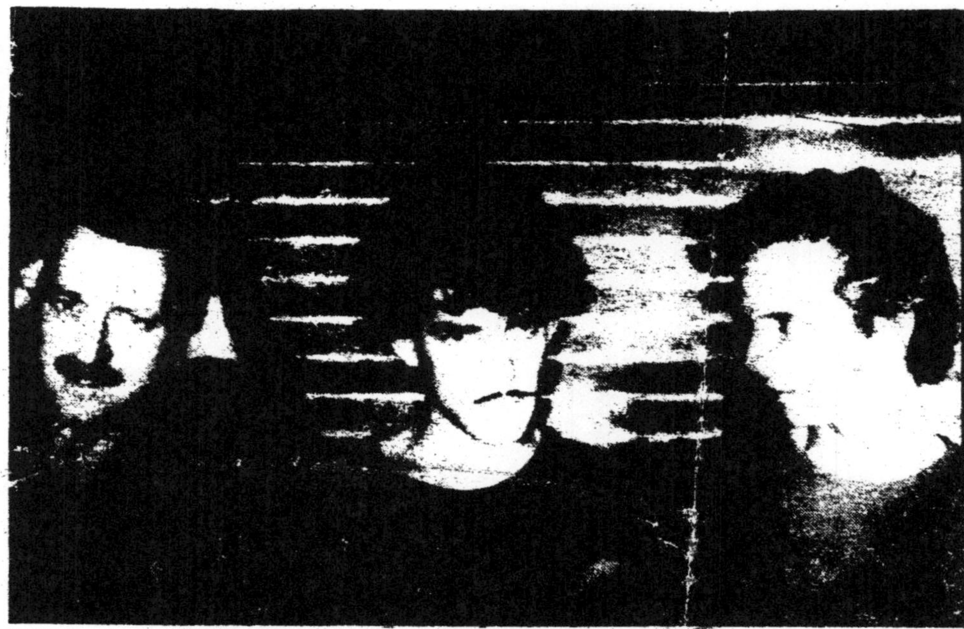

YELLO, the wacky listener's long mac band

Funloving futurists

Luckily for them and us, they instill these songs with the verve long since surgically removed from the Tangs.

Beneath the swarm of musical styles ('Stantztrigger' for example consists of a manic percussion montage reminiscent of the locomotive section of Can's 'Peking O') there is a unifying philosophy to Yello's music. So, they shouldn't be thought of as the Ralphian Barron Knights. Like the R*s*d*nts, they're too aware of the music around them to stay in one style, so they spread their funny, funky, and febrile personality across a wide range of music. They have the wit and pizazz to become the cuckoo (no jokes about clocks please) in the R*s*d*nt's nest.

JOHN GILL

Album-Kritik in der wöchentlichen britischen Musikzeitschrift *Sounds.*

Album review from the British music weekly Sounds.

Charts und Playlist der Radiostation KSCU FM89, Santa Clara, Kalifornien, USA.

Charts and playlist, Radio KSCU FM89, Santa Clara, California, USA.

KSCU FM 89
TOP 20

Music Director - Harold Pestana

November 28-December 12, 1980 *New/add

	Artist	Album	Label	Side, cut
1	*Blondie	Autoamerican	Chrysalis	1,4;1,2
2	*Any Trouble	.....	Stiff America	1,1;1,2
3	The Hitmen	Aim For The Feet	Urgent/CBS	2,1;1,1
4	*999	The Biggest Tour In Sport	Polydor	2,1;2,2
5	XTC	Black Sea	Virgin/RSO	1,2;1,4
6	Rockpile	Seconds Of Pleasure	Columbia	1,1;1,3
7	Romantics	National Breakout	Nemperor	1,1;1,5
8	various	Yes Nukes	Rhino	all
9	*Jimmie Mack & The Jumpers	.....	RCA	1,1;2,1
10	*various	Rodney On The Roq	Poshboy	2,5;2,1
11	Police	Zenyatta/Mondatta	A&M	1,1;1,4
12	*Wippo	.....	mManmade	1,1
13	*Ian Lloyd	3WC	Atlantic	1,4;1,2
14	*Ian Gillan	Glory Road	Virgin/RSO	2,1
15	Impatient Youth	45	.....	1,2;1,3
16	*Kid Courage	45	A.P.E.	1,1;2,1
17	*The Hoovers	45	Airstrip	2,1;1,1
18	*Jon Anderson	Song Of Seven	Atlantic	1,4
19	*Desmond Dekker	Black & Dekker	Stiff America	1,3;2,1
20	*Golden Earring	Long Blond Animal	Polydor	1,1;1,3

Significant Airplay

Artist	Album	Label	Side, cut
*Jona Lewie	On The Other Hand	Stiff America	1,2;2,1
*Yello	Solid Pleasure	Ralph	2,4
*Roy Buchanan	My Babe	Waterhouse	1,1;1,2
Donnie Iris	Back On The Streets	MCA	1,1;1,2
The Korgis	Dumb Waiters	Elektra/Asylum	1,5
The Kings	...Are Here	Elektra/Asylum	2,4
*Blotto	Hello, My Name Is....	Blotto	2,1;1,1
*Vktms	45	415	2,1
*REO Speedwagon	Hi Infidelity	Epic	1,1;21
*Visage	EP	Polydor	2,2;2,1
*Human Sexual Response	Fig. 14	EaT	1,1;1,3

New!: Talking Heads, Ziggurat, Kwame, Billy Thorpe, Wall Of Voodoo,
(Warner) (Robox) (Polydor)(Elektra) (
and a special Christmas single from NRBQ (Rounder).

Notes

WOW! A lot of new music is out that is GOOD! Keep it coming.... I still feel bad about the sudden death of John Lennon. He's in my prayers ...We will still be on during Christmas, so I'll still be reporting on schedule.... We do have a country show once a week done by Kevin Vogelsang and late night jazz shows all week here, in case you've forgotten.... Now we are also reporting to D.I.Y. Magazine, so look for us in their latest edition....We've had some giveaways lately for John Abercrombie at San Jose State and the Modern Humans i n Fremont....If any of you have some videos worthy of showing, please let us knowso we can show them...
BYE...

PO BOX 1207 SANTA CLARA, CALIFORNIA 95053

(408) 984-4413

Poster für Yello und The Residents von Ralph Records.

Ralph Records poster for Yello and The Residents.

52

Fotosession mit Bruno Bänziger, 1980.

Photo shoot with Bruno Bänziger, 1980.

53

Text zur ersten Single bei Ralph Records, «Bimbo», von Dieter Meier säuberlich auf seiner Hermes «Baby» getippt.

Lyrics for the first Ralph Records single, 'Bimbo', neatly typed out by Dieter Meier on his trusty Hermes 'Baby' typewriter.

54–55

Ausschnitt vom Cover der Single «Bimbo».

Detail from the cover of the 'Bimbo' single.

YELLO-NEW RALPH ARTIST!
NEWRALPHARTIST
YELLO
This first album from Switzerland's electronic masters is packed with such a vast array of rhythmic noises that you'll never know whether you're supposed to visit space city or dance the plastic off your shoes (a particularly dastardly decision when coolness is essential). Nevertheless, this record spins nicely on the brain. BUY IT.
YELLO
SOLID PLEASURE
NEW!-FROM THE RESIDENTS!
THE RESIDENTS COMMERCIAL ALBUM
40 1-minute songs about love & hate
New singles from Ralph Records!
There's TUXEDOMOON'S song to the Doppelganger, DARK COMPANION, coupled with the second version of 59 TO 1, heard first on their album, "Half Mute." MX-80 SOUND presents parts one and two of O TYPE, a sneak preview of their movie soundtrack, a melodic, macabre mixture of message and beat.

27A
26A

S T A N D A R D   W H I T E   B I M B O

No No

Don't wanna be standard

I wanna be special

No No standard

Bombo, Bimbo, Bimbo ....

I wear a white hmat, ~~white gloves~~ and white shoes

I sip manhattens but not for the booze

I hear hip music ...ain't got the blues

Fist in my pocket ~~I~~ don't wanna lose

I try so hard

Let me be smart

Look at myself in the window of a drugstore

look in my eys

Look at myself in the window of a toystore

ain't got the seize

Never ever gonna be smarty ... me

Never ever gonna be smarty me

Standard ... that's all I realy am

Special.... I am my only fan

Taht's so hard for me to take

Silly to walk around a fake   (Bombo Bimbo Bimbo)

Look at myself in the window of a drugstore .... ain't got the seize

Look at myself in the window of a toystore   .... ~~xixfxxgxixx~~ look in my eys

Oh Oh it's so sad

Oh Oh it frives me mad

Special that's all I wanna be

Standard o what a silly me

I don't want..... to be standard standard

I I I am so smart

I I try so hard

To be special

«Bimbo»-Kritiken aus den USA.

'Bimbo' reviews from the USA.

Yello Plays 'Bimbo'

From page five

R&B song called "Bimbo." This cut, from their first LP, "Solid Pleasure," is backed with a demented cut entitled "I.T. Splash." This sound is too evil for their debut disc.

ENTERTAINMENT EDITOR'S NOTE: Snakefinger's making a movie from his latest single, "The Man In The Dark Sedan"... **Tuxedomoon & MX-80 Sound** are also planning "videos," while **The Residents** will soon be releasing a series of "minute movies." SO-WHAT?-DEPT.: For the non-believers out there, here is a miniscule sampling of magazines and papers who review Ralph Records: **Rolling Stone, Creem, The Washington Post, High Times, Record World, The New York Times,** etc! Remember "Ralph's" motto -- **"Buy or Die!"** • • • • **.. Here's a chance to sample the goodies! For a 7-inch EP Sampler of four LPs by The Residents, Snakefinger, etc., send $1.00 (post. & hand.) along with your name & address to: ALMOST FREE/Ralph Records/444 Grove St./San Franc./CA. 94102... AND DON'T FORGET! Tell 'em "W." sent ya!**

"Bimbo"!

By W. Scott Phoenix
Entertainment Editor

It's "underground artist time" again! Subjects: The new singles by **Tuxedomoon, MX-80 Sound** and a trio to Swiss electronic experimentalists named **Yello.**

Tuxedomoon's single "Dark Companion" takes a different, somewhat humorous look at politics: "Another round for my dark companion... The endless prattle of politicians rings in my ears. ..." The single contains great vocals.

The flip-side is a reworking of one of their best songs, "59 to 1." It's still pessimistic and still great.

MX-80 Sounds's latest 45" is the first two parts of a movie soundtrack entitled "O Type." The heavy metal heads have changed their approach a bit with this record. It's strange, semi-militaristic, yet still electric. I can't wait for the flick.

Yello, last but not least, has released an electronic

See Yello ... page six

NOVEMBER 12, 1980
THE PENNSYLVANIA STATE UNIVERSITY
VOL. 30 NO. 5

Jay Clem
c/o Ralph Records
444 Grove St.
San Fran. CA. 94102

57

Beitrag von Yello zum Ausstellungskatalog *Saus und Braus*, Strauhof Zürich, 1980. Die wegweisende, von Bice Curiger kuratierte und von Peter Fischli und Claudia Schifferle mit einem Plakat versehene Multimediaausstellung/Show gab den Zürcher Post-Punks einen Fokus und erwies sich als eine der wichtigsten Veranstaltungen in der Schweizer Kunstszene der 1980er-Jahre.

Yello's contribution to the Saus und Braus *exhibition catalogue, Strauhof, Zürich, 1980. The multimedia exhibition, curated by Bice Curiger and advertised with a poster designed by Claudia Schifferle and Peter Fischli, gave Zürich's post-punks a new focus, and turned out to be one of the most important events in the Swiss art world of the 1980s.*

Гражданин Союза Советских Социалистических Республик
летчик-космонавт Валерий Федорович БЫКОВСКИЙ.

Kolaborazion with Swiss Technik Musichian comerades YELLO is very good.

sincerely

Anatoli Lucashevich SZT
First rec. Engeneere UW
Luna 10 Studio, Moskau

YELLO

Ein Rätsel: Was ist schweizerischer Herkunft und in den Billboards der Staaten und England (noch vor Blondie, Bowie, Specials etc.) vertreten? Krokus. Nein – schon mal was von *Yello* gehört? Yello, die Band aus Zürich, die vor 4 Jahren bei Ralph Records (San Francisco) anklopfte und dort auf begeisterte Ohren stiess . . .

Nun, man käme der Gruppe von **Boris Blank** (electronics & backing vocals), **Dieter Meier** (vocals) und **Carlos Peron** (Tapes) sicher nicht gerecht, schenkte man ihr nur aufgrund der Plattenumsätze Aufmerksamkeit. Yello, um es vorwegzunehmen, produzieren jene Musik/Klangstrukturen, die üblicherweise aus dem morbiden Akron, Los Angeles/San Francisco und dem untergangsgeweihten Birmingham den Weg zu uns finden. Der Zusammenhang zwischen der Umwelt und ihrer Reflexion in der Musik ist dort gegeben.

Yello wirkt aber in einem anderen Umfeld. Sie sind keine Arbeitslosengang, nicht durch negative Sozialindikatoren geprägt/geschädigt, dennoch stellen sie Soundfragmente/Collagen im Stil der Friscoer **Residents** her. Boris Blank meint dazu, dass sie ihre Musik ohne Konzept *(«Yello ist eine Nicht-Konzeptband – man hockt zusammen, beredet eine Idee, und irgendwann sind backingtapes da.»)* und viel Freude und auch Intellekt angehen. Oder anders gesagt: Das Erfassen der komplizierten Elektronik und deren Einsetzen zur Klangbildung mit Freude und Gefühl ergibt die Yello-Musik (Fun loving futurs).

. . . Ein krasser Gegensatz zum No-future-Gefühl? Ein klares *Ja* von Boris Blank. Yello ist keine eigentliche Techno-wave-Band, sondern vielmehr eine zeitgemässe Rockband. Als solche lieben sie nicht nur sehr kalte Klänge/Töne, sondern auch ganz warme *(«entweder Grönland oder Sahara, dazwischen liegt nichts!»)*. Das Ganze hat sich in dem Sinn verändert, als keine eigentlichen Musikinstrumente wie Gitarre, Schlagzeug etc. verwendet werden, sondern eben der Synthi . . . schliesslich haben die Beatles damals auch ihre Gitarren elektrifiziert, und heute werden sie sogar von den puritanischen Folk-Bands benützt. So einfach ist das.

Boris geht sogar soweit in der Annahme, dass in wenigen Jahren der Siegeszug des Synthis beendet sein wird und neue Elemente kommen werden, alles andere hat etwas mit Nostalgie und Kunstsüffisanz zu tun *(«wer sich in 10 Jahren noch Stones hinter die Ohren klemmt, ist wirklich selber schuld»)!*

Na, ein bisschen überheblich ob des einsetzenden Erfolgs? Selbstsicher gibt Carlos Peron zu verstehen, dass Nicht-Yello-Musik durchaus ihre Berechtigung hat und auch im bevorstehenden Synthi-Zeitalter sicher wieder eingesetzt wird, so vermutlich vor allem die klassische Musik. Bei ernsthafter Musik möchte Yello allerdings nicht experimentell eingreifen.

Der interessanteste Aspekt an ihrer Musik ist aber, dass nicht nur blosse technische Novitäten manifestiert werden, sondern dass ein kollektives Umdenken erfolgen soll. Griffe man immer wieder zu denselben Rock-Riffs aus vergangenen Tagen, würde man vermutlich keine Erweiterung des menschlichen Denkprozesses herbeiführen. Der Synthi ermöglicht indessen den Aufbau einer ganz anderen Gefühlswelt (Umweltverständnis). Angesichts der drohenden ökologischen Katastrophe ein wichtiger Beitrag, der aber vielleicht Gefahr läuft, als der letzte Schrei gedankenlos konsu-

Genesis

Ein früher Presseartikel aus der Schweiz in der Zürcher Jugendzeitschrift *21i*, 28. Oktober 1981.

An early Swiss feature in the Zürich teenage magazine 21i, *28 October 1981.*

«Bostich»-Notenblätter und -Text, herausgegeben vom Neue Welt Musikverlag.

Sheet music and lyrics for 'Bostich', published by Neue Welt Musikverlag.

Bostich (N'est ce pas)

B. BLANK / D. MEIER

(c) 1982 by NEUE WELT MUSIKVERLAG GMBH, München
All rights reserved

Fotokopiert mit Genehmigung des Verlag
NEUE WELT MUSIKVERLAG GMB
München

Bostich ②
F#m C#m
RUSH, PUSH, CASH.
N'EST-CE PAS?
F#m C#m To Coda.
(no chord) (G#m) D#m
I KNOW YOU THINK I'M CRAZ-Y — I'M GON-NA
Emaj7
ASK YOU ALL THE SAME I KNOW YOU'RE JUST A MACH-INE I WAN-NA
D#m
DANCE WITH YOU THAT'S MY GAME 'COS — EV-RY-BOD-Y —
G#m D#m
NEEDS SOME-BOD-Y — SOME-TIMES SOME-TIMES. I

Bootsch

G#m
KNOW YOU'RE MADE OF STEEL YOU GON-NA DANCE THAT'S ALL I FEEL
D#m
I KNOW YOU'RE THE ONE SO PLEASE PLEASE PLEASE COME ON I
Emaj 7
KNOW YOU'RE GONN-A KEEP THE BEAT YOU GON-NA DANCE WITH ME AND NEED NO FEAR I WAN-NA
D#m
SEE YOU DANCE YOU GON-NA FOLL-OW ME PLEASE DON'T LEAVE ME A-LONE MAKE
D#m/A
D#m/F#
D#m/G#
UP YOUR MIND I'M NOT THE KIND WHO'S GON-NA USE THE PHONE
G#m
N'EST-CE PAS - EV-'RY-BOD-Y NEEDS SOME-BOD-Y

Einladungskarte von Stiff Records zur Release-Party der Maxi-Single «You Gotta Say Yes to Another Excess», Danceteria, New York, 12. Oktober 1983.

Invitation from Stiff Records America to the launch party for the 12-inch single 'You Gotta Say Yes to Another Excess', Danceteria, New York, 12 October 1983.

64–65

Fotos aus *Cut – Magazin für Wohlklang*, 1983, Bruno Bänziger.

Photos from Cut – Magazin für Wohlklang*, 1983, Bruno Bänziger.*

YELLO

66–69

Video-Stills vom ersten Yello-Video
The Evening's Young, 1981.

Stills from the first Yello music video, for
The Evening's Young, *1981*.

70

«Reaction report»
zu «You Gotta Say Yes To Another Excess», UK, 1983.

*'Reaction report'
for 'You Gotta Say Yes to Another Excess', UK, 1983*

71

Dieter Meier und Boris Blank, ca. 1981.
Foto: Laura Levine.

*Dieter Meier and Boris Blank, around 1981.
Photo: Laura Levine.*

Rush Release Promotions

Reaction Report

(L.P)

RECORD: YOU GOTTA SAY YES TO ANOTHER EXCESS ARTIST: YELLO

NAME: STEVE WILLIAMSON AREA: REDDITCH - WORCESTERSHI

CLUB: REDDIES CODE NUMBER: 018-00000 17814

REACTION	Personal	Audience
Excellent	✓	✓
Very Good		
Good		
Fair		
Average		
Poor		

CHART POTENTIAL ✓
L.P CHART TOP 10 [✓]
TOP 30 [__]
TOP 50 [__]
TOP 75 [__]
DISCO CHART [__]
SPECIALIST [__]

Are you returning it to any charts? NO

Are your local dealers stocking it? YOU BET THEY ARE

If not will they be ordering it? —

Is your local radio station playing it? NOT SURE

ANY REQUESTS?
YES [✓] MORE THAN AVERAGE AMOUN
NO [__]

Additional Comments?

IF I HAD TO COMMENT ON EVERY TRACK I'D BE HERE FOR EVER THIS ALBUM IS BRILLIANT FROM PRODUCTION OF THE L.P. TO THE QUALITY OF THE VINYL ITS PRESSED ON IM SURE IF MY PUNTERS ARE ANYTHING TO GO BY THEN ITS A POSSIBL NO 1 FOR L.P. CHARTS - I CAN'T (HONESTLY PUT IT DOWN ITS BEING PLAYED AT HOME AL DAY AND WORK ALL NIGHT.

I REALLY AM PROUD TO HAVE THE L.P. IN MY COLLECT THANK YOU ALL

65 Bedford Hill
London SW 12
(01) 675-4916/7
Directors: Ian & Nick Titchener

YELLO

72–73

Das Magazin *Live Music*, 1982.

Live Music *magazine, 1982.*

Frühe Entwürfe von Jim Cherry für das Cover von *Claro Que Si.*

Jim Cherry's early design drafts for the cover of Claro Que Si.

F4

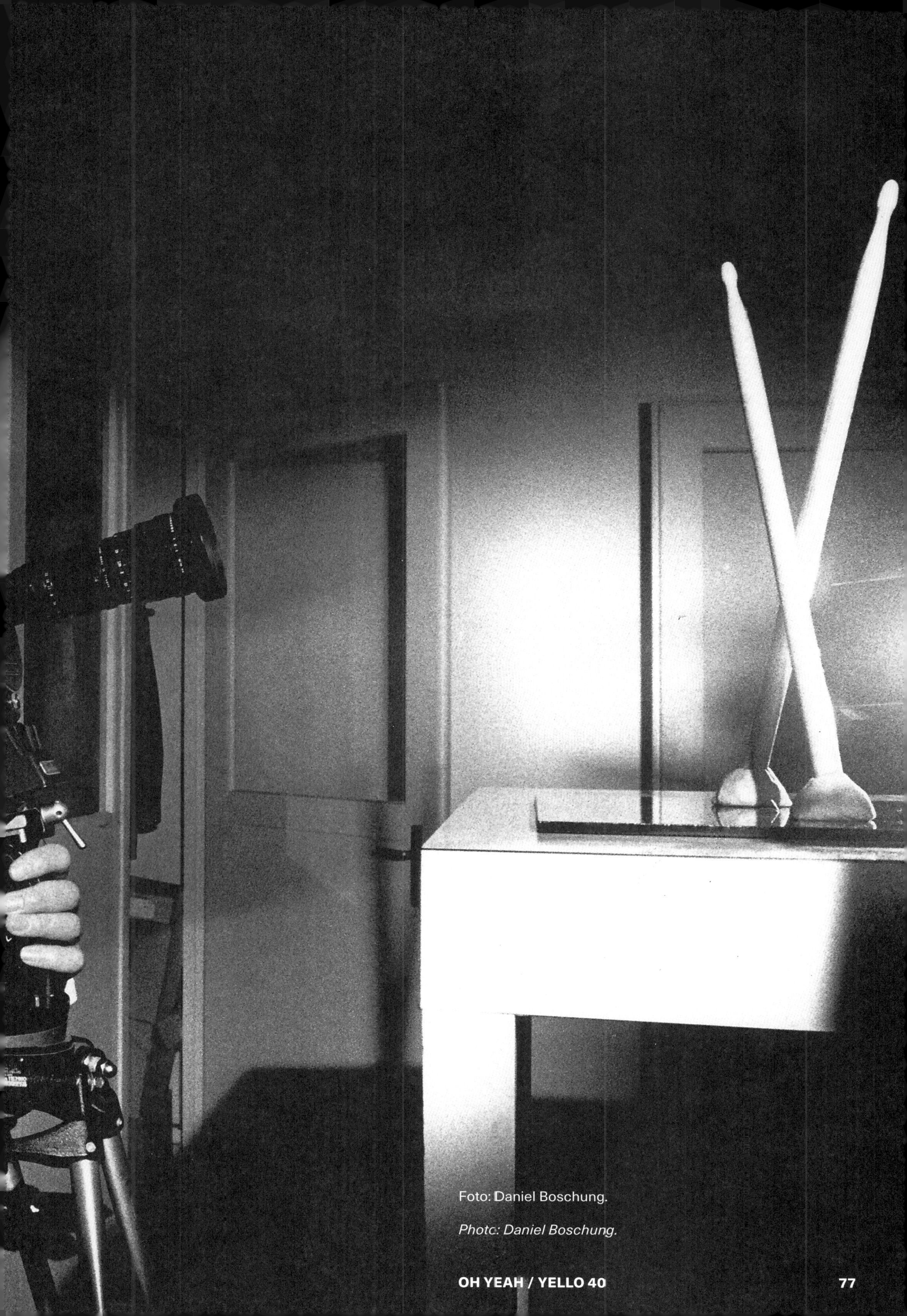

Foto: Daniel Boschung.

Photo: Daniel Boschung.

76–77

Dieter Meier mit seiner Beaulieu-16-mm-Filmkamera.

Wie für all seine früheren Experimentalfilme verwendete Dieter Meier auch für die ersten Yello-Videos eine 16-Millimeter-Kamera. Die Beaulieu war zwar für Amateure gedacht, hatte aber den grossen Vorteil, dass die Belichtung vom ersten Moment an, wenn man auf den Knopf drückte, stimmte. Bei den professionellen Kameras vergingen jedes Mal mehrere Frames, bis es so weit war. Die Beaulieu war ein wichtiges Element in der frühen Yello-Ästhetik. Damit wurde auch das Video zu «Pinball Cha Cha» gedreht. Die Männchen wurden mittels simplen Stop-Motion-Schritten zum Tanzen gebracht. Man fotografierte sie, bewegte sie ein wenig und machte eine weitere Aufnahme. «Es war toll, als das Video in die permanente Sammlung des Museum of Modern Art in New York aufgenommen wurde», sagt Dieter Meier. «Endlich merkten meine Eltern, dass ich nicht komplett meschugge war.»

Dieter Meier with his Beaulieu 16-mm movie camera.

As with all the experimental films he had made, Dieter Meier used a 16-mm camera to shoot Yello's early music videos. The Beaulieu was regarded as an amateur camera. However, it had a massive advantage over the so-called professional cameras in that the exposure was perfect from the moment the button was pressed; professional cameras took several frames before it was set. The Beaulieu was an important part of the early Yello aesthetic. The little dancing men in 'Pinball Cha Cha' were a simple stop-motion animation. One single frame was shot, the little men were moved a little, and another shot taken. Meier: 'It was great when the music video became part of the Museum of Modern Art collection in New York. At last, my parents realised that what I was doing wasn't entirely bonkers.'

The Fight – Dieter schlägt Boris und umgekehrt.
Fotos: Bruno Bänziger.

The Fight*: Dieter beats Boris, and vice versa.*
Photos: Bruno Bänziger.

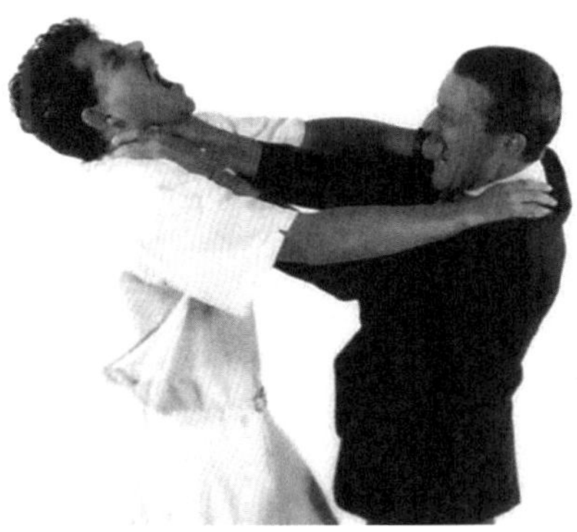

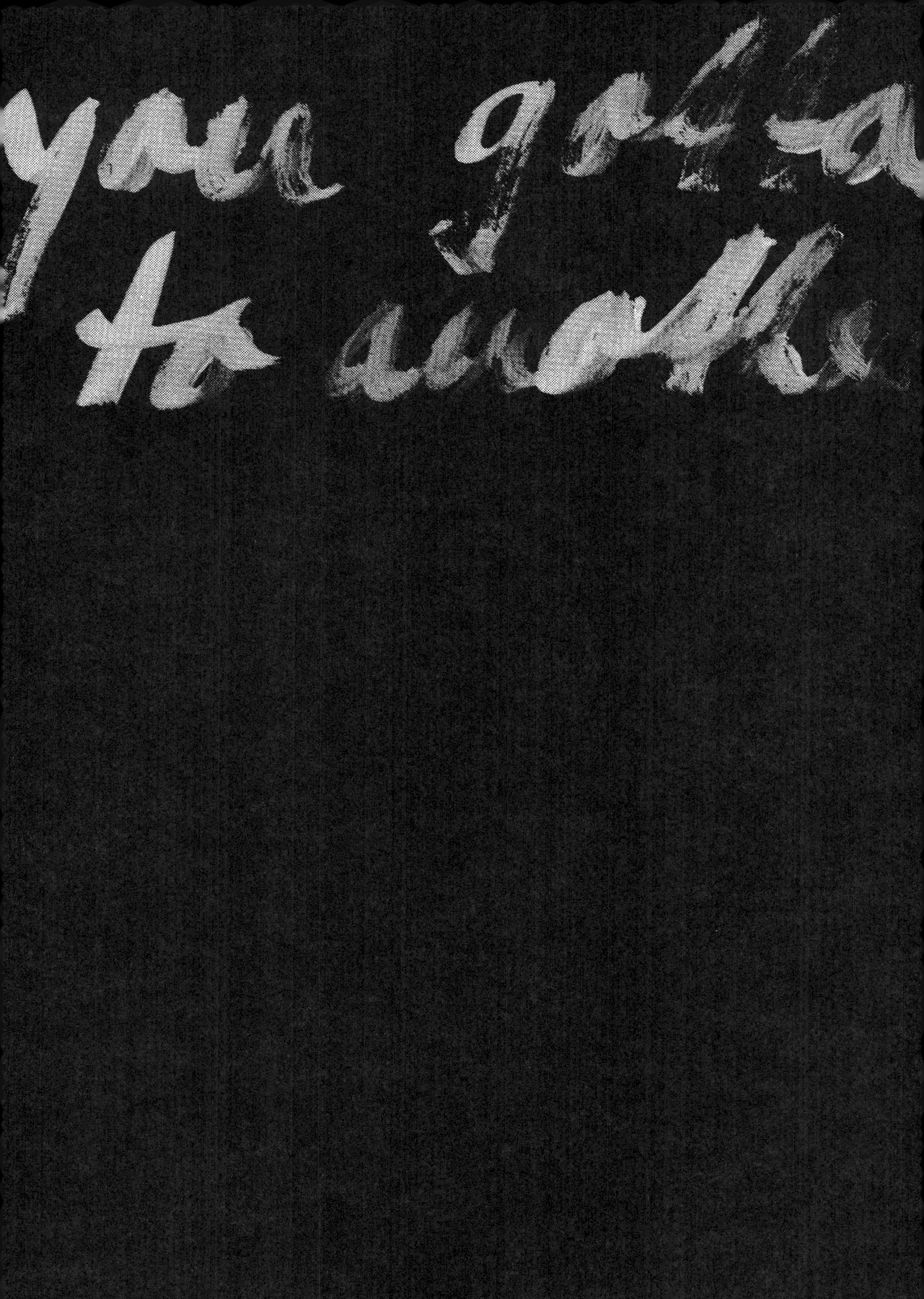
you gotta

You Gotta Say Yes to Another Excess,
Flyer von Dieter Meier, 1983.

You Gotta Say Yes to Another Excess,
flyer by Dieter Meier, 1983.

Boris Blank.

Boris Blank.

I KNOW
I LOVE YOU
YELLO
NEW SINGLE
I LOVE YOU

(C) 1983 NEUE WELT MUSIKVERLAG GMBH, München
Alle Rechte vorbehalten
All Rights reserved

R.H. Ms. 01-674 4184

84

Poster in Godzilla-Grösse zur Single «I Love You», Stiff Records, New York, 1983.

Godzilla-sized poster announcing the 'I Love You' single, Stiff Records, New York, 1983.

85–87

Noten und Text von «I Love You», 1983.

Sheet music and lyrics for 'I Love You', 1983.

INTRO: (Repeat)

VERSE: You know I need it to ride in your car
I'm always with you wherever you go

This is essential
The way your drive is just sensational
I hate to love you
Love you all the same
You know baby driving is a serious game
I love you
I know
I love you
I know
You gonna get me a heart attack
Stop it
Hold it
Hold it back

(fade on 'C')

88

Reaction report zu «I Love You», UK, 1983.

Reaction report for 'I Love You', UK, 1983.

89

Fotosession mit Bruno Bänziger, 1983.

Photo shoot with Bruno Bänziger, 1983.

Rush Release Promotions

Reaction Report

RECORD: I LOVE YOU ARTIST: YELLO

NAME: daved kay AREA: merseyside

CLUB: national djservice CODE NUMBER: E 018 000015750

REACTION	Personal	Audience
Excellent	X	
Very Good		X
Good		
Fair		
Average		
Poor		

CHART POTENTIAL

TOP 10 [__]

TOP 30 [X]

TOP 50 [__]

TOP 75 [__]

DISCO CHART [__]

SPECIALIST [__]

Are you returning it to any charts? kgw electric 11

Are your local dealers stocking it? ?

If not will they be ordering it? ?

Is your local radio station playing it? yes sir

ANY REQUESTS?

YES [X]

NO [__]

Additional Comments?

what can I say except

all three trax → FIRST CLASS

65 Bedford Hill
London SW 12
(01)675-4916/7
Directors: Ian & Nick Titchener

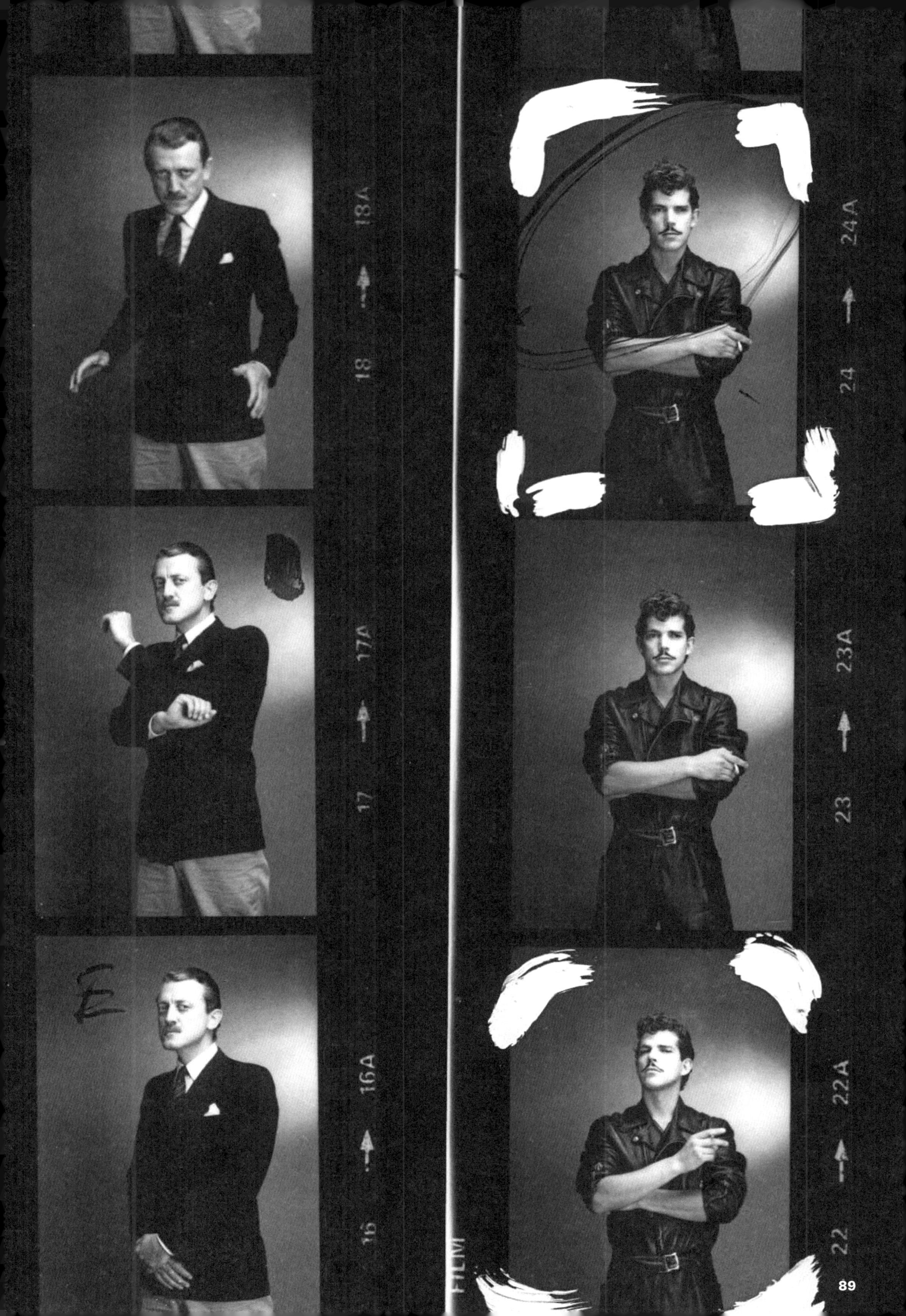
18A
18
17A
17
16A
16
24A
24
23A
23
22A
22
FILM

Vor der Roten Fabrik, 1983. / *Outside the Rote Fabrik, 1983.*

YE

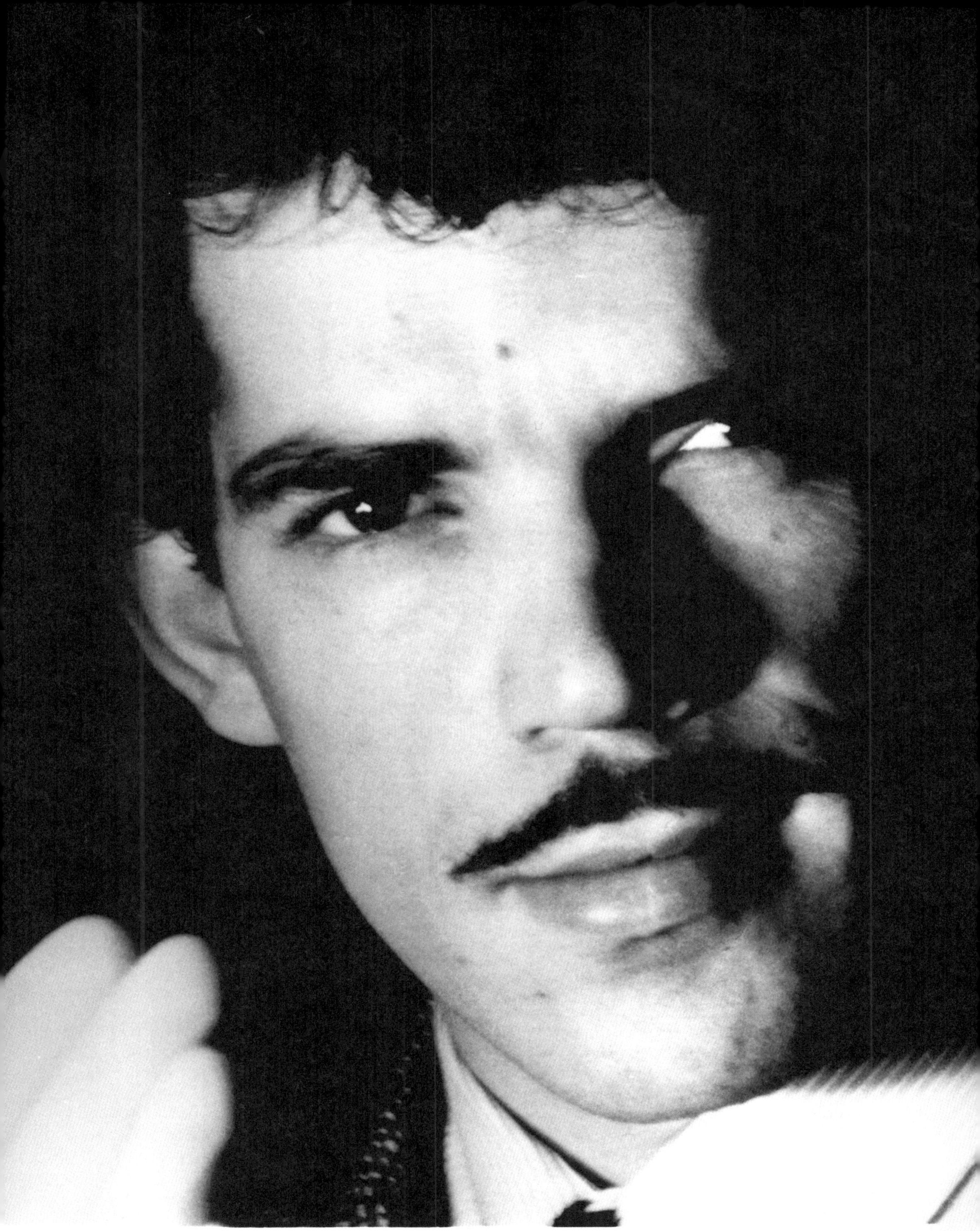

Pressefoto von Do It Records, 1982.

Do It Records publicity shot, 1982.

Ian Tregoning hatte Physik studiert und in Plattenläden gearbeitet, bevor er mit seinem Bruder sowie dem Produzenten Robin Scott das Indie-Label Do It Records gründete. Dank dem ersten Album von Adam & the Ants und dem von Scott unter dem Namen M veröffentlichten Welthit «Pop Muzik» stand die Firma bald auf einem soliden Sockel. Es war harte Arbeit. «Jede Punkband in Europa schickte uns ihre Demos, und alle tönten sie gleich», erinnert sich Tregoning. Da legte ein Freund eine Platte auf, die er soeben von den Residents aus San Francisco zugeschickt bekommen hatte. Es war *Solid Pleasure*. «Nur schon bei der Erinnerung an den Moment kriege ich Gänsehaut», sagt Tregoning vierzig Jahre später in seinem Studio in London. «Die Musik packte mich sofort. What the fuck is this!» Als die Nadel bei «Bostich» angelangt war, wusste er: Mit dieser Band muss er arbeiten. Nach endlosen Irrwegen mit ungültigen Telefonnummern bekam er drei Monate später endlich Dieter Meier an den Draht, der in Berlin gerade seinen ersten Spielfilm *Jetzt und Alles* drehte. «Wir verstanden uns sofort. Nach einer Stunde sagte Dieter endlich: ‹Ian, ich muss auflegen, ich bin gerade am Duschen.›»

Yello hatte bereits die Arbeit am zweiten Album aufgenommen und zeigte sich wenig begeistert, als Tregoning nochmals auf «Bostich» zu sprechen kam. Das Stück war kaum zwei Minuten lang, und er war überzeugt, dass eine längere Version stärkere Resonanz auslösen würde. Mit dem Versprechen, für die Sessions selber aufzukommen, holte er die Band zwei Tage ins Studio. In der neuen Maxi-Single-Version schlug «Bostich» in der afro-amerikanischen Klubszene New Yorks ein wie ein Blitz. Damit begann die Karriere von Yello erst richtig.

Am 31. Oktober 1982 gegen 22 Uhr 30 – «ich weiss es noch ganz genau» – sass Ian Tregoning am Schreibtisch und rechnete zusammen, wie viel all die Projekte kosten würden, die er für die nächsten 18 Monate geplant hatte. Er kam auf eine halbe Million Pfund. «Ich hörte eine Stimme im Hinterkopf, und sie stellte die Frage: ‹Wofür würdest du dieses Geld ausgeben, wenn es nur nach dir ginge?› Ich wusste die Antwort sofort: Ich würde es in Yello investieren.» In der Folge investierte er kein Geld, sondern Einsatz. Um die Gunst der Stunde auszunützen, zog er sogar nach New York. Eines Tages kam er mit einem Freund auf den neuen Film von Regisseur John Hughes zu sprechen, *Ferris Bueller's Day Off*. Man tue sich schwer, die richtige Musik für den grossen Ferrari-Moment zu finden. Tregoning griff in die Tasche und überreichte eine neue Yello-Aufnahme. Am nächsten Tag kam der Anruf: «Let's do the deal.» Der Song hiess «Oh Yeah».

Auch nachdem er seine Aufgabe als Manager, Inspiration und Mädchen für alles gegen Ende der 1980er-Jahre niedergelegt hatte, spannte Tregoning immer wieder mit Yello zusammen, so für das Album *Toy*, die Live-Show in Berlin sowie *Electrified*, das Solo-Album von Boris Blank. Blank: «Für uns ist Ian Tregoning einer der ganz wichtigen Menschen und Partner gewesen – und ist es immer noch.»

Ian Tregoning had studied physics and worked in record shops before he, together with his brother Max and the producer Robin Scott, founded the indie label Do It Records in London. Thanks to Adam and the Ants' first album and the worldwide hit 'Pop Muzik', released by Scott under the name M, the company soon found itself on a solid footing. It was hard work. 'Every punk band in Europe sent us their demo, and they all sounded the same,' Tregoning recalls. One day, a friend put on a record that had recently arrived in a package sent by The Residents from San Francisco. It was Solid Pleasure*. 'Just remembering that moment still gives me goose-bumps,' Tregoning says forty years later in his studio in London. 'The music grabbed me immediately. "What the fuck is this!"' By the time the needle reached 'Bostich', he was absolutely certain that this was a band he had to work with. There followed a wild goose chase involving countless incorrect phone numbers until, finally, three months later, he managed to locate Dieter Meier in Berlin, where he was shooting his first feature film,* Jetzt und Alles*. Tregoning: 'We understood each other immediately. After an hour Dieter said, "Ian, I have to hang up, I'm in the middle of taking a shower."'*

Yello, having already started work on their second album, were considerably less than enthusiastic when Tregoning insisted on talking about 'Bostich' again. The track was barely two minutes long; Tregoning was convinced that a longer version would create a much greater buzz. Promising to pay for the sessions himself, he persuaded the band to return to the studio. The extended 12-inch version of 'Bostich' hit the African-American clubs in New York like an earthquake. This was the real beginning of Yello's career.

On 31 October 1982 at around 10.30 p.m. – 'I remember it very clearly' – Ian Tregoning sat at his desk and calculated how much all the projects he had planned for the next eighteen months would cost. 'The figure I arrived at was in the region of half a million pounds. I heard a little voice in the back of my mind: "What would you do with all this money," the voice asked, "if it was totally up to you how to spend it?" I knew the answer immediately. I would invest it in Yello.' As it turned out, instead of money he would invest time. First off, to make use of the opportunities opened up by the success of 'Bostich', he moved from London to New York. One day a friend who was working with the film director John Hughes mentioned in passing their difficulties in finding the right music to go with the Ferrari scene in their new movie, Ferris Bueller's Day Off*. Tregoning reached into his pocket and handed over a brand new Yello track. The next day the phone rang: 'Let's do the deal.' The track was called 'Oh Yeah'.*

Even though Tregoning stood down in the late 1980s from his role as Yello's manager, motivator and general jack-of-all-trades, he has never entirely dropped out of the band's orbit, collaborating, for instance, on the album Toy*, the live show in Berlin, and* Electrified*, the Boris Blank solo project. Blank: 'Ian Tregoning was one of Yello's most important people and partners – and he still is.'*

Foto: Boris Blank, 1995. / *Photo: Boris Blank, 1995.*

Fotos von Bruno Bänziger fürs Cover
des Albums *You Gotta Say Yes to Another Excess*, 1983.

Bruno Bänziger's photos for
the You Gotta Say Yes to Another Excess *album cover, 1983.*

Video-Dreh für *I Love You* mit Patrizia Fontana.
Foto: Bruno Bänziger.

I Love You *music video shoot, with Patrizia Fontana.*
Photo: Bruno Bänziger.

Anton Corbijn lässt seine magische Kamera spielen.

Photographer Anton Corbijn applying his moody magic.

102–105

Video-Stills von *I Love You*.

Stills from the I Love You *music video.*

Boris, «Lost Again».

Boris, 'Lost Again'.

Noten und Text zu «Lost Again».

Sheet music and lyrics for 'Lost Again'.

(C) 1983 NEUE WELT MUSIKVERLAG GMBH, München
Alle Rechte vorbehalten
All Rights reserved

B.H. Mm 01-674 4184

109–112

Video-Stills aus *Lost Again*, mit Jenny Wright.

Stills from the Lost Again *music video, with Jenny Wright.*

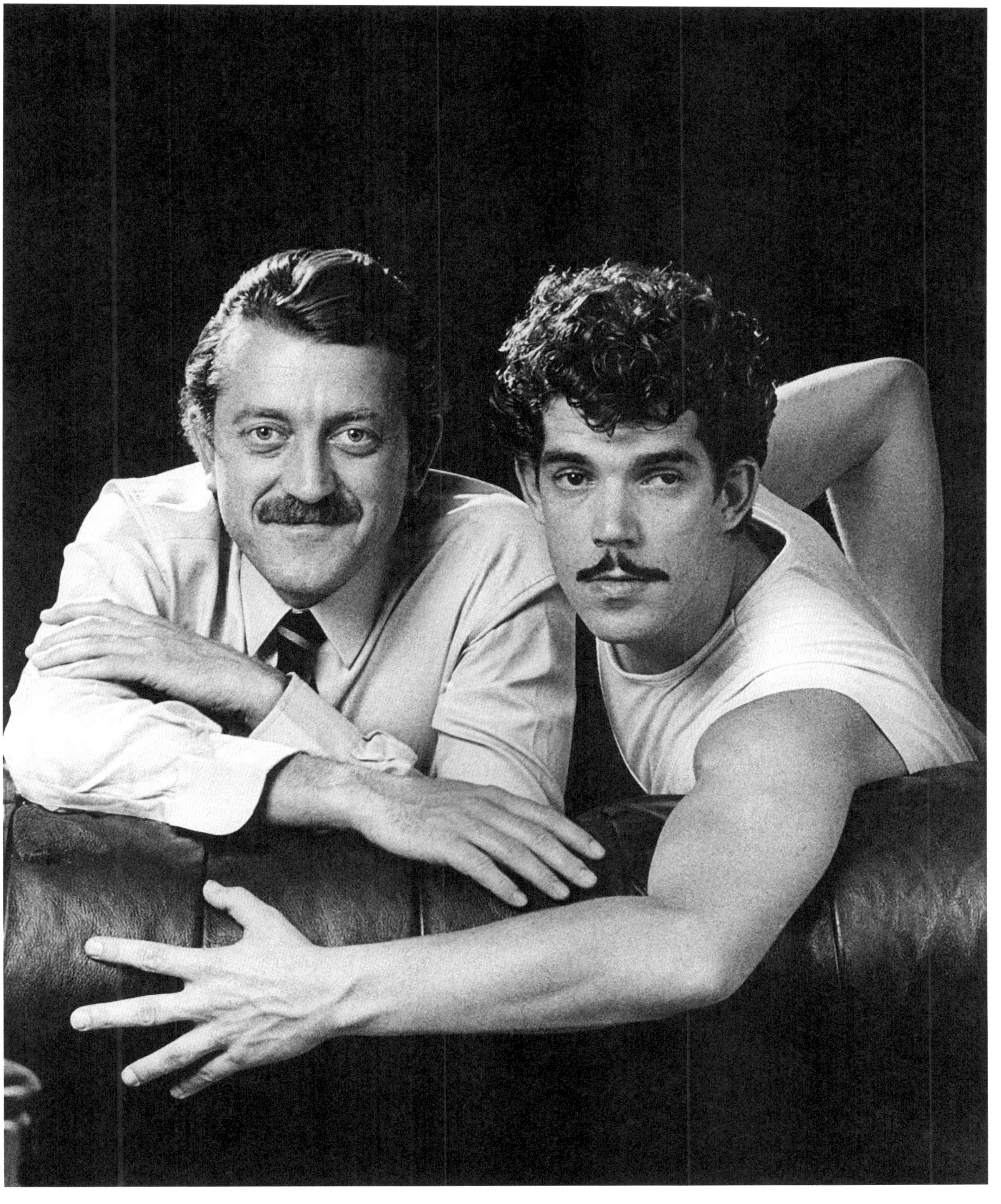

Dieter Meier und Boris Blank in New York. Der Name des Fotografen ist leider im Nebel der Zeit verloren gegangen, aber Boris Blank erinnert sich gut an die Session: «Jeder Finger musste ganz genau stimmen. Dieter ist fast durchgedreht.»

Dieter Meier and Boris Blank in New York. The name of the photographer is lost in the mists of time, but Boris Blank remembers the session well: 'Each finger had to be arranged just so. Dieter very nearly lost it.'

MASK OF THE YELLO PERIL

ANK INFO
TER DATA

hello to Yello, who are not
ch, but also stars of *NME's*
Those who have seen their
ng will be pleased to know
video for their new single 'I
ch these stills are taken.
ello composer Boris Blank
n the passenger seat of his
toriously lousy driver, she
aution, responding simply
you". Sweet, but she's not
onalist. What happens next
rotruding part is pointing
revealed in due course.
zarre, you should see what
ch TV. Shy to a fault, Boris
s Peron set up their synths
outers and left the stage to
nce artist Dieter Meier, who
ke a dead cat" ad infinitum.
dness does bear fruit, and
f sounds grow their exotic
the low tones of the erotic
rked up from a pig's grunt.
a Cha' has two solid Boris
belches at its base.

BORIS BLANK & DIETER MEIER 1982 – 1983

Yello in der britischen Musikzeitschrift *New Musical Express*, 28. Mai 1983. Fotos: Anton Corbijn.

Yello in the UK's New Musical Express, *28 May 1983. Photos: Anton Corbijn.*

Anton Corbijn in den 1980er-Jahren.

Anton Corbijn in the 1980s.

Der holländische Fotograf und Filmregisseur Anton Corbijn, bekannt für seine stimmungsvollen Schwarz-Weiss-Aufnahmen, war über Ian Tregoning zu Yello gestossen und begleitete das Duo auf der Kuba-Reise, Veranstaltungen und Partys.

The Dutch photographer/film director Anton Corbijn, famous for his slightly moody black-and-white shots, was put in touch with Yello by Ian Tregoning. He would accompany Dieter Meier and Boris Blank on the Cuba trip, and to some events and parties.

Zeichnung von Dieter Meier; der *You Gotta Say Yes ...* -Stempel ist im Yello-Archiv abgelegt.

Drawing by Dieter Meier; the You Gotta Say Yes ... *stamp is filed away in the Yello archive.*

Noten und Text zu «Heavy Whispers».

Sheet music and lyrics for 'Heavy Whispers'.

(C) 1983 NEUE WELT MUSIKVERLAG GMBH, München
Alle Rechte vorbehalten
All Rights reserved

R.H. Mss. 01-674 4184

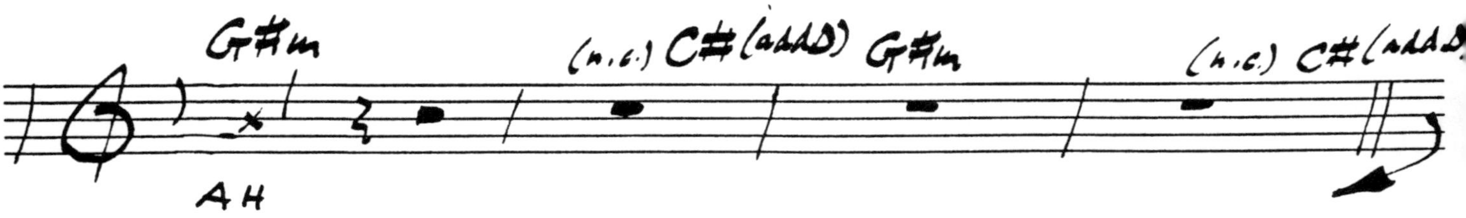

VERSE 2: AH, AH ....
PLEASE STOP TO CRY BABY CRY
OR TELL ME WHY BABY WHY
I NEED TO KNOW BABY KNOW
WHY IS IT SO BABY SO.
OH, OH, OH, OH BABY PLEASE
I BEG YOU DOWN ON MY KNEES
WHY DON'T YOU SMILE BABY SMILE
NOT IN A WHILE BABY WHILE, AH, AH

INSTR: Synth: Gm / A7 / Gm / Cm / Gm / Cm / D7 / Cm
Gm / A7 / Gm / Cm / Gm / Cm / D7 / Cm /
Gm / A7 / Gm / Cm / Gm

VERSE 3: AH. BABY THE TRUTH BABY TRUTH
HAS TO BE SMOOTH BABY SMOOTH
WHY DON'T YOU FLY BABY FLY
PLEASE TELL ME WHY BABY WHY
I HAVE TO KNOW BABY KNOW
DON'T LET ME GO BABY GO
WHY DON'T YOU SMILE BABY SMILE
NOT IN A WHILE BABY WHILE.

Dieter Meier isst Fleischkäse vom Metzger Bär vor der Abreise nach New York. Als Tisch dient die Motorhaube von Boris Blanks Plymouth.

Dieter Meier gathering strength for the flight to New York with a portion of Fleischkäse *('meat-cheese') from Metzger Bär (a local delicacy that has absolutely nothing to do with cheese). The bonnet of Boris Blank's Plymouth serves as a table.*

120–121

Boris Blank am Keyboard seines geliebten Fairlight CMI Samplers, 1983.

Boris Blank showing off his beloved Fairlight CMI sampler, 1983.

Foto: Koni Nordmann. / *Photo: Koni Nordmann.*

Als Teenager entdeckte Boris Blank die Magie der Geräusche. Er liebte das Echo in Höhlen, das Blubbern von Milch, wenn man mit dem Strohhalm hineinblies, und den mysteriösen Twang von Metallfedern, wenn man daran zupfte. Mit der Leidenschaft eines Sammlers trug er ein Archiv von Klängen zusammen, die er mit der Akribie eines Uhrmachers und dem Auge eines Kunstmalers in Musik verwandelte. Die ersten beiden Yello-Alben waren Soundcollagen, die vor allem mit Tonband, Rasierklinge und Klebstreifen gezimmert worden waren. Nun kam der Fairlight CMI Sampler auf den Markt, ein revolutionäres, in Australien entwickeltes Instrument, das es erlaubte, jegliche Art von Geräuschen einzufangen und digital zu bearbeiten. Für Blank war es das Gerät seiner Träume. Er gehörte zu den ersten Musikern in Europa, die damit arbeiteten, und *You Gotta Say Yes to Another Excess* war das erste Yello-Album, bei dessen Entstehung es die führende Rolle spielte. «Am Anfang war jeder Klang ein Experiment, jeder Ton eine Offenbarung. Man musste nicht mehr drei Minuten lang aufs Bongo trommeln, sondern man machte ein Sample und spielte damit so lang, wie man wollte. Ich erinnere mich genau an den Moment, als ich merkte, wie einfach es war, die Stimme höher oder tiefer zu schalten. Plötzlich konnte ich singen wie eine Frau. So entstand ‹I Love You›.»

Boris Blank was in his early teens when he discovered the magic of sound. He loved the echo in caves, the bubbling of milk when you blew into it through a straw, and the mysterious twang of metal springs when you plucked at them. With the passion of a collector, he assembled an archive of sounds which he transformed into music with the precision of a watchmaker and the eye of a painter. The first two Yello albums were sound collages crafted mostly with tape, razor blade and sellotape. Now the Fairlight CMI Sampler arrived on the market, a revolutionary instrument developed in Australia that made it possible to capture any kind of sound and process it digitally. For Blank, it was the device of his dreams. He was among the first musicians in Europe to work with the Fairlight, and You Gotta Say Yes to Another Excess *was the first Yello album to benefit from the new technology. Blank: 'In the beginning, every sound was an experiment, every note a revelation. You no longer had to bash your bongos for the full three minutes of a track. You simply made a sample and let that play as long as you needed it. I remember the exact moment when I realised how easy it was to make a voice higher or lower. Suddenly I could sing like a woman. That's how "I Love You" was born.'*

Dieter Meier. Foto: Yvon Baumann.

Dieter Meier. Photo: Yvon Baumann.

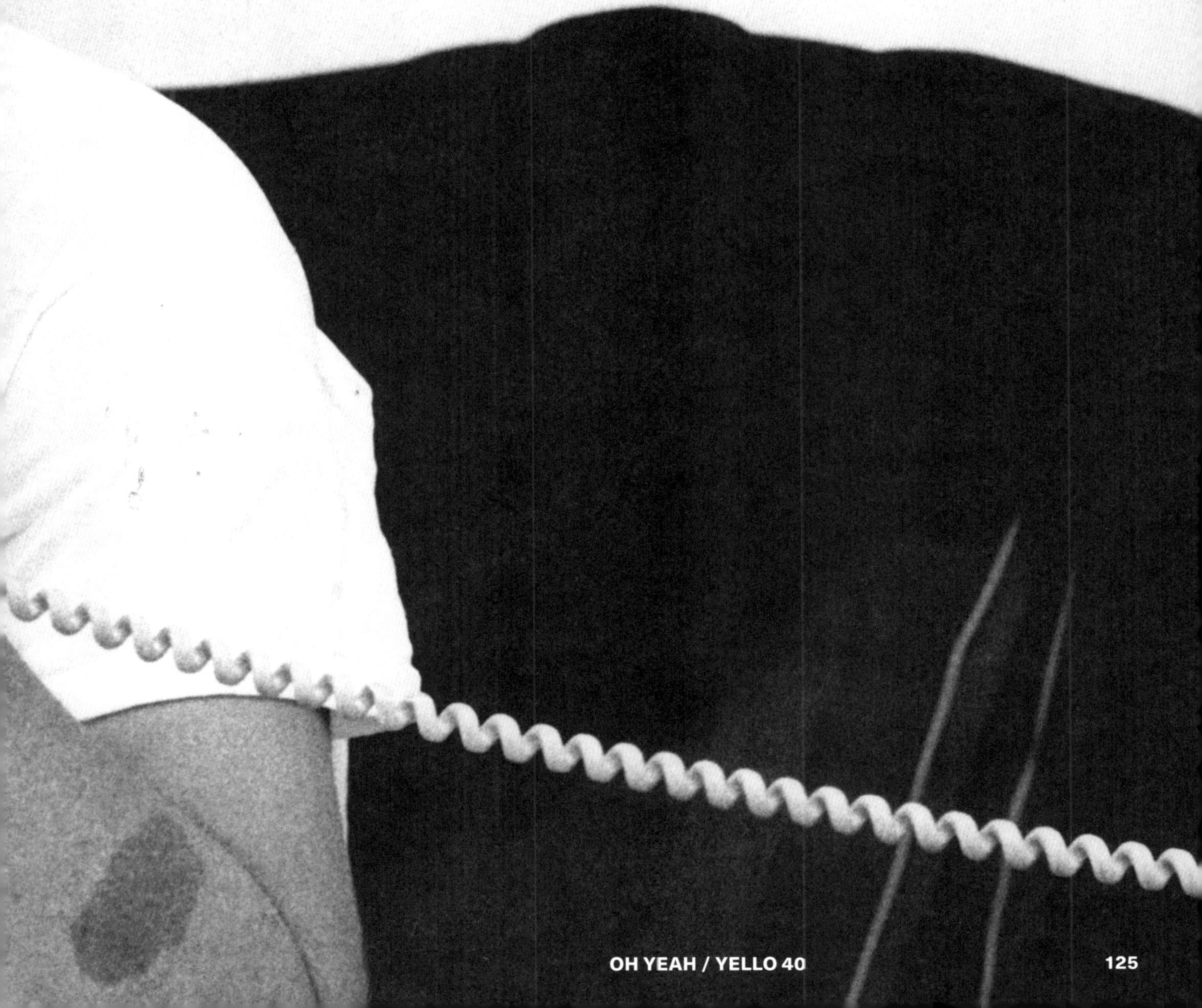

Die Mutter von Dieter Meier stellte ein Fotoalbum mit Bildern vom Live-Auftritt von 1983 im New Yorker Roxy Club zusammen. Leider traute der Buchbinder den Anweisungen nicht und verpasste Yello ein zusätzliches «W». Es wurde mit einem goldenen Schmetterling zum Verschwinden gebracht.

Dieter Meier's mother had created an album of photos from Yello's performance at the Roxy Club in New York. Unfortunately, the bookbinder distrusted the instructions he had received, and added a 'W' to Yello. A golden butterfly fluttered to the rescue.

YELLO

New York

1983

Frankie Crocker hatte «Bostich» häufig in seinem New Yorker Radioprogramm gespielt. Auf diese Weise mauserte sich die Single zum Underground-Hit in den frühen Hip-Hop-Klubs mit vornehmlich afro- und lateinamerikanischem Publikum. Als die Nachricht von diesem Phänomen Zürich erreichte, beschloss Boris Blank, einen Augenschein zu nehmen. «Ich kippte aus den Schuhen. All diese Menschen, die wie verrückt zu unserer Musik tanzten und es natürlich viel besser konnten als wir selber!»

Irgendwie geschah es dann, dass sich Yello dazu überreden liess, sich für zwei Shows im sagenumwobenen Roxy Club buchen zu lassen. «Wir hatten keine Ahnung, was uns da erwartete», erinnert sich Blank. Der Laden war zum Bersten gefüllt. Als Bühne diente ein Boxring mitten auf dem Tanzboden. In der Garderobe drang die Meldung durch, dass am Eingang allerhand Messer und Schusswaffen beschlagnahmt worden waren. Afrika Bambaataa trat als Erster in den Ring und heizte das Publikum mächtig auf. Blank: «Nur schon das Zuschauen verwandelte mich in ein nervöses Wrack. Als die Reihe endlich an uns war, brachte ich es vor lauter Zittern fast nicht fertig, den ersten Knopf zu drücken.» Kaum hatte Yello losgelegt – peng! Totale Dunkelheit. Sämtliche Sicherungen durchgebrannt. «Ich dachte: Das ist es. Unser letztes Stündchen hat geschlagen.» Aber es kam alles anders. Als die Elektrizität endlich wieder in Gang gebracht wurde, reagierte das Publikum genauso enthusiastisch wie bei Afrika Bambaataa. «Welch eine Erinnerung!»

Frankie Crocker had been playing 'Bostich' on his WBLS radio show in New York, and the track had become a hit in the very early hip-hop clubs, clubs with mostly African-American crowds. When news of this unexpected turn of events reached Zürich, Boris Blank decided to take a look for himself. 'I was absolutely flabbergasted. All these people dancing like crazy to our music! And, of course, they were much better at it than us.'

Someone somehow managed to persuade Yello to let themselves be booked for two shows at the Roxy Club. Boris Blank: 'We had no idea what to expect ...' The place was packed to the rafters. A boxing ring in the middle of the dance floor served as the stage. Word reached the dressing room that a wide array of knives and firearms had been confiscated at the doors. Afrika Bambaataa was on first. He worked the crowd into a frenzy. Blank: 'Just watching them reduced me to a nervous wreck. By the time it was our turn to go on stage I was so jittery I barely managed to hit the button to get started.' No sooner had their performance begun, when bang! Total darkness. All of the fuses blown. 'I thought: "This is it, we're dead!"' But when the electricity was at last restored, the crowd's reaction to Yello was just as enthusiastic as it had been for Afrika Bambaataa. 'What a memory!'

129–133

Yello an der Seite von Gastgeberin Dianne Brill live im Roxy Club, New York, 2. und 3. Dezember 1983. Fotos: Bruno Bänziger.

Yello with their host, Dianne Brill, live at the Roxy Club, New York, 2 and 3 December 1983. Photos: Bruno Bänziger.

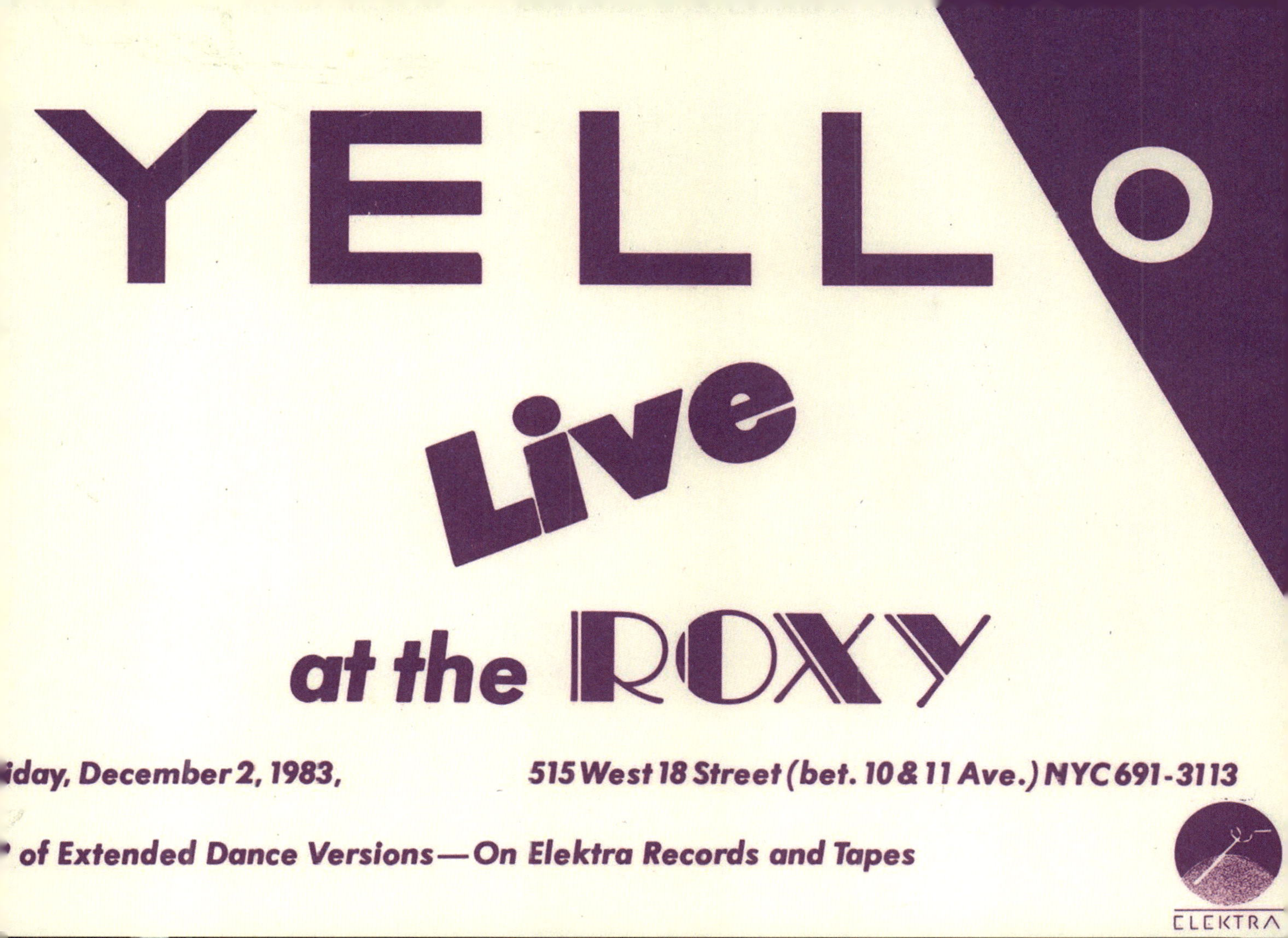
YELLO
Live
at the ROXY
iday, December 2, 1983,
515 West 18 Street (bet. 10 & 11 Ave.) NYC 691-3113
of Extended Dance Versions—On Elektra Records and Tapes
ELEKTRA

134–135

Bericht aus New York im *Musikexpress Sounds*, 1984.
Foto: Bruno Bänziger.

Report from New York in Musikexpress Sounds*, 1984.*
Photo: Bruno Bänziger.

BORIS BLANK & DIETER MEIER 1983

YELLO

New York, Roxy

Für die beiden Schweizer Boris Blank und Dieter Meier (Tape-Spezialist Carlos Peron blieb zu Hause) war ihr allererster Live-Auftritt eine ganz spezielle Erfahrung: Im Roxy verkehren etwa fünf Prozent Weiße, 15 Prozent Puerto-ricaner und 80 Prozent Schwarze. Für ein solches Publikum war der Auftritt einer weißen Band aus der Schweiz („wo die Schokolade und die Uhren herkommen") schlichtweg eine Sensation.

Zwei Wochen lang wurde das Konzert im Radio angekündigt –

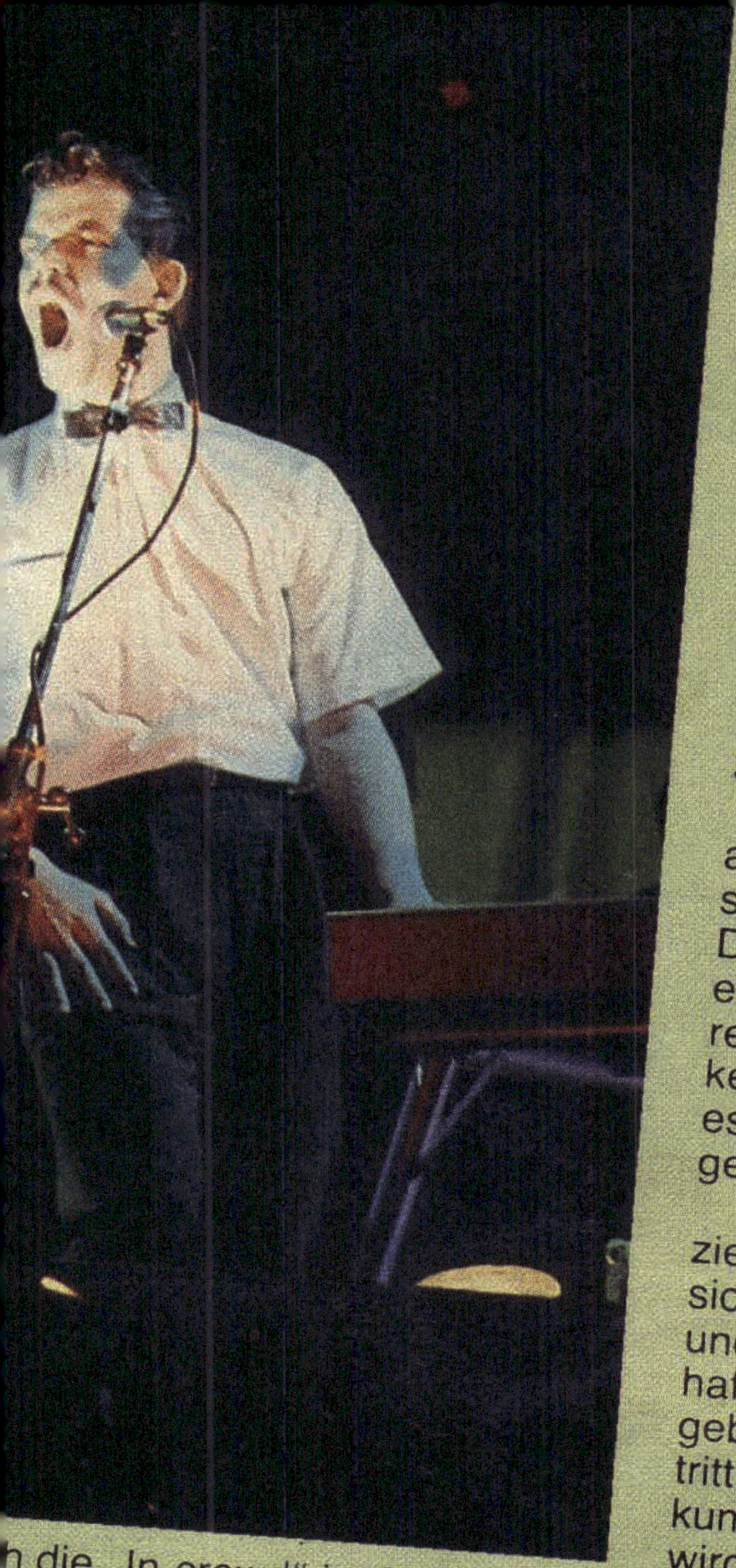

h die „In-crowd“ im Roxy warte-
oller Ungeduld. Der Club, der
derzeit von einer Rollschuh-
o in einen Tanzclub verwandelt,
am Freitagabend mit 3000
t schwarzen, energiegelade-
Besuchern fast gefüllt.
war eine typische Freitag-
mit unzähligen Breakdancers
er South Bronx und Harlem.
r, die meisten waren gekom-
men, um vorher und nachher d Top-Künste von DJs wie Afric Bambaataa zu genießen, aber e gab durchaus auch einige Yello Fans. Wie etwa Discjockey Islam der – wie er mir sagte – alle Platter der Schweizer Gruppe besitzt unc dem Kommenden mit Spannung entgegensah.

Boris Blank, der vor dem Auftritt fürchterlich nervös war, flüsterte mir zu: *„Ich bin noch nie in meinem Leben live aufgetreten und komme mir hier vor wie auf einem anderen Stern.“*

Dann der Auftritt. Boris, anfangs allein auf der Bühne, beginnt mit seinem Zauberberg aus Triggern, Drum-Maschinen und Bandgeräten elektronische Laute aus einer anderen Welt zu produzieren. Ein Tukkern, Blubbern und Stampfen, wie es dieses Publikum wohl noch nie gehört hat.

Mit einem im Hintergrund projizierten Film über gewaltige Explosionen erscheint dann Dieter Meier und beginnt augenblicklich, roboterhaft Worte und Laute von sich zu geben. Der bizarre theaterhafte Auftritt hat auf das New Yorker Publikum eine erstaunliche Wirkung und wird mit „Yello“-Rufen und einem großen Applaus bestätigt.

Ich frage Boris nach dem Ende des Konzertes, wie er sich nach seinem Bühnendebüt fühle. Er antwortet mit einem ungläubigen Lächeln: *„Ich hätte nie und nimmer gedacht, daß unsere Musik hier im Roxy ankommen würde. Ich glaube, New York is ready for us.“*

Michael Flum

Einladung zur Plattentaufe von *You Gotta Say Yes to Another Excess* in New York.

Invitation to the New York launch party of You Gotta Say Yes to Another Excess.

Karte von Dianne Brill.

Postcard from Dianne Brill.

KISSES, BORIS,
MILLIONS OF
KISSES ...
XXX

Dieter Meier, Rote Fabrik, 1984.

Dieter Meier, the Rote Fabrik, 1984.

GROSS-KUNDGEBUNG
SEEPROMENADE
DONNERSTAG
20. SEPT.
13.30h
Die grosse Drachentöterschau von Wolf Biermann
Freilichtspiele Chur 1984 Arcas

Foto: Anton Corbijn.

Photo: Anton Corbijn.

142–145

Video-Stills aus *Bostich*, 1984
in New York gedreht.

Stills from the Bostich *music video, shot in 1984 in New York.*

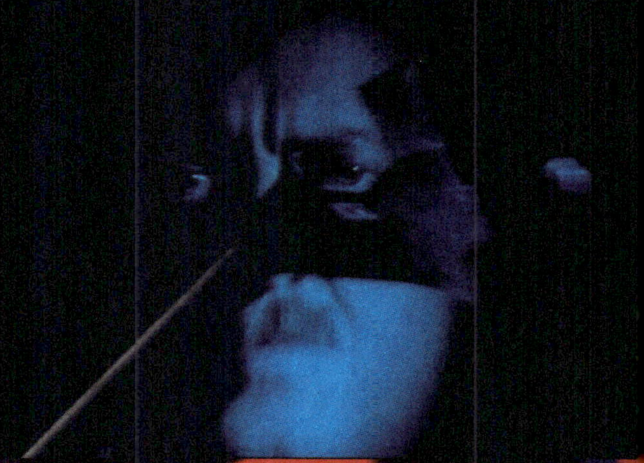

BORIS BLANK & DIETER MEIER 1985

Anton Corbijn (links) und Ian Tregoning auf dem Flugplatz von Gander (Neufundland), wo das Flugzeug auf dem Weg nach Havanna aufgetankt wurde. Die Air-Cubana-Piloten mussten die Dollars für den Sprit in Cash hinblättern.

Anton Corbijn (left) and Ian Tregoning on their way to Havana, on a refuelling stop at Gander Airport, Newfoundland. The Air Cubana pilots were made to pay for the fuel in cash.

Video-Dreh in Havanna, 1985.

Die Idee für den Dreh war kühn: Ohne Storyboard oder Drehbuch würde man nach Kuba reisen und sich von den Gerüchen und Bildern inspirieren lassen. Das resultierende Tohuwabohu entlockte Anton Corbijn den unsterblichen Ausruf: «Dieter, this is total chaos!» Die tropischen Temperaturen, die intensiven Farben und die geradezu barocke Stimmung von Havanna und dem Club Tropicana passten perfekt ins Video zur Single «Desire». Auch als Auto- und Motorrad-Fans kamen Dieter und Boris auf ihre Rechnung.

Boris Blank erzählt: «Im Video sieht man, wie ich Dieter abhole vom Schiff. Es war ganz früh am Morgen, bei Sonnenaufgang. Wir hatten einen Buick aus dem Jahr 1952 ausgeborgt, der gleiche Jahrgang wie ich. Wenn man damit 300 Meter gefahren ist, hat er gekocht und man musste Wasser nachgiessen. Die Kamera war fixiert, ich musste genau an der richtigen Stelle stoppen, eine Zigarette anzünden und aufs Schiff schauen, wo Dieter auf die Treppe trat. Das war verdammt schwierig, denn man musste hart auf die Bremse treten, sonst passierte nichts. Wir mussten die Szene mindestens zwanzig Mal wiederholen, bis ich den Stopp richtig hinkriegte. Der Kameramann, Avelino hiess er, war vollkommen verrückt. Ich brauste die Malecon hinunter, Dieter neben mir, der hat drauflosfabuliert und mit den Händen gefuchtelt, und vorn auf der Motorhaube sass Avelino mit seiner 16-Millimeter-Kamera und hat uns gefilmt. ‹Bori, Bori, rodamos, rodamos!›, hat er gerufen. ‹Wir drehen, wir drehen.› Dies bei 60 km/h.»

Music video shoot in Havana, 1985.

The idea was bold: Yello and Anton Corbijn would set off for Cuba without so much as a storyboard or a script, and let inspiration be guided by the scents and impressions around them. The result was mayhem, summed up by Corbijn with the immortal line: 'Dieter, this is total chaos!' The tropical temperature, the intense colours and the quasi-Baroque atmosphere of Havana and the Club Tropicana was perfect for the Desire *music video. What's more, Dieter and Boris, classic motoring enthusiasts both, fully appreciated the rich selection of vintage cars and motorbikes cruising the streets.*

Boris Blank: 'In the music video you see me picking Dieter up from the port. It was very early in the morning, at sunrise. We had borrowed a 1952 Buick, the same vintage as me. You barely drove 300 metres before the engine overheated and you had to top up the water. My task was to pull up at exactly the right spot in front of the camera, which could not be moved, light a cigarette and look up at the boat where Dieter was stepping out onto the stairs. This was much more difficult than it sounds, because you had to step hard on the brakes for anything at all to happen. We had to repeat the take at least twenty times before I got it right. The cameraman, Avelino, was completely crazy. I was racing down the Malecon, Dieter next to me, spinning his yarns and throwing his arms about, and on the bonnet in front of us sat Avelino with his 16-mm camera, without any kind of safety harness, filming away. "Bori, Bori, rodamos, rodamos!" he cried, "We're shooting, we're shooting." This at 60 kilometres an hour!'

148–151

Fotos: Michael Roemer.

Photos: Michael Roemer.

HM-6649

BOORIS BLANK & DIETER MEIER 1985

Foto: Anton Corbijn.

Photo: Anton Corbijn.

BORIS BLANK & DIETER MEIER 1985

Wrack eines Schiffs in der Nähe von Varadero. Foto: Michael Roemer.

Shipwreck near Varadero. Photo: Michael Roemer.

BORIS BLANK & DIETER MEIER 1985

Fischen in der Nähe von Havanna.
Fotos: Paul Grau.

Fishing near Havana.
Photos: Paul Grau.

160–165

Fiesta, La Bodeguita del Medio, La Habana.

Fotos: Anton Corbijn. / *Photos: Anton Corbijn.*

CRISTAL
Stephen

Stephen

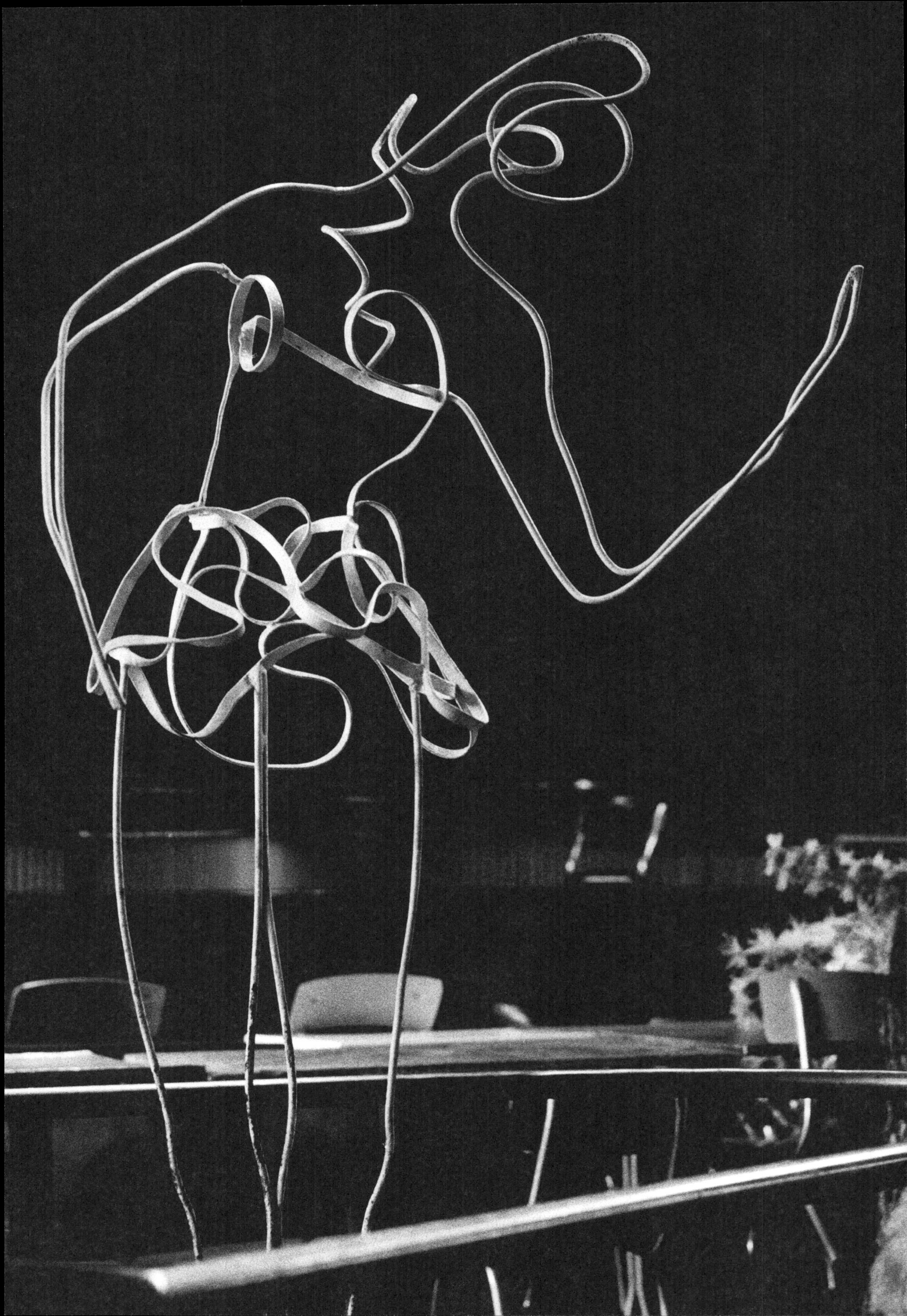

BORIS BLANK & DIETER MEIER 1985

166–167

Club Tropicana.
Foto: Ian Tregoning.

At the Club Tropicana.
Photo: Ian Tregoning.

BORIS BLANK & DIETER MEIER 1985

Fragenkatalog per Telefax an Ian Tregoning
von Juan Cabanas, Empresa Cubana Radio y TV.

Questionnaire sent to Ian Tregoning
by Juan Cabanas from Empresa Cubana Radio y TV.

266511 ELEKTR G
266511 ELEKTR G
511600 TVC CU

LA HABANA, 13 DE ABRIL DE 1985

GRUPO YELLO
ATTON : IAN TREGONING
=====================
53269 SUIZA
266511 INGLATERRA.-

RE: YELLO VIDEO-FILM EN CUBA

NECESITAMOS PARA PODER GARANTIZAR SU VISITA A CUBA EL DIA 5/5/85 NOS RESPONDAN A LA MAYOR BREVEDAD POSIBLE LAS SIGUIENTES PRECISIONES :

1) DATOS PARA VISA : NOMBRE, DIRECCION PARTICULAR
FECHA Y LUGAR DE NACIMIENTO
NO. DE PASAPORTE
FECHA EXPEDICION/FECHA EXPIRACION

2) SEGUN SU TELEXS SON 6 PERSONAS

3) NO PODEMOS FILMAR EN 35MM, SOLO TENEMOS EQUIPOS DE 16MM. ADEMAS MENOS COSTOSO Y USUALMENTE EN EL MUNDO SE GRABA EN 16MM Y SE TRANSFIERE POSTERIORMENTE DE 16MM A 35MM. ESTO LO PUEDEN HACER EN LONDRES FACILMENTE.

4) SEGUN ACORDAMOS EN LONDRES, EL SONIDO SE LO INSERTAN USTEDES POSTERIORMENTE . A QUE SONIDO SE REFIEREN EN SU TELEXS? PENSAMOS QUE SEA SONIDO DE REFERENCIA.

5) NECESITAMOS UN LISTADO PRECISO DE SUS NECESIDADES, EN CUANTO A PERSONAL, EQUIPOS YSERVICIOS TECNICOS QUE REQUIEREN.

6) NECESITAMOS INFORMACION SOBR LO QUE DESEAN HACER Y SI TIENEN UN GUION O IDEA PRELIMINAR ELABORADO. SIN ESTOS DETALLES IMPOSIBLE DARLE EL PRESUPUESTO Y COSTOS EN GENERAL.

7) EL ESTUDIO QUE SOLICITAN CONQUE OBJETIVO? QUE FACILIDADES DEBE TEBER EL ESTUDIO

DESEAMOS ACLARAR QUE SEGUN DISPOSICIONES TECNICAS Y SINDICALES NUESTROS EQUIPOS SE APORTAN CON EL PERSONAL QUE LOS OPERA. NO BRINDAMOS EQUIPOS SIN OPERADORES.

8) NECESARIO COMUNIQUEN A LA EMPRESA BRITANICA QUE DEBEN ABONAR 5,000 USD POR LOS DERECHOS DE FILMACION EN CUBA Y QUE NECESITAMOS DATOS COMPLETOS DE VISA, ALOJAMIENTO, . TRANSPORTE Y SERVICIOS QUE REQUIEREN.

AL TANTO DE SUS NOTICIAS,

MARIO MARTINEZ/JUAN CABANAS
EMPRESA CUBANA DE RADIO Y TV
INTERTV.-

511600 TVC CU
266511 ELEKTR G
.....

170–173

Video-Stills aus *Desire.*

Stills from the Desire *music video.*

TROPICANA

Monique und Patrizia,
die Ehefrauen von Dieter und Boris.

*Dieter and Boris's wives,
Monique and Patrizia.*

Im Yello-Studio, Rote Fabrik, 1985.
Foto: Koni Nordmann.

The Yello Studio, the Rote Fabrik, 1985.
Photo: Koni Nordmann.

Arbeitsmethode

«Als musikalische Treibkraft von Yello ist für mich das Musikmachen wie die Nahrung für den Stoffwechsel, der mich am Leben erhält. Ich brauch die Musik tatsächlich zum Überleben. Es geht kein Tag vorbei, an dem mich nicht irgendein Geräusch inspiriert, etwas daraus zu machen. Es gibt sehr viele verschiedene Frequenzen, die in der Musikwelt vorkommen, all diese Bassfrequenzen, diese Schlagwerkinstrumente, die können ersetzt werden durch jedwelche Geräusche, die uns jeden Tag umgeben. Mit denen kann man Musik machen, und das ist meine Welt.»

Boris Blank, *Pure Audio Recordings Blog*, 26. März 2021

«Die modularen Moog-Synthesizer haben mich schon früh fasziniert. In den 1970er-Jahre war ich ganz süchtig nach dem ARP 2600, und ich spielte auch mit dem kleinen EMS A AKS-Synthesizer herum, mit dem man lustige, zufallsgenerierte Sound-Sequenzen produzieren konnte. Für mich waren die Überraschungen und die neuen Sounds und Abfolgen von Klängen, die man mit diesen Maschinen herstellen konnte, viel wichtiger als die Frage, ob ich die Technologie dieser Systeme vollständig verstand.»

«Obwohl die spätere Musik von Yello vor allem mit Samplern generiert wurde, sind Synthesizer und die Suche nach neuen Sounds mit der heutigen Generation von Synthesizer-Plug-ins ein grundlegender Aspekt und eine wichtige Antriebskraft für meine musikalische Kreativität. Es ist für mich immer sehr wichtig gewesen, in die Molekularstruktur eines Klanges einzudringen, um ihn zu verändern und seine DNS zu modifizieren, bis der gewünschte Charakter hervortritt.»

«Ein essenzieller Teil meiner Kompositionsarbeit mit Yello besteht darin, die verschiedenen Sound-Elemente zu arrangieren. Dazu gehören Synthesizer-Sounds genauso wie Samples, Perkussion, Drums, Dieters Stimme und akustische Instrumente.»

«Seit den 1970er-Jahren verfolge ich ganz genau die neuesten Errungenschaften in der Musiktechnologie. Ich bin offen für alles, was auf dem Markt erscheint. Natürlich ist Modularität auch mit Instrumenten möglich, die im Computer stecken. Mein Credo ist dies: Ob die Werkzeuge analog oder digital sind, die Hauptsache besteht darin, dass die Freude an der kreativen Arbeit nicht im Akademischen verloren geht.»

Boris Blank, *A Guide to Modular Works* von Rolf-Dieter Lieb / Ulf Kaiser, Oktober 2009

«Die Transparenz unserer Klanggebäude ist mir sehr wichtig. Die Frequenzen – Bass, Mitte, Höhe – müssen sorgfältig getrennt werden, so dass tatsächlich das Gefühl von Dreidimensionalität entsteht. Für mich ist jedes Stück wie eine Klangwelt samt den ihr eigenen Menschen, Pflanzen und Tieren. Diese Räumlichkeit liegt mir sehr am Herzen. Ich wünsche mir, dass man der Versuchung nicht widerstehen kann, sich mit der Musik auf eine Wanderung zu begeben und sich laufend von neuen Eindrücken in den Bann ziehen zu lassen. Das zu erreichen erfordert viel administrative Fleissarbeit. Das hat wenig mit Kreativität zu tun und macht mir nicht besonders viel Spass. Aber sie ist unerlässlich für mein Verständnis von Sound.»

«In dieser Vorstellung von Sound gründet auch die gemeinsame Arbeitsmethode von Dieter und mir. Im Studio tritt Dieter in diese kaleidoskopartigen Klangwelten ein und lässt sich von den Bildern, die er sieht, zum Schreiben seiner Texte inspirieren. Wie ein Schauspieler auf der Bühne nimmt er in jedem Stück eine neue Rolle ein. Damit ist die Welt von Yello komplett.»

Boris Blank, 8. Juni 2021

Working Method

As the musical driving force behind Yello, making music is like food for the metabolism to keep me alive. I actually need music to survive. Not a day goes by without some kind of sound inspiring me to make something out of it. There are a great many different frequencies in the world of music. All these bass frequencies, the percussion, everything can be replaced by any other kind of noise from our environment. Making music out of these, that's my world.

Boris Blank, Pure Audio Recordings blog, *26 March 2021*

Those walls of Moog modular synthesisers naturally piqued my interest early on. In the 70s I was hooked on the ARP 2600 and also played around with the small EMS Synthi AKS modular synthesiser, which by chance made funny sequences. For me, the surprises and the discovery of new sounds and sequences with these machines were always more important than a complete understanding of the underlying technology of such systems.

Even though Yello's later completed works primarily involved samplers and synthesisers and the search for new sounds, today's generation of synthesiser plug-ins are an essential aspect and driving force of my musical creativity. For me, it has always been very important and special to penetrate into the molecular structures of a sound in order to change and modify its DNA until the desired character emerges.

An essential part of my composition work with Yello consists of arranging the most diverse sound elements. Synthesiser sounds play just as much a part as samples, percussion and drum sounds, Dieter's voice and acoustic instruments.

From the 70s onwards I have cultivated an ongoing desire for new developments in music technology. Today I'm just as open to all new innovations that appear on the music market. Of course, modularity is also possible with instruments inside the computer. For me, the credo is: Whether it's analogue or digital, the main thing is that the joy of creative work does not get lost in academia.

Boris Blank in A Guide to Modular Works *by Rolf-Dieter Lieb and Ulf Kaiser, October 2009*

The transparency of our sound constructs is very important to me. The frequencies – bass, middle, treble – must be carefully separated so that the feeling of three-dimensionality can actually arise. For me, each piece is like a sound-world complete with its own people, flora and fauna. This kind of spatiality is very close to my heart. I hope that it's impossible to resist the temptation to go on a journey with this music, impossible not to be captivated by a constant stream of new impressions. To achieve this aim requires a lot of administrative diligence. This type of work has little to do with creativity and I don't particularly enjoy it. But it is essential to my understanding of sound. Our joint working method is also based on this idea of sound. In the studio, Dieter enters these kaleidoscopic soundworlds and lets the images he sees inspire him to write his lyrics. Like an actor on stage, he takes on a new role in each piece. That's when the Yello world is complete.

Boris Blank, 8 June 2021

Dieter Meier und Boris Blank singen «Yeloooooohhh».
Foto: Yvon Baumann.

*Dieter Meier and Boris Blank singing 'Yeloooohhh'.
Photo: Yvon Baumann.*

YELLO "OH YEAH" (SINGLE & VIDEO VERSION)

(Boris Blank / Dieter Meier)

OH YEAH
OH YEAH
OH YEAH
THE MOON - BEAUTIFUL
THE SUN - EVEN MORE BEAUTIFUL
OH YEAH
OH YEAH
OH YEAH

BEAUTIFUL
OH YEAH OH YEAH

SUCH A GOOD TIME
A REALLY GOOD TIME } nur Videoclip-Version

OH YEAH
OH YEAH
OH YEAH
THE MOON - BEAUTIFUL
THE SUN - EVEN MORE BEAUTIFUL
OH YEAH
OH YEAH
OH YEAH

Text von «Oh Yeah».

Lyrics for 'Oh Yeah'.

Boris Blank demonstriert für den *Stern* das Sampling mit dem Fairlight. Foto: René Burri.

Boris Blank demonstrating the Fairlight sampling process to the German magazine Stern. *Photo: René Burri.*

184–189

Video-Stills aus *Oh Yeah*
mit Dieter Meiers Tochter Eleonore.

Stills from the Oh Yeah *music video, with Dieter Meier's daughter Eleonore.*

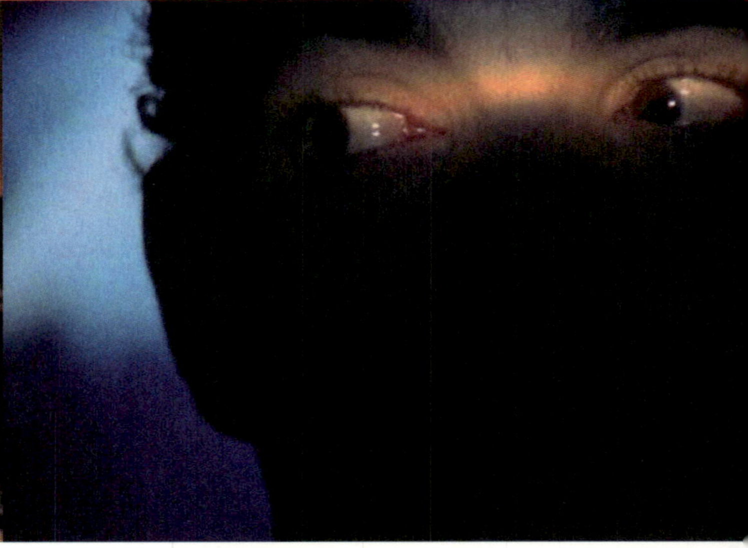

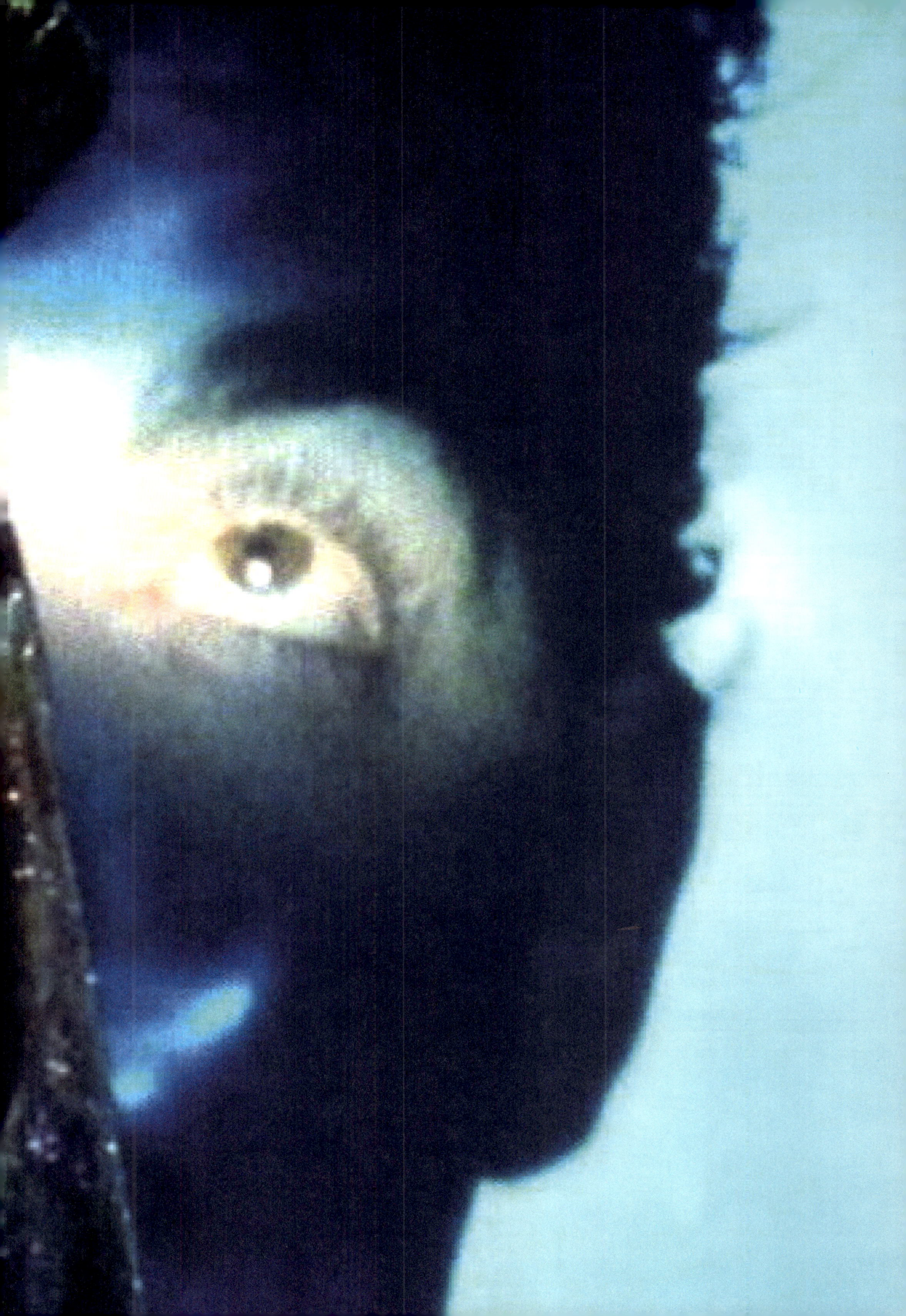

Noten zu «Oh Yeah».

Sheet music for 'Oh Yeah'.

Brief vom Musikverlag.

Letter from the music publisher.

WARNER BROS. MUSIC GMBH GERMANY
MUSIK UNSERER ZEIT VERLAG GMBH
NEUE WELT MUSIKVERLAG GMBH

Mauerkircherstraße 5
8000 München 80
Telefon (089) 98 49 91
Telex 5 215 177

Herrn
Dieter Meier
Aurorastr. 78

CH-8032 Zürich

München, den 13.5.1985

Sehr geehrter Herr Meier,

in der Anlage übersenden wir Ihnen Kopien der Leadsheets für die Titel auf der YELLO LP "STELLA", die wir in London anfertigen ließen. Wir bitten Sie nun, diese zu überprüfen und gegebenenfalls zu vervollständigen. Bitte geben Sie uns so bald als möglich Bescheid, damit wir die Leadsheets an unsere Partnerfirmen verschicken können.

Vielen Dank für Ihre Mühe.

Mit freundlichen Grüßen
WARNER BROS. MUSIC GMBH GERMANY

Hildegard Riedler

Hildegard Riedler

Anlage

Geschäftsführer: Edward C. Heine · Eingetragen im Handelsregister München, HRB 56981 · A Warner Communications Company

Goldene Schallplatte für *Stella*, überreicht in der Zürcher Widder-Bar von Lys Assia, der Gewinnerin des ersten Eurovision Song Contest im Jahr 1956 mit dem Lied «Refrain».

A gold record for Stella, *handed over in the Widder Bar in Zürich by Lys Assia – the winner in 1956 of the first Eurovision Song Contest with a song called 'Refrain'.*

Gold für *1980–1985 The New Mix in One Go*, mit Louis Spillmann, Wolf-Dieter Gramatke, Ossi Drechsler im Hintergrund.

Another gold record, this one for 1980–1985 The New Mix in One Go, *with Louis Spillmann, Wolf-Dieter Gramatke and Ossi Drechsler in the background.*

Louis Spillmann – Motto: «I'm the best, fuck the rest» – eine Schlüsselfigur in der Geschichte von Yello. Aufgewachsen in einem idyllischen Dorf in der Nähe von Zürich, hätte er eigentlich in London Wirtschaft studieren sollen. Aber seine wahre Zukunft begann mit einem Gelegenheitsjob in der Schweizer Abteilung von Phonogram Records. Am ersten Arbeitstag holte er Black Sabbath am Flugplatz ab, am zweiten Jethro Tull. Neun Jahre später wurde er als Geschäftsführer nach Hamburg geholt, um den Ruf der Firma als altmodische Schlagerfabrik aufzubessern. Als Erstes trat er mit The Residents in Kontakt, die zuoberst auf seiner Wunschliste standen. Die Band schickte ihm einen Stapel Ralph-Records-Platten, darunter *Solid Pleasure*. Schon das Froschbaby auf dem Cover fand er genial. Dann entdeckte er den Hinweis, dass das Album in einem Zürcher Studio entstanden war. Niemand in seinen Kreisen hatte je von dieser Band gehört. Erst ein Indie-Platten-Händler in Zürich konnte ihm eine Telefonnummer geben. Boris Blank erinnert sich gut an den Anruf. Kurz vor Weihnachten sei es gewesen, wenig später sass man in Hamburg im Büro von Spillmann und unterzeichnete den Vertrag. «Spillmann war noch ein echter Label-Chef. Er hatte das Gespür dafür, eine Band von Grund auf zu führen und gedeihen zu lassen, ohne ihr irgendwelche Vorschriften zu machen. Und er hat immer irrsinnig tolle Geschichten erzählt, wie er mit Elton John herumgehängt ist zum Beispiel, oder wie er Lemmy beim literweise Wodka-Saufen zugeschaut hat.»

Louis Spillmann – motto: 'I'm the best, fuck the rest' – is another key figure in the history of Yello. Born and bred in an idyllic village near Zürich, he was still planning to study economics in London when he took on what he thought was a temporary job in the Swiss branch of Phonogram Records. His task on his first day at work was to pick up Black Sabbath from the airport. On the second day it was Jethro Tull. Nine years later, he arrived in Hamburg as a managing director. His mission was to radically overhaul the German wing of the company, which had picked up a terrible reputation as the home of dodgy, old-fashioned Schlager singers. His first move was to contact The Residents, who were top of his wish list. In return, the band sent him a stack of Ralph Records albums. One of these was Solid Pleasure. *Spillmann thought everything about the album was genius, starting with the frog baby on the cover. He was even more astonished when he read in the small print that it had been recorded in Zürich. Alas, none of his Swiss friends had heard of Yello. Only after some serious sleuthing did he find a record dealer who was able to pass him a telephone number. Boris Blank remembers the call well. It arrived just before Christmas. In no time at all they were sitting in Spillmann's Hamburg office to sign the contract. Blank: 'Spillmann was one of the great old-school label bosses. He had the good sense to let a band develop at their own pace, and without imposing any rules. Plus, he had an inexhaustible reservoir of ludicrously great stories to tell about hanging out with Elton John, for example, or watching Lemmy drink pints of vodka.'*

The Museum of Modern Art

Department of Film

July 24, 1985

Dieter Meier
Yello Video Europe
Aurorastrasse 78
8033 Zurich

Dear Dieter Meier:

We are pleased to announce our selection of Pinball Cha-Cha as part of the Museum's exhibition entitled "Music Video: The Industry and Its Fringes," which will be on view September 3 - 30 in the Video Gallery. The show will feature seldom seen as well as popular works, and will offer an overview of twenty years of change and experimentation in the field.

The exhibition will conclude the festivities of the Film Department's 50th Anniversary Celebration. A press release will be forthcoming. We thank you for your contribution to what promises to be an interesting and entertaining exhibition.

Sincerely yours,

Keith C. Johnson

Keith C. Johnson (on behalf of Barbara J. London)
Video Department

11 West 53 Street, New York, N.Y. 10019-5486 Tel: 212-708-9400 Cable: MODERNART Telex: 62370 MODART

Das Museum of Modern Art, New York, zeigt das Yello-Video *Pinball Cha Cha*. Später wurde dieses in die permanente Sammlung aufgenommen.

The Pinball Cha Cha *music video on display at the Museum of Modern Art, New York. It was later acquired for MOMA's permanent collection.*

195–198

Video-Stills aus *Pinball Cha Cha*.

Stills from the Pinball Cha Cha *music video.*

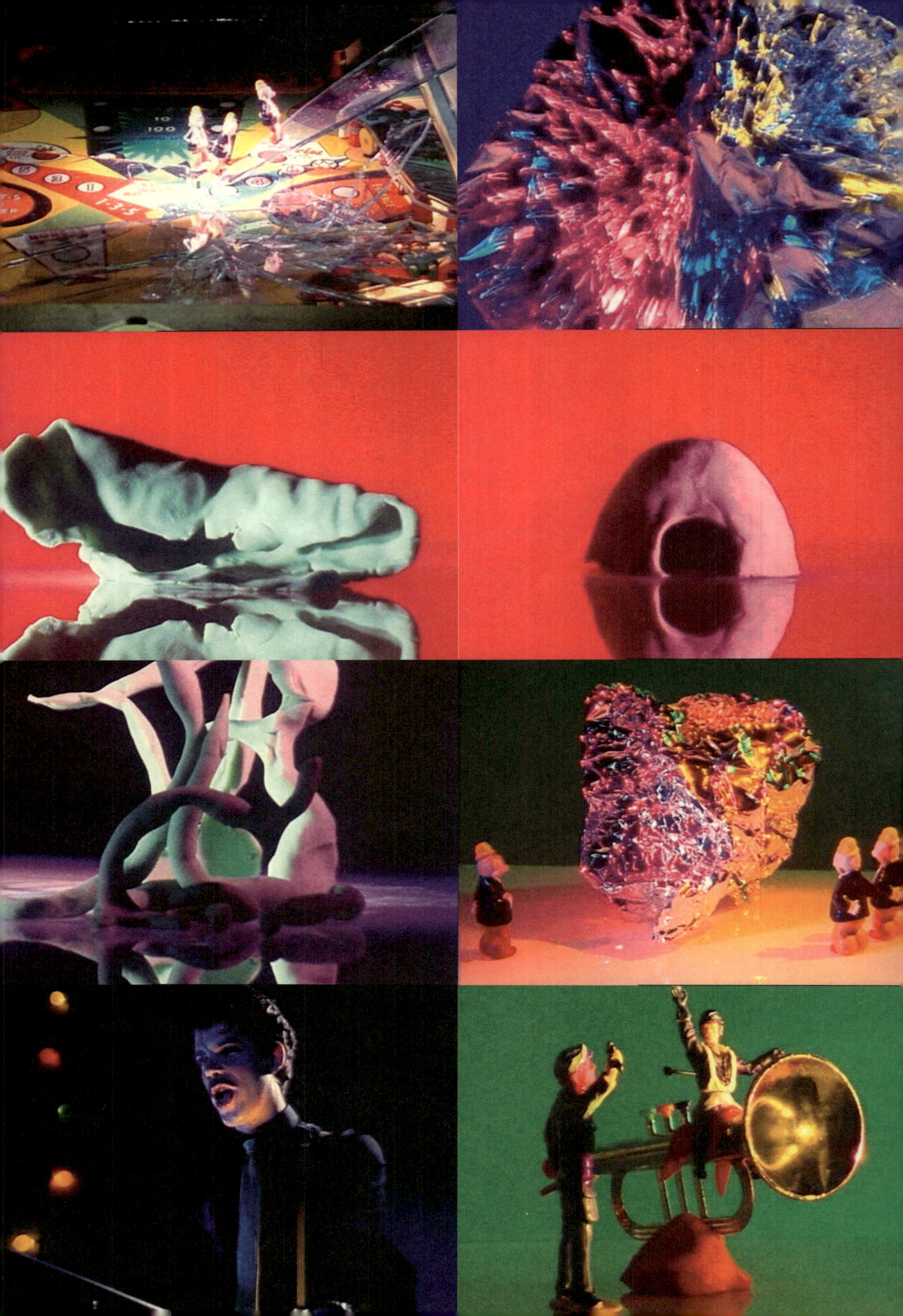

3 4 4
CAN PLAY
HAYBURNERS
HAYBURNERS
FINISH
PINBALL BAR

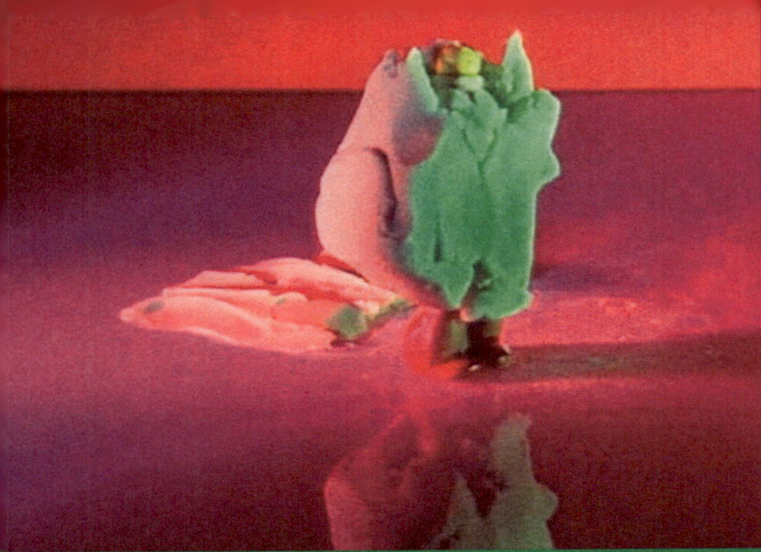

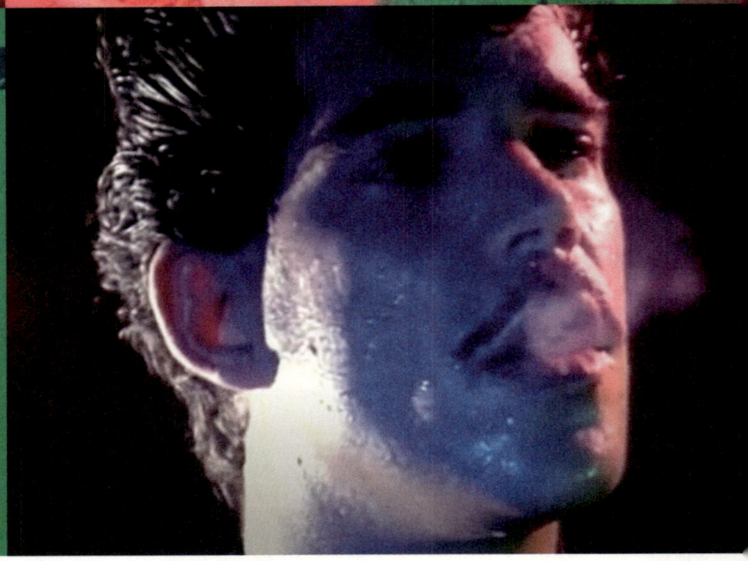

200–201

Probe für Video *Vicious Games*, Rote Fabrik, 1985.
Fotos: Daniel Boschung.

Rehearsal for the Vicious Games *music video, the Rote Fabrik, 1985. Photos: Daniel Boschung.*

202–205

Video-Stills aus *Vicious Games*,
mit Mirjam Montandon, Rote Fabrik, 1985.

Stills from the Vicious Games *music video, with Mirjam Montandon, the Rote Fabrik, 1985.*

Foto-Shooting für eine Mode-Illustrierte.
Boris Blank: «Es war immer lustig, sich ein bisschen zu verkleiden.»

Photo shoot for a fashion magazine.
Boris Blank: 'It was always fun to dress up.'

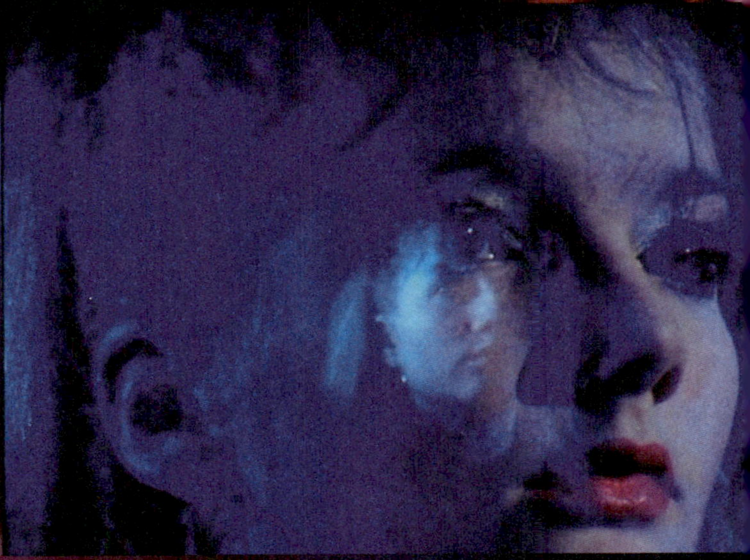

Originalentwurf für das Cover von *One Second* von Ernst Gamper.

Ernst Gamper's original artwork for the One Second *album cover.*

208–209

Fotosession in der Tropfsteinhöhle «Höllloch» bei Baar, Zug. Foto: Charles Seiler.

Photo shoot in a dripstone cave, Höllloch, near Baar, Zug. Photo: Charles Seiler.

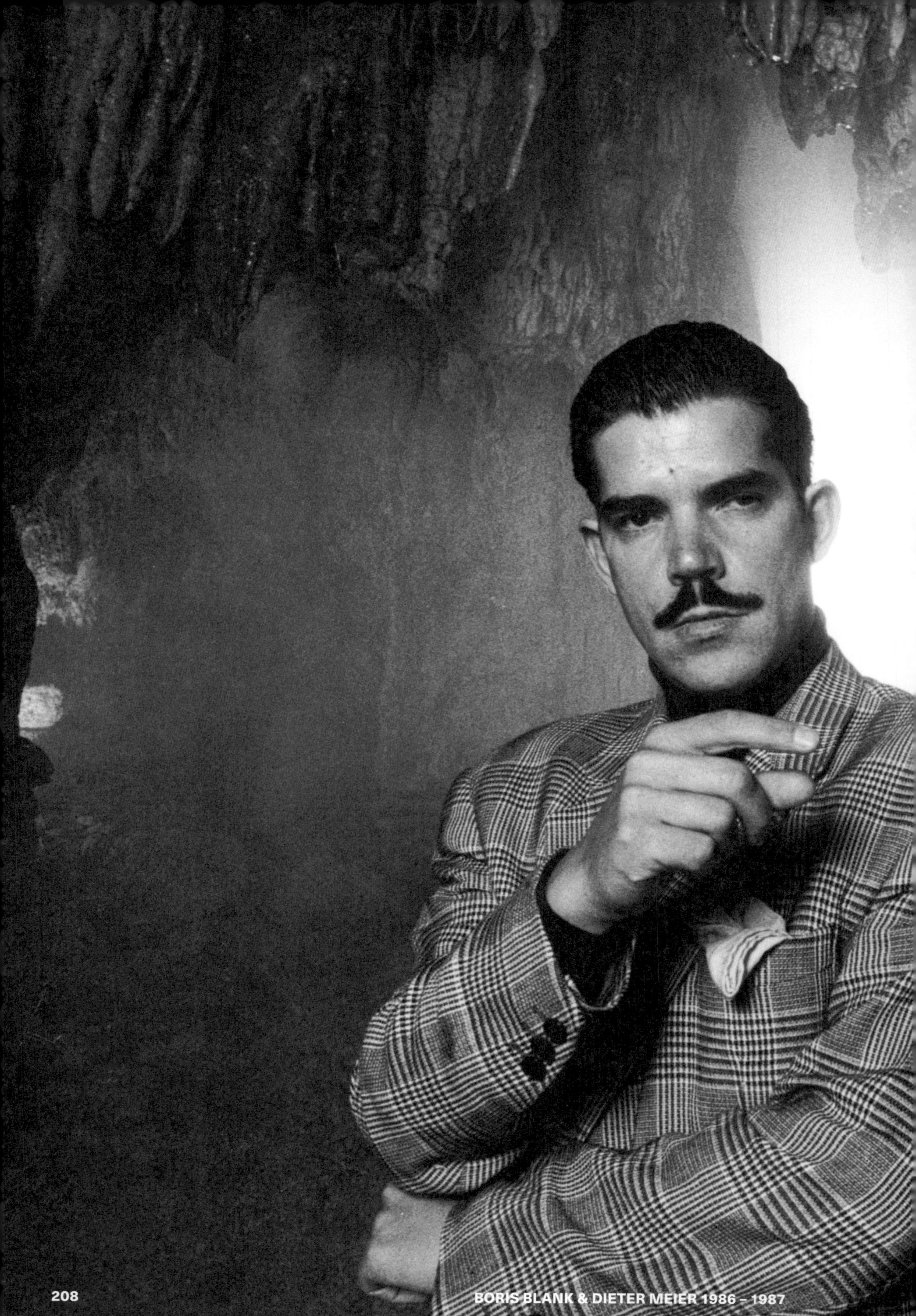

Monique Meier am Stranc. Foto: Dieter Meier. / *Monique Meier on the beach. Photo: Dieter Meier.*

212–216

Video-Stills aus *Goldrush*, mit Patrizia Fontana, Edi Oleschak sowie Ian Tregoning als Mephisto, 1986.

Stills from the Goldrush *music video, with Patrizia Fontana, Edi Oleschak, and Ian Tregoning as Mephisto, 1986.*

212, 214, 215

Fotos: Daniel Boschung.

Photos: Daniel Boschung.

213, 216

Fotos: Anton Corbijn.

Photos: Anton Corbijn.

3:48 Single-EDIT

G O L D R U S H

Ain't got no gold
So you get no show
So come on with me
And give it to me
Give it to me

(Gold, gold gold gold)

This is your show
And it's all in here
So why don't you stay
I give it to you
Give it to you

(Give me your gold
Give me your gold)

You gotta a nugget in your pocket
Gotta a nugget in your hand
Gotta a nugget in your pocket
Gotta a nugget for a grand
So forget your hesitation
Take it as an invitation
Nuggets for a great confusion
Nuggets for a great illusion

Clouds Love
Stars Colors

(Gold, gold
Take it into the night
guitar solo)

Blue moon is walking
Big slips are smoking
Big time disaster
My heart gets faster
My pot is melting
Doctors consulting
Destiny - give it to me
Destiny - give it to me

(Give me your gold
Gold ...)

~~Blue moon is walking~~
~~Big slips are smoking~~
~~Big time disaster~~
~~My heart gets faster~~
~~My pot is melting~~
~~Doctors consulting~~
~~Destiny - give it to me~~
~~Destiny - give it to me~~

(Give me your gold... Gold)

Text «Goldrush».

Lyrics for 'Goldrush'.

2

This is your life
And you got to know
It's just one more show
It's fantasy
Give it to me
Fantasy
Give it to me

3

3

You got a nugget in your pocket
Got a nugget in your hand
Got a nugget in your pocket
Got a nugget for a grand
So forget your hesitation
Take it as an invitation
Nuggets for a great confusion
Nuggets for a great illusion

~~(Gold gold~~
~~Take it into the night)~~

Clouds - love
Stars - colors

(Gold
mamama...
Guitar solo
Take it into the night)

Gold
fold

216, 219, 220, 221

Fotos: Anton Corbijn, 1986.

Photos: Anton Corbijn, 1986.

HELLO ☐ INVOICE ☐ REQUEST ☐ SPIELEREI ☐

ANTON CORBIJN,
BASEMENT,
132 LIVERPOOL ROAD,
LONDON N1 1LA,
UNITED KINGDOM.

TEL: 01-607 8001

ZE FAMOUZ

Skizze für eine Bildszene von Anton Corbjin.

Sketch by Anton Corbijn for a photo set.

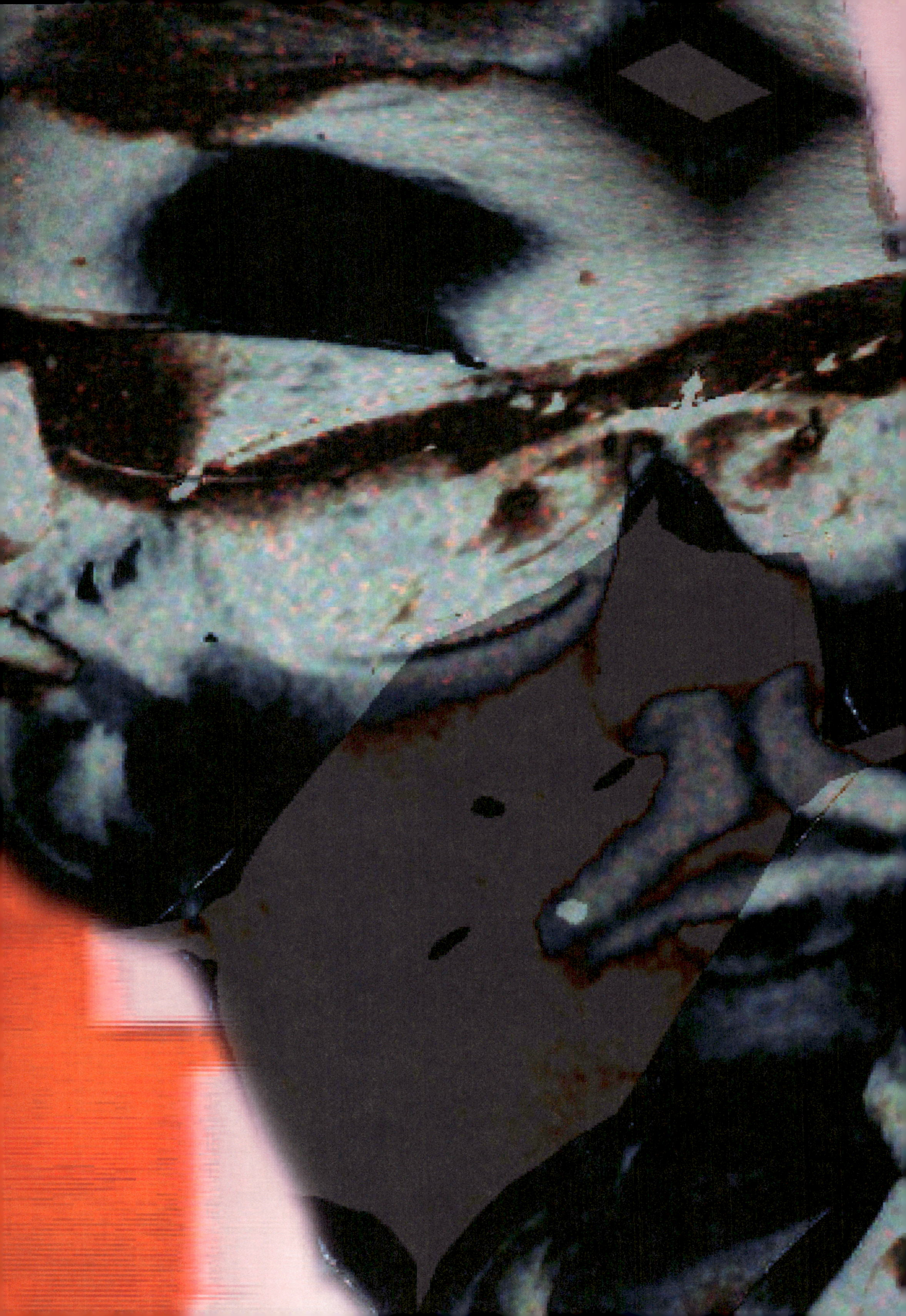

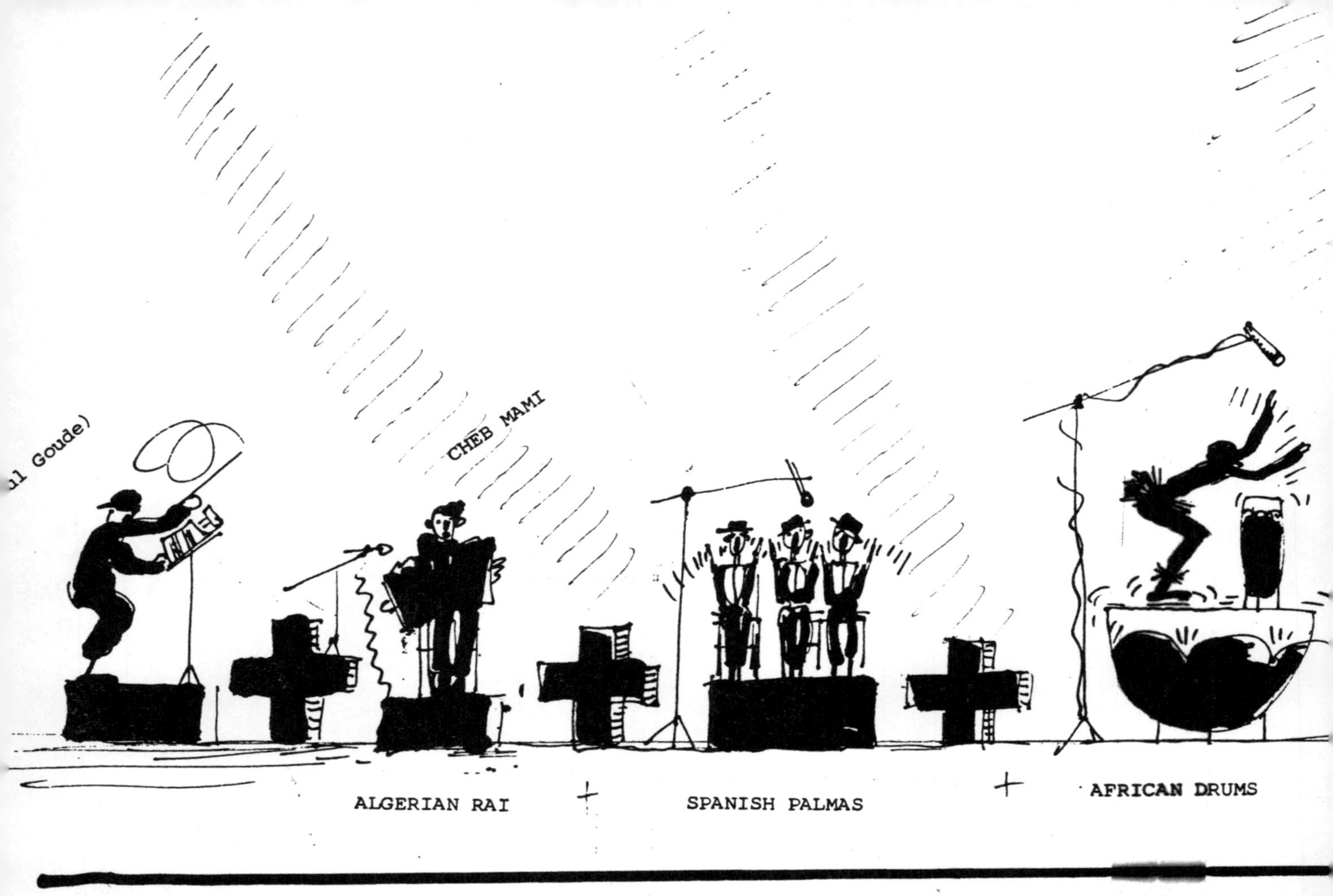

AS THE MUSICAL INTRODUCTION TO "
SLOWLY TRAVELS TO REVEAL, ONE B
MOVEMENT STOPS AS IT REACHES FA

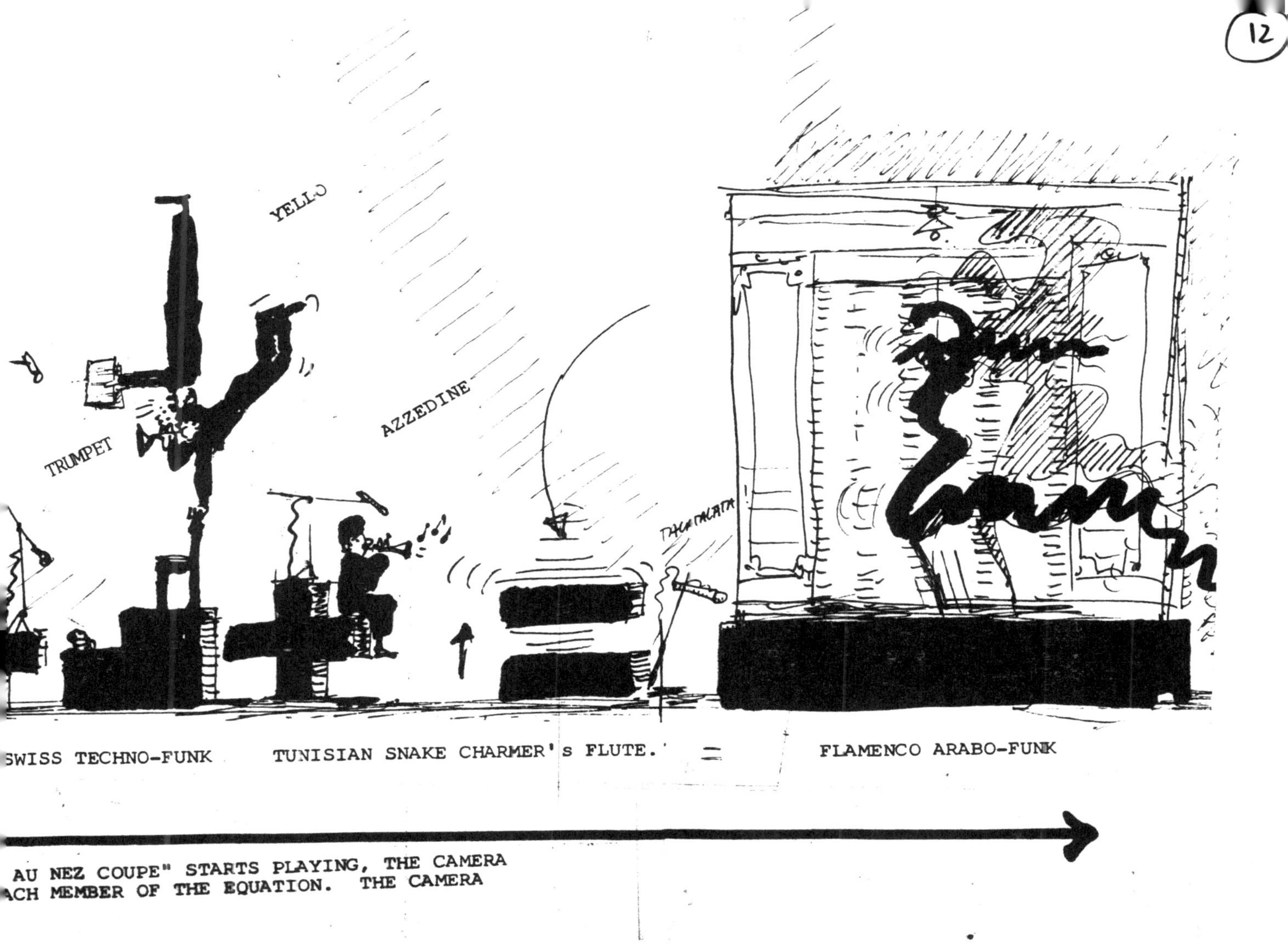

Storyboard von Jean-Paul Goude für ein Musical mit Yello, das leider nie realisiert wurde. Yello und Goude arbeiteten bei einigen Commercials zusammen.

Storyboard by Jean-Paul Goude for a Yello musical, which was unfortunately never made. Yello and Goude, however, did collaborate on several commercials

Boris Blank mit Contrabass.
Fotos: Christian Jungwirth.

Boris Blank with double bass.
Photos: Christian Jungwirth.

flugplan für Herren Dieter Meier und Boris Blank

1987

12.Okt.	ab Zuerich an New York (JFK)	12.30 Uhr 16.00 Uhr	SR 100 Boeing 747
Sitzplätze :	2J/2K Raucher/Gang u. Fenster		
	ab J.F.Kennedy Airp. an East 60 th Sreet	open	Helikopter
15.Okt.	ab East 60 th Street an J.F.Kennedy Airp.	open	Helikopter
16.Oct	ab New York (JFK) an Zürich	18.00 Uhr 06.35 Uhr	SR 101 Boeing 747
	ab Zürich an Hamburg	open	

Sie sind ausserdem fuer den 16.Oktober auf der SR 101 und auf der SR 111 (via Genf) von New York nach Zürich gebucht.(Warteliste)

Freigepäck : Piece Concept

Wir wünschen Ihnen einen angenehmen Flug und einen erfolgreichen Aufenthalt in New York.

Menzell Reisebüro

Sven Sturm

Hamburg,07.Okt.1987
ÄNDERUNGEN VORBEHALTEN

Promotrip-Flugplan Zürich – New York
(inklusive Helikopter-Flug nach Manhattan).

Schedule for promo trip from Zürich to New York, including helicopter ride to Manhattan.

Dieter Meier im Video *Call It Love*, 1987.
Foto: Daniel Boschung.

Dieter Meier in the Call It Love *music video, 1987. Photo: Daniel Boschung.*

Kapellmeister Borislav Blancovic in *Call It Love*.
Foto: Daniel Boschung.

Maestro Borislav Blancovic in Call It Love
Photo: Daniel Boschung.

Video *Call It Love*.
Foto: Daniel Boschung.

Call It Love *music video.*
Photo: Daniel Boschung.

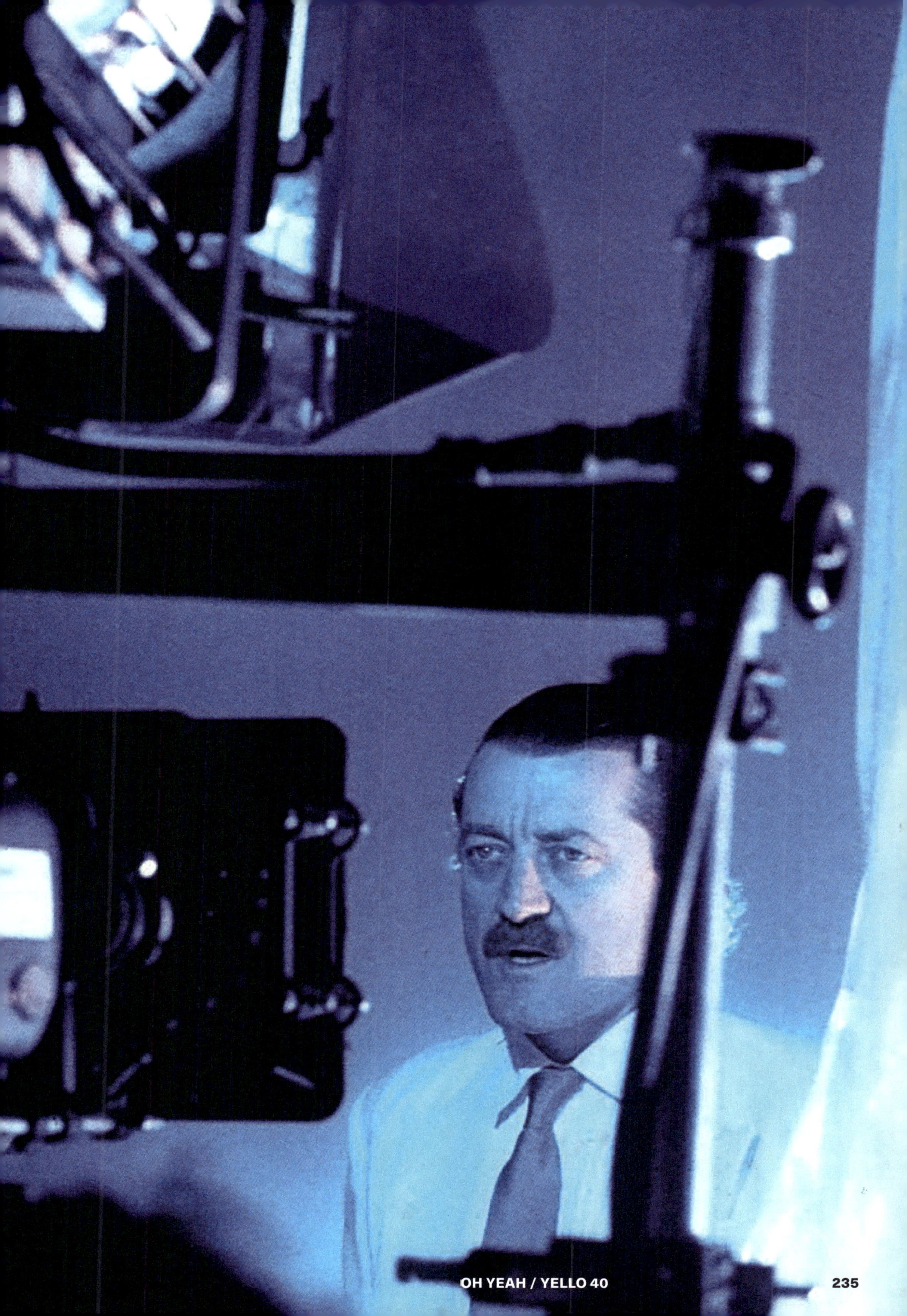

Restaurant français Cocktail Bar Terrasse
Tel. 01/251 70 10 Telex 816398 Telegramm: Rivehotel

HOTEL BELLERIVE AU LAC ZÜRICH

Fam. Simmen
Propriétaire
Utoquai 47
8008 Zürich

Lions member

IN RYTHMN DIVINE

YOU KNOW THAT THESE TEARS
HAVE KEPT ME AWAKE
THE LONGER YOUR GONE
I'LL HUNGER AND SHAKE
FROM WARSAW TO ROME
I WAIT OUT OF TIME
WITH YOU IN MY HEART
THE RYTHMN DIVINE.

SO WON'T YOU COME CLOSE
BRING THIS TO AN END
WITH EACH WINTER ROSE
MY LOVE I WILL SEND
SO TENDER THE NIGHT
WHEN YOU HOLD ME TIGHT
WITH YOU IN MY HEART
THE RYTHMN DIVINE

SAID WITH A DOUBLE SCOTCH
IN HAND.

↓

TALKING: YOU KNOW THAT THESE TEARS
HAVE BATHED ME IN BLUE
BUT I'LL LEAD MY LIFE
THE WAY I LOVE YOU
WITH YOUR HEART AND MINE
THE RYTHMN DIVINE.

YOU KNOW THAT THESE TEARS
HAVE KEPT ME AWAKE
THE LONGER YOUR GONE
I'LL HUNGER AND SHAKE
FROM WARSAW TO ROME
I WAIT OUT OF TIME
WITH YOU IN MY HEART
THE RYTHMN DIVINE THE RYTHMN DIVINE THE RYTHMN DIVINE

Billy Mackenzies handgeschriebener Songtext zu «The Rhythm Divine» im Hotel Bellerive Au Lac, 1987.

Billy Mackenzie's hand-written lyrics for 'The Rhythm Divine', Hotel Bellerive au Lac, 1987.

237–239

Fotosession im Hyde Park, London.
Fotos: Andrew Catlin.

Photo shoot in Hyde Park, London.
Photos: Andrew Catlin.

Shirley Bassey mit Prinz Hubertus von Hohenlohe im Yello-Studio, 1987.

Shirley Bassey with Prince Hubertus von Hohenlohe at the Yello Studio, 1987.

Die Verbindung mit Billy Mackenzie hatte Ian Tregoning angeregt. Als er die Musik von Yello hörte, packte ihn eine solche Begeisterung, dass er seine katastrophale Flugangst überwand und in den Flieger nach Zürich stieg. Boris Blank: «Billy Mackenzie hat mich emotional extrem berührt. Er war wahnsinnig schnell im Entwickeln von Ideen. Er konnte eine Melodie singen und gleich darauf mehrere Harmonien übereinander legen. Und er konnte sich gut in andere Musiker hineindenken. Für «The Rhythm Divine» hat er die Vorlage geliefert. Eingedacht in die Tonlage von Shirley Bassey hat er die Leadstimme eingesungen und einen Text geschrieben, der perfekt zu ihrer Ausstrahlung passte. Den Kontakt zu Shirley Bassey hatte Prinz Hubert von Hohenlohe hergestellt, nachdem er Yello für eine Sendung im österreichischen Fernsehen interviewt hatte. Als Bassey dann ins Yello-Studio kam, um den Song aufzunehmen, war Billy Mackenzie so nervös, dass er in den Wald spazieren ging. Bei seiner Rückkehr war alles schon fertig.» Bis zu seinem tragischen Tod arbeiteten Mackenzie und Yello immer wieder zusammen. Jedes Mal deckte Mackenzie Blank und Meier mit feinen Kleidern aus der Boutique seiner Familie in Dundee ein.

The connection with Billy Mackenzie from the Scottish band the Associates was set up by Ian Tregoning. Mackenzie was so bowled over by what he heard from Yello that he forced himself to overcome a catastrophic fear of flying and board a plane for Zürich. Boris Blank: 'Billy Mackenzie was a deeply emotional man, and his presence was inspirational. He was insanely fast at developing ideas. He could sing a melody and then immediately put several harmonies on top. He was also able to think in other voices, as it were. Providing the demo recording for 'The Rhythm Divine', he sang in the pitch of Shirley Bassey and wrote lyrics that perfectly complemented her style and charisma. The contact with Bassey had come through Prince Hubertus von Hohenlohe after he had interviewed Yello for Austrian television. When Bassey arrived in our studio to record the song, Billy Mackenzie was so nervous he went off for a walk in the nearby woods. By the time he returned, everything was done.' On and off, Mackenzie and Yello would work together until Mackenzie's tragic and untimely death in 1997. Whenever he arrived in Zürich, he brought with him a suitcase full of fine clothes for Boris and Dieter from his family's boutique in Dundee.

Recording-Session mit Shirley Bassey in Zürich, 1987, mit Hubertus von Hohenlohe und Billy Mackenzie, der die Guide-Melodie und den Text zu «The Rhythm Divine» schrieb. Foto: Felix von Muralt.

Recording session with Shirley Bassey in Zürich, 1987, with Hubertus von Hohenlohe and Billy Mackenzie, who wrote the guiding melody and the lyrics for 'The Rhythm Divine'. Photo: Felix von Muralt.

Fotos: Felix von Muralt. / *Photos: Felix von Muralt.*

Video-Dreh für *The Rhythm Divine*, 1987.
Foto: Christian Jungwirth.

The Rhythm Divine *music video shoot, 1987.
Photo: Christian Jungwirth.*

248–249

Foto-Shooting in München vor der TV-Sendung «Formel Eins», 1987. Foto: Christian Jungwirth.

Photo shoot in Munich before the recording of the TV show 'Formel Eins', 1987. Photo: Christian Jungwirth.

DATE 190687

SUBJECT

TECHNICAL DATA

© christian jungwirth
a-8010 graz, friedrichg. 6, T. 78774

Foto-Shooting auf der Quaibrücke in Zürich für *Elle*.
Fotos: Alberto Venzago, 1988.

Photo shoot for Elle *magazine on Zürich's Quai Bridge.*
Photos: Alberto Venzago, 1988.

Foto von der Parkgarage Bellevue,
mit dem Lincoln Continental Mark IV.
Foto: Alberto Venzago.

*Photo from the Bellevue underground car park,
with Boris's Lincoln Continental Mark IV.
Photo: Alberto Venzago.*

Dieter Meier im Billiard-Salon Schlauch
in der Zürcher Altstadt. Fotos: Alberto Venzago.

*Dieter Meier in the Schlauch pool hall
in Zürich's Old Town. Photos: Alberto Venzago.*

YELLO T i e d U p (Single & Video Version) 3:30

Kalué

Tied up, tied up

Shake it up
Beat on the beat
Shake it up
The bababumba beat

Stay out

Get together
Beat after beat
Congas calling
In the city heat
Kick the gong
Hit the bell
Shift your body
You're doing it well
Kick the gong
Beat up the beat
Back to hell
And to the city heat

It's the african queen
who got the summer night crown
It's the african queen
the hottest lady in town
It's the african queen
who keeps me on my feet
It's the african queen
the bababumba beat

Never ever call my name
All you need is love
Take my heart and hold me tight
Forever forever

Gulemo Dilemma
Gulemo Dilemma

Kick the gong
Beat up the beat
Back to hell
Into the city heat
Hit the bell
Roll down the street
Tie me up
The bababumba beat
Take the beat
Take the fight
Take me back into the ring tonight

255–256

Songtext «Tied Up».

Lyrics for 'Tied Up'.

Kalué Kalué

(guitar solo)

Keep it cool
Keep low your mind
Shift the beat
You're one of a kind
Kick the gong
Beat up the beat
Back to hell
Into the city heat
Hit the bell
Roll down the street
Tie me up the bababumba beat
Take the beat
Take the fight
Take me back into the ring tonight

It's the african queen
Who got the summer night crown
It's the african queen
The hottest lady in town
It's the african queen
Who keeps me on my feet
It's the african queen
The bababumabeat

Never ever call my name
All you need is love
Take my heart
And hold me tight
Forever   forever

(c) 1988 All rights reserved

257–262

Video-Stills *Tied Up*, 1989.

Stills from the Tied Up *music video, 1989.*

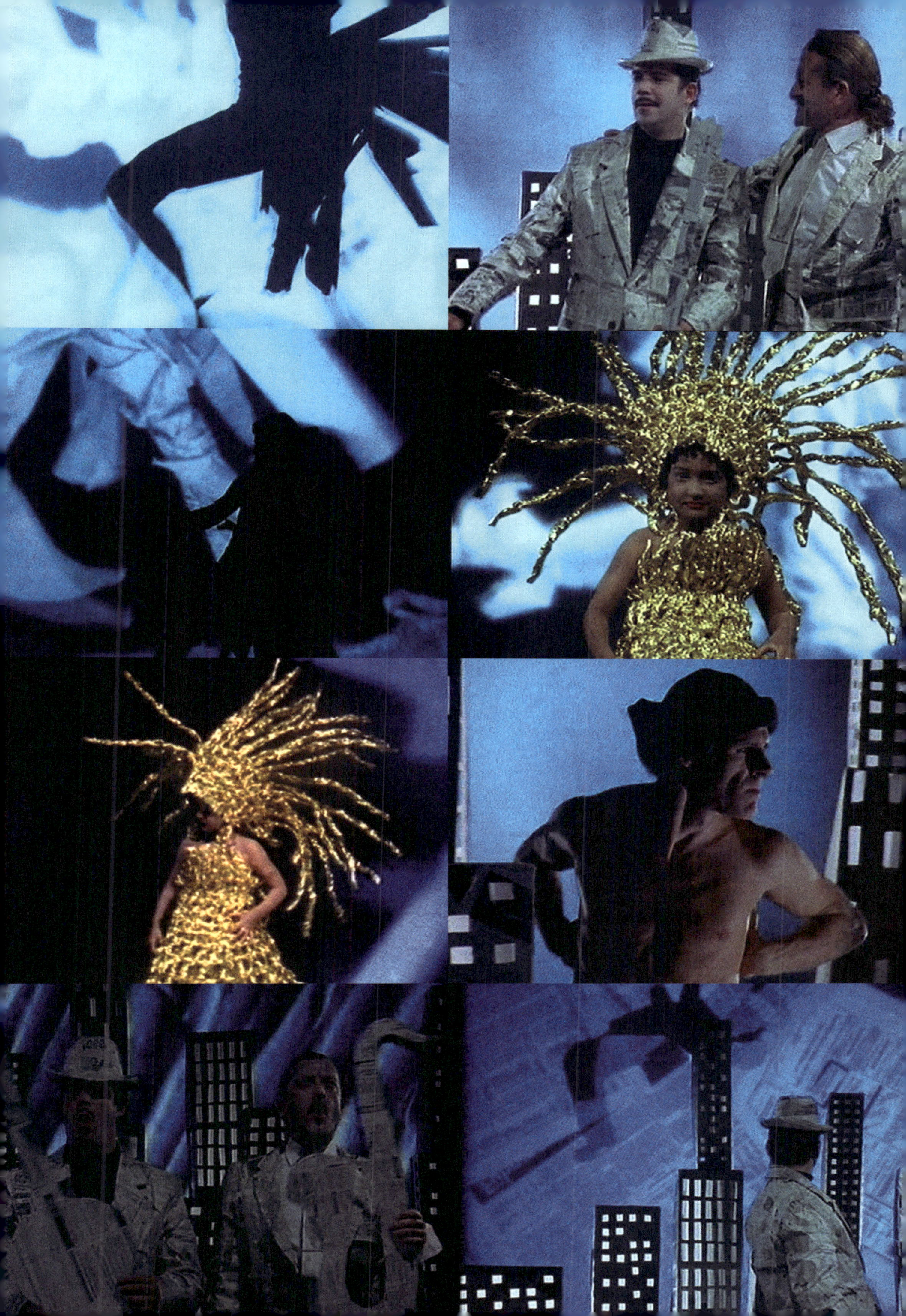

263–266

Text von «The Race».

Lyrics for 'The Race'.

YE L L O "THE RACE" Video-Version

1. Shout

2. Count on me, I'm gonna win the race
   Count on me, I'm gonna win the race

3. Rumbadibumtheriglingdum
   Rumbadibumtheriglingdum

4. Shut the door, keep down the stuff (leise)
   Shut the door, keep down the stuff (lauter)

5. Are you ever gonna push me
   Let me run or let me do
   I need it and I'm ready
   And I haven't got a clue

6. Any track is turning
   But the race is in my head
   I am chasing the illusion
   But the stopping drives me mad

7. Time is running out
   And the illusion fades away
   Time is running out
   Another day is on its way

8. On the fast lane of the street I'm driving
   Sometime, somewhere I'm arriving, every day and every night

9. Another day is ready
   Coming up to drive me mad
   Cos' I haven't got a notion
   Got a clue I need it bad

10. ~~(verhallt)~~ Gimmie a br

11. Another sun was shining
   And he knew he wasn't great
   He didn't have a target
   But he knew he coul[d]n't wait

12. Are you ever gonna push me
   Let me run or let me do
   I need it and I'm ready
   And I haven't got a clue

13. Any track is turning
   But the race is in my head
   I am chasing the illusion
   But the stopping drives me mad

14. (Speech) Ladies and Gentlemen, this [illegible] ly Mac [illegible]osky ....

Another day is ready fxxxhim

ready for him me   coming up to make me run

Ready for the guy who wants to wixx be

Cause I havent got a notion and this is that makes me

Is this my face is this the race

Another sun was shining

and he knew that he was great

He didn't have a target

but he knew he couldn't wait

Push Me

This is my face I am ready for the race

Are you ever gonna   ARE YOU EVER GONNA

They only got to take me   let me run and let me

andxIxwillxtellxthemxwhatxtoxdo   got to tell me what to do

I need it am strong I am ready and I haven't got a clue

Ixknowxtheyraceyxyxitxisxmyxfacex

gimme the space I want the race

Let me run   Ixamxthexone and let me sing give me a reason to begin

Another sun is shining

gimme a clue   Is thi the race Is t is my face

Who's ever gonna tell me whatxtoxdo blue is blue

need the speed

let me compete

But the race is in my head

Everything ~~Every~~ Any

~~Magick~~ track is turning ~~isxturning~~ ~~and is s peding~~ in my head

~~For runing~~ Heading without looking ~~evry~~ stop wuold make me sad

But

All in my

~~it's in~~ my head

fades away

Time is runing out and the illusion ~~shows it's end~~

and Braisn bend

One more day and one more night ~~tixes~~ in Bars is ~~whatxixspend~~ illusions

alone with dreams

the race is

Any track is turning but ~~from racing in~~ my head

I am atacking the illusion ~~evry stop would make me mad~~

~~Any stopping~~ drives me mad

BUT THE STOPPING DRIVES ME MAD

ANY STOP ~~SENT~~ ~~DRIVE ME MAD~~

DRIVING ME MAD

Any track is turning but the race is my head

I am atacking the illusion ~~an~~ but the stopping drives me mad

Another day is ready comin up to drive me mad

Cause I haven't got a notion got a clue I need it bad

Boris Blank traute seinen Augen nicht, als ihm Dieter Meier die Villa am Zürichberg zeigte, die er mit der Absicht erworben hatte, im Gartengeschoss ein neues Studio einzurichten. Er kannte das Haus gut. In einem vergangenen Leben hatte er als Fernsehmechaniker gejobbt und auf diesem Haus die Antenne montiert. Blank: «Ich konnte mich gut erinnern, wie ich auf dem Dach stand, auf den verwilderten Garten hinunterblickte und dachte: ‹Wie herrlich!› Ein älterer Chirurg wohnte dort, ein weltbekannter Ohrenspezialist. Manchmal musste ich vorbeigehen, um ihm die neue Fernbedienung zu erklären.» Das neue Studio hatte alles, was Blank brauchte: ein Mischpult mit 48 Kanälen, eine separate Kabine für Schlagzeug- und Gesangsaufnahmen sowie einem Panoramafenster, das auch im Regen offen bleiben konnte, denn es lag geschützt unter der Terrasse. Blank: «Ich könnte mir keinen schöneren Arbeitsort vorstellen. Man kann hier komplett in die eigene Welt eintauchen. Man hört nur die Vögel, und manchmal wandert ein Fuchs vorbei.»

Boris Blank couldn't believe his eyes when Dieter Meier showed him the villa he had bought high up in the hills above Zürich with the intention of setting up their studio on the ground floor. He knew the house well. In one of his past lives he had been a television technician, installing aerials all over Zürich. 'I remember standing on the roof of that very house and looking down on the garden, which had been left pretty much to its own devices, and thinking "How wonderful!" An elderly doctor lived there, a worldwide authority in ear surgery. He'd ask me round to explain the remote to him.' The new studio had everything Blank's heart desired, from a forty-eight-channel mixing desk to a separate recording booth for drums and vocals, as well as first-rate sound proofing. It also had a large front window, which – as it was hidden away under a terrace – could be left open even in the rain. 'I couldn't imagine a more beautiful place to work. You can totally immerse yourself in your world here, with only the birds for company and the odd fox or deer wandering past.'

Das Yello-Studio am Zürichberg.
Foto: Alberto Venzago.

*The Yello Studio on Zürichberg.
Photo: Alberto Venzago.*

268–273

Video-Stills von *The Race*, mit Patrizia Fontana, 1988.

Stills from The Race *music video, with Patrizia Fontana, 1988.*

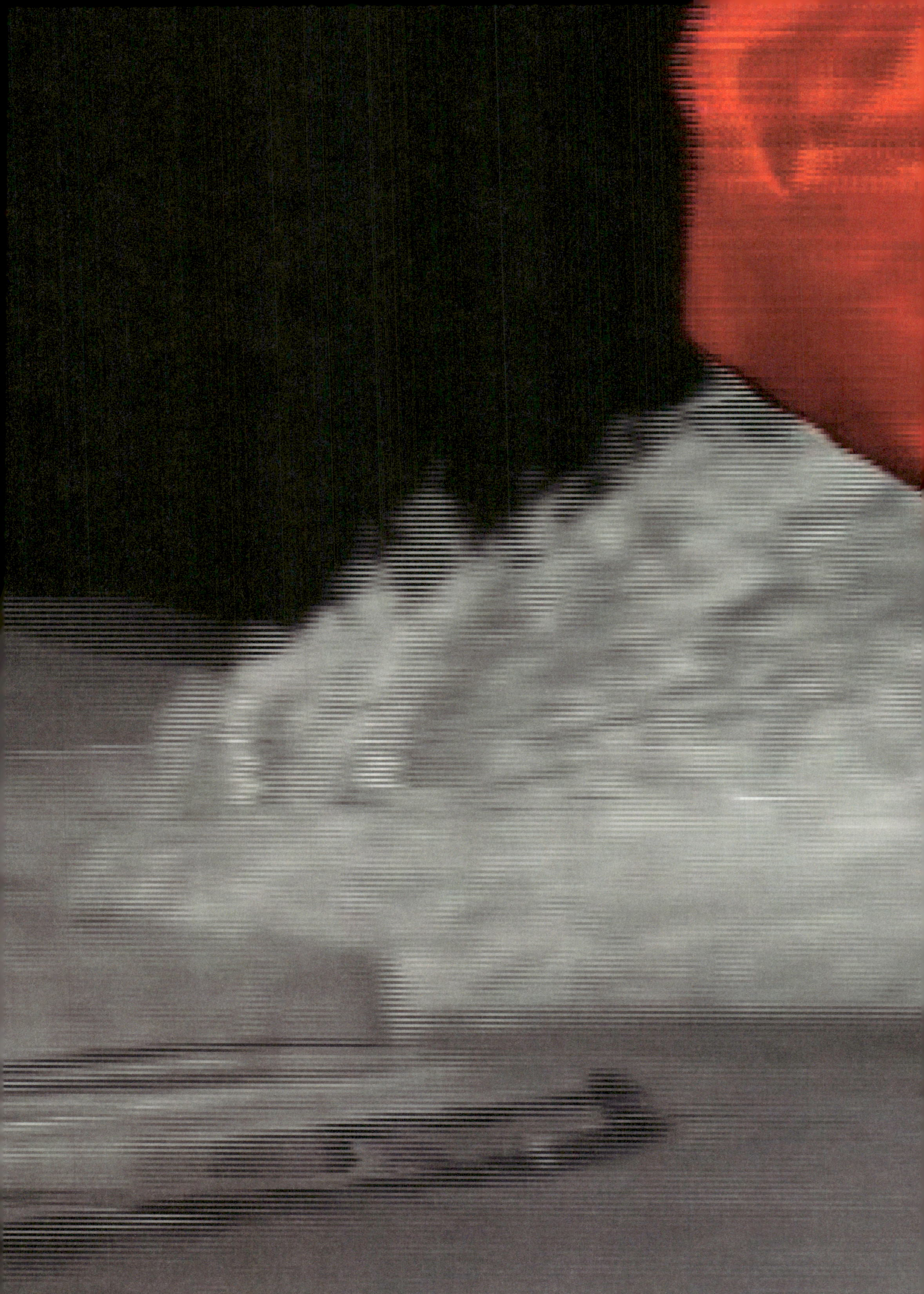

Original-Zeichnung für das Cover von *Flag* von Ernst Gamper.

Ernst Gamper's original drawing for the Flag *cover.*

Video-Stills aus *Blazing Saddles*, 1989.

Stills from the Blazing Saddles *music video, 1989.*

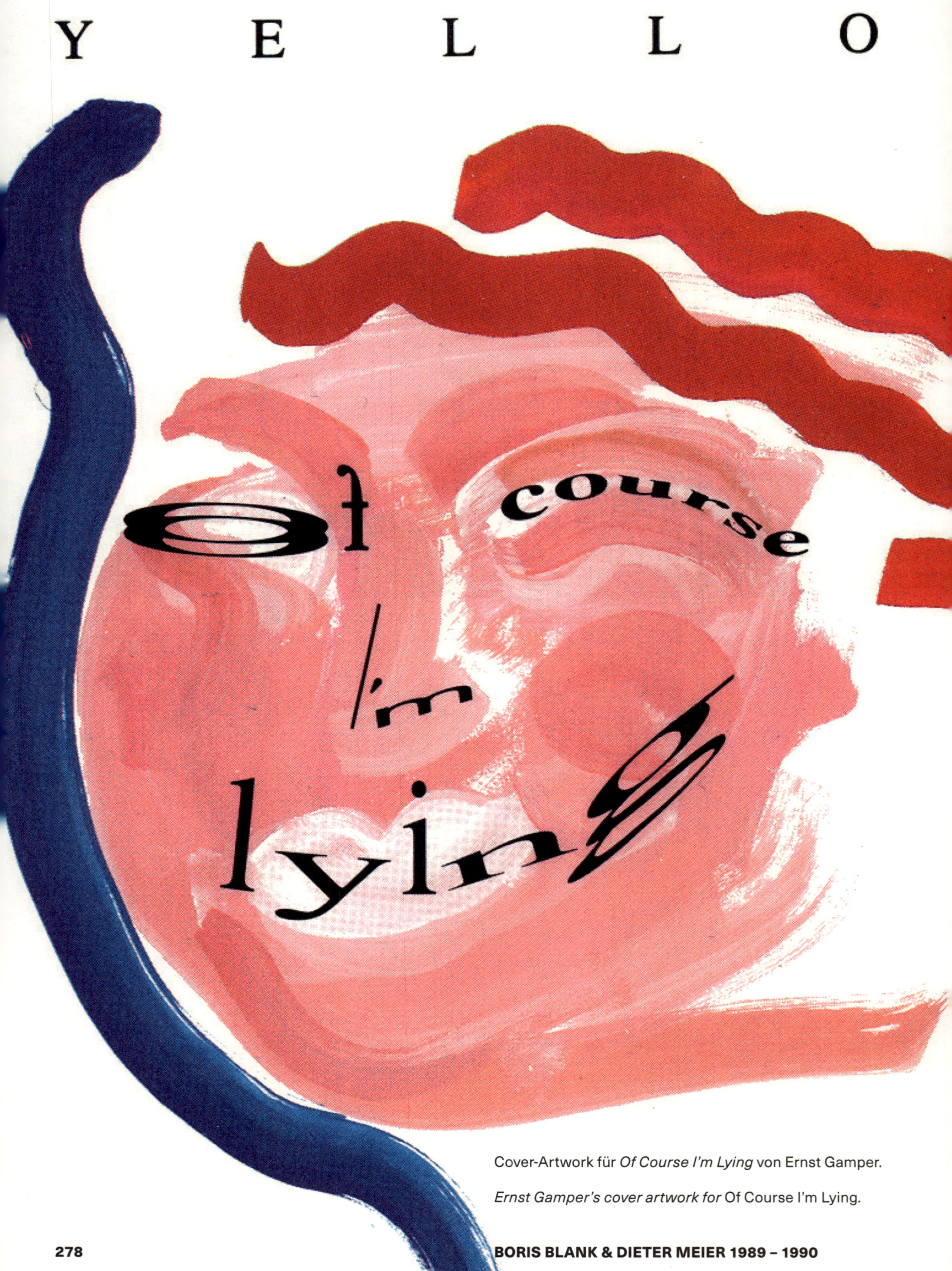

Cover-Artwork für *Of Course I'm Lying* von Ernst Gamper.

Ernst Gamper's cover artwork for Of Course I'm Lying.

Y E L L O

" O f   C o u r s e   I ' m   L y i n g "

(Music: Boris Blank / Lyrics: Dieter Meier)

Single- & Video-Version

Her name is Julie
When she took me on a ride in her old Chevrolet
Straight into a dusty sundown
And Julie, going to make up one of her stories
She couldn't believe it
When I told her how much I love her lies
And how much I love her games

Riding on the highway
We're going much too far
You're lying so much better
When you drive a car
You're lying into the sundown
Some look into my face
You're lying, I love it
You're lying, I love it
You're lying, I love it
You're lying

I love your games
I love your lies
I love your games
Look in my eyes
Take me in your arms and hold me tight just for tonight
I need no truth, I love your lies, you hide me from the night
Your lying, I'm buying, I'm buying every word
I love your lies, I love your games

Take me to the ballroom
We're dancing through the night
I'm in your arms, I love your lies
They make me feel so light
You're lying to the shadow
Some look into my face
You're lying, I love it
You're lying, I love it
You're lying

Telefax
An Christel Gautenbrink
Ref. Nr.
Von P. Vitzthum
Datum 5.4.93
Seiten 2
Post-it™ 7643/D

Songtext von «Of Course I'm Lying».

Lyrics for 'Of Course I'm Lying'.

(Yello, Of course..... / Continued)

Julie stopped her car
The sun had gone and left one of these dark red skies
She looked in my eyes
And with a smile in her face
She said: Of course I'm lying
But I think I love you

(2) Riding on the highway
We're going much too far
You're lying so much better
When you drive a car
You're lying into the sundown
Some look into my face
You're lying, I love it
You're lying, I love it

(X)

281–285

Video-Dreh für *Of Course I'm Lying*.
im verschneiten Arosa. Fotos: Christian Jungwirth.

Of Course I'm Lying *music video shoot in snow-covered Arosa. Photos: Christian Jungwirth.*

Z1300

Boris' Kawasaki Z1300.

Boris's gleaming Kawasaki Z1300.

ALPINA-

Fotosession auf einem Schrottplatz für die *Schweizer Illustrierte*. Fotos: Charles Seiler. Das Design der Anzüge stammt von Ines Boesch, die für Monique Meiers Mode-Label En Soie arbeitete.

Photo shoot in a scrapyard for Schweizer Illustrierte *magazine. Photos: Charles Seiler. The suits were designed by Ines Boesch for En Soie, Monique Meier's fashion label.*

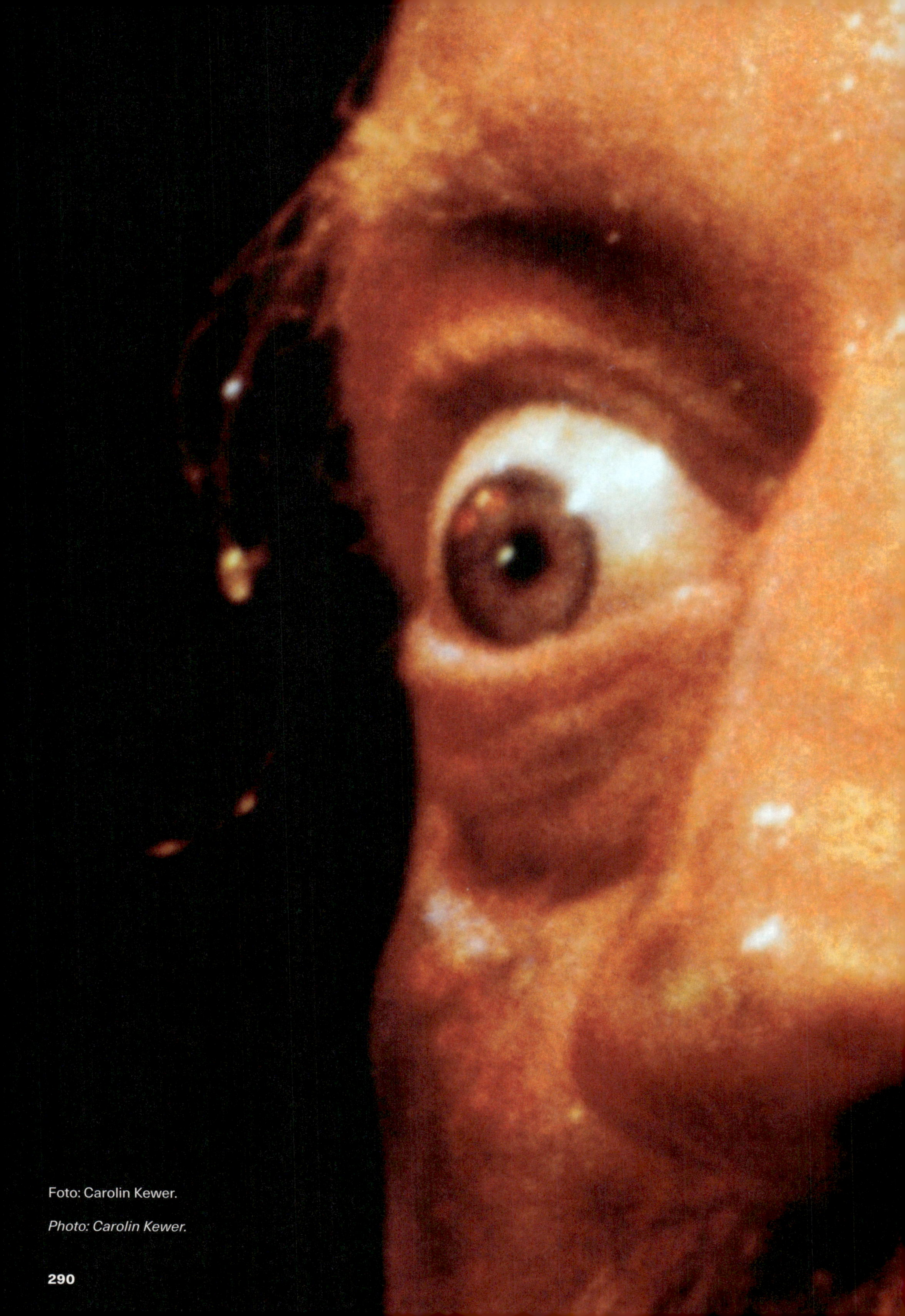

Foto: Carolin Kewer.

Photo: Carolin Kewer.

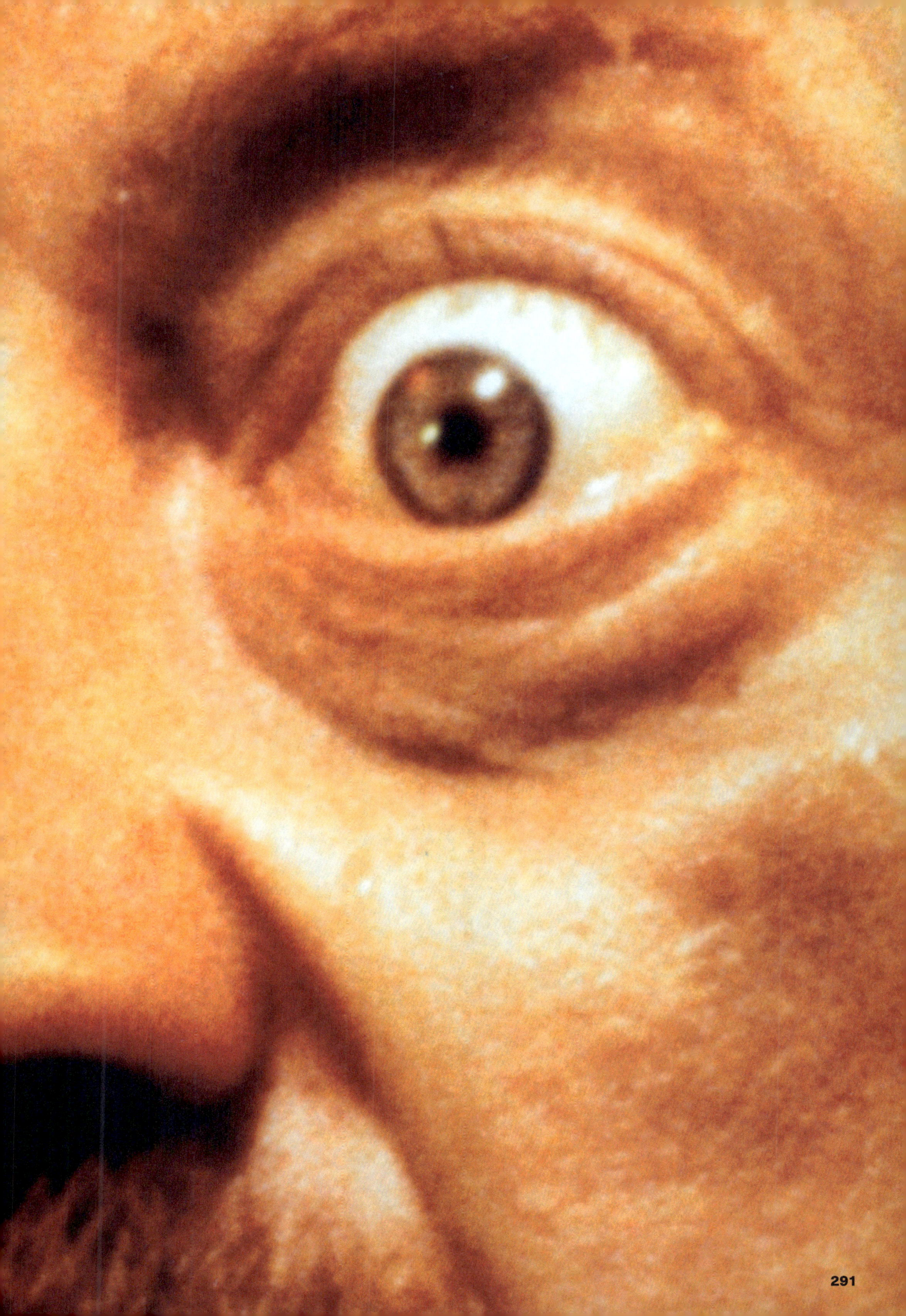

292–295

Video-Stills aus *Jungle Bill*, 1991.

Stills from Jungle Bill *music video, 1991.*

Boris Blank: «Wir probten für unseren Auftritt am Abend im Palais. Die grossen Leuchter brannten noch nicht, da zeigte Boris Nizon ins Dunkel und sagte: ‹Ist das nicht …› Tatsächlich, dort sass er, ganz allein an einem Tischchen. Ich ging zu ihm hin und sagte: ‹Hey, dein Gesicht kenn ich doch. Was machst du denn hier?› Er sagte: ‹I love Yello. «The Race» is my favourite song. I just wanted to see your rehearsal.› Unseren Award bekamen wir später von Ursula Andress überreicht. Das war ein feiner Tag für Klein-Boris!»

Boris Blank: 'We were rehearsing for our performance that evening at the Palais. The big chandeliers were not yet lit when Boris Nizon pointed into the darkness and said: "Isn't that…" Sure enough, there he was, sitting all alone at a little table. I went up to him and said, "Hey, I know your face. What are you doing here?" He said, "I love Yello. 'The Race' is my favourite song. I just wanted to see your rehearsal." Later on, our award was presented to us by Ursula Andress. A fine day all round for little Boris!'

Ringo Starr bei den Proben für den Yello-Auftritt bei den World Music Awards 1991 in Monte Carlo. Foto: Boris Nizon.

Ringo Starr at Yello's rehearsal for their performance in Monte Carlo at the World Music Awards 1991. Photo: Boris Nizon.

Hauptprobe: Boris schiesst auf Dieter, der das Projektil mit den Zähnen auffängt und wieder ausspuckt.

Dress rehearsal: Boris fires a shot at Dieter who catches the projectile in his teeth, and spits it out.

Zweiter Akt: Levitation mit Hula-Hoop-Ring. / *Act two: levitation with hula hoop.*

Boris Blank und Patrizia on the road.

Boris Blank and Patrizia on the road.

Boris und sein Ferrari 328 GTS, plus Dieter Meier von hinten.

Boris and his Ferrari 328 GTS, plus Dieter Meier from behind.

Foto-Shooting für *Bolero* im Zirkus Conelli in Zürich. Foto: Peter Gallina.

Photo shoot for Bolero *magazine at Circus Conelli in Zürich. Photo: Peter Gallina.*

Video-Dreh für *Do It*.

Video shoot for Do It.

Video-Dreh für *Do It*, mit Eleonore, Anna und Sophie Meier.

Video shoot for Do It, *with Eleonore, Anna and Sophie Meier.*

314–317

Video-Stills aus *Do It*.

Stills from the Do It *music video.*

DO IT

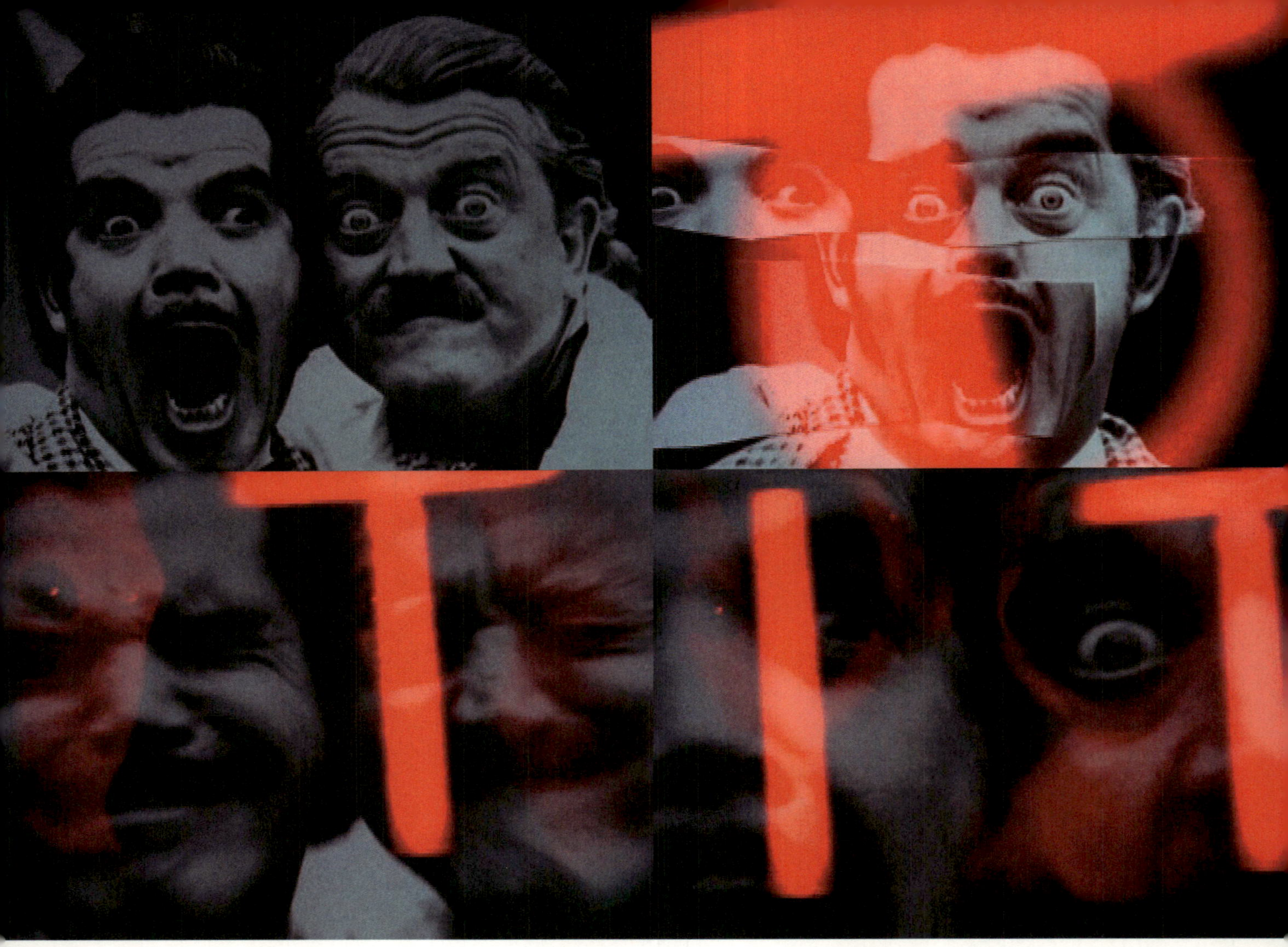

DO IT

Bilder für Video-Animationen.
Photos for the music video animations.

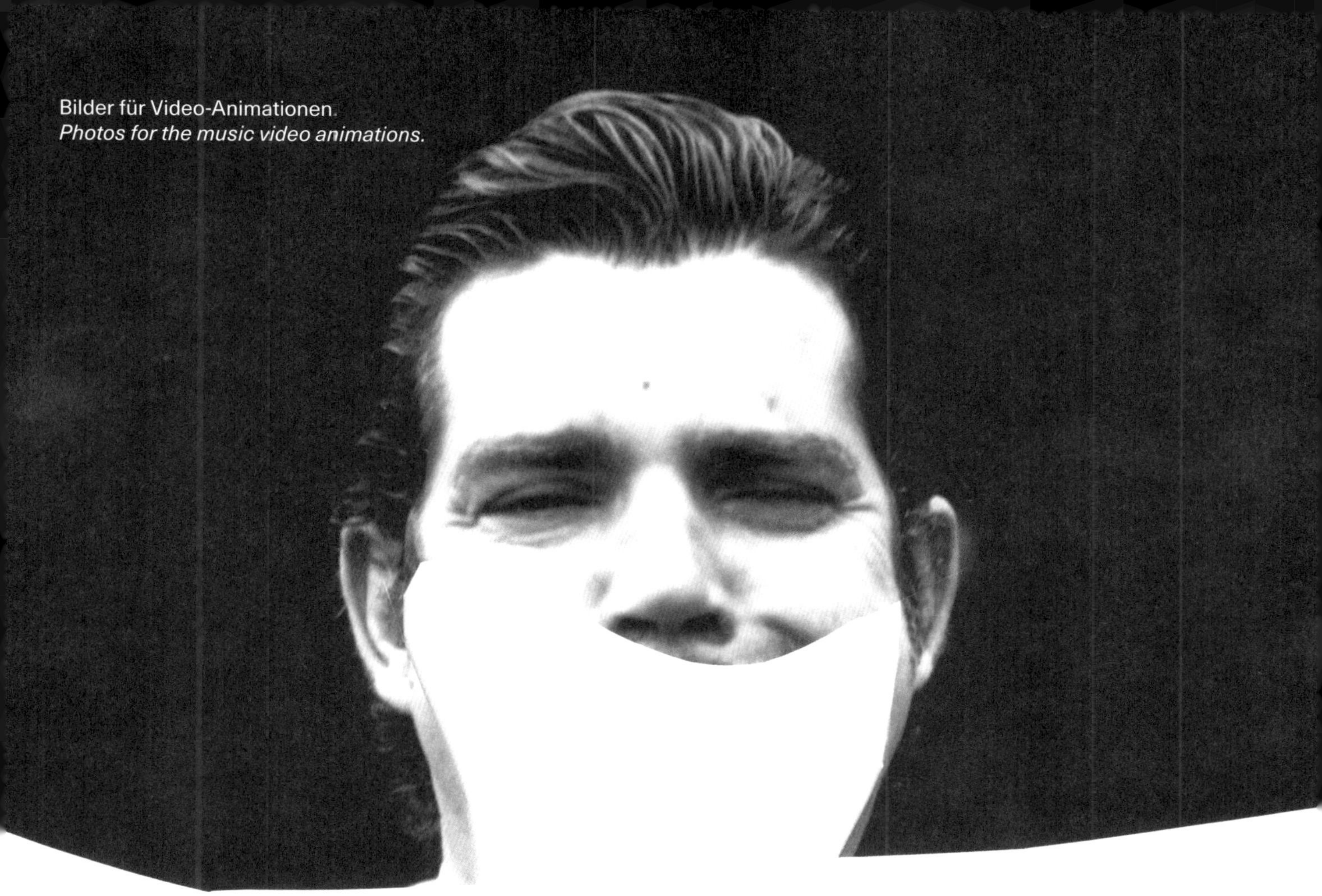

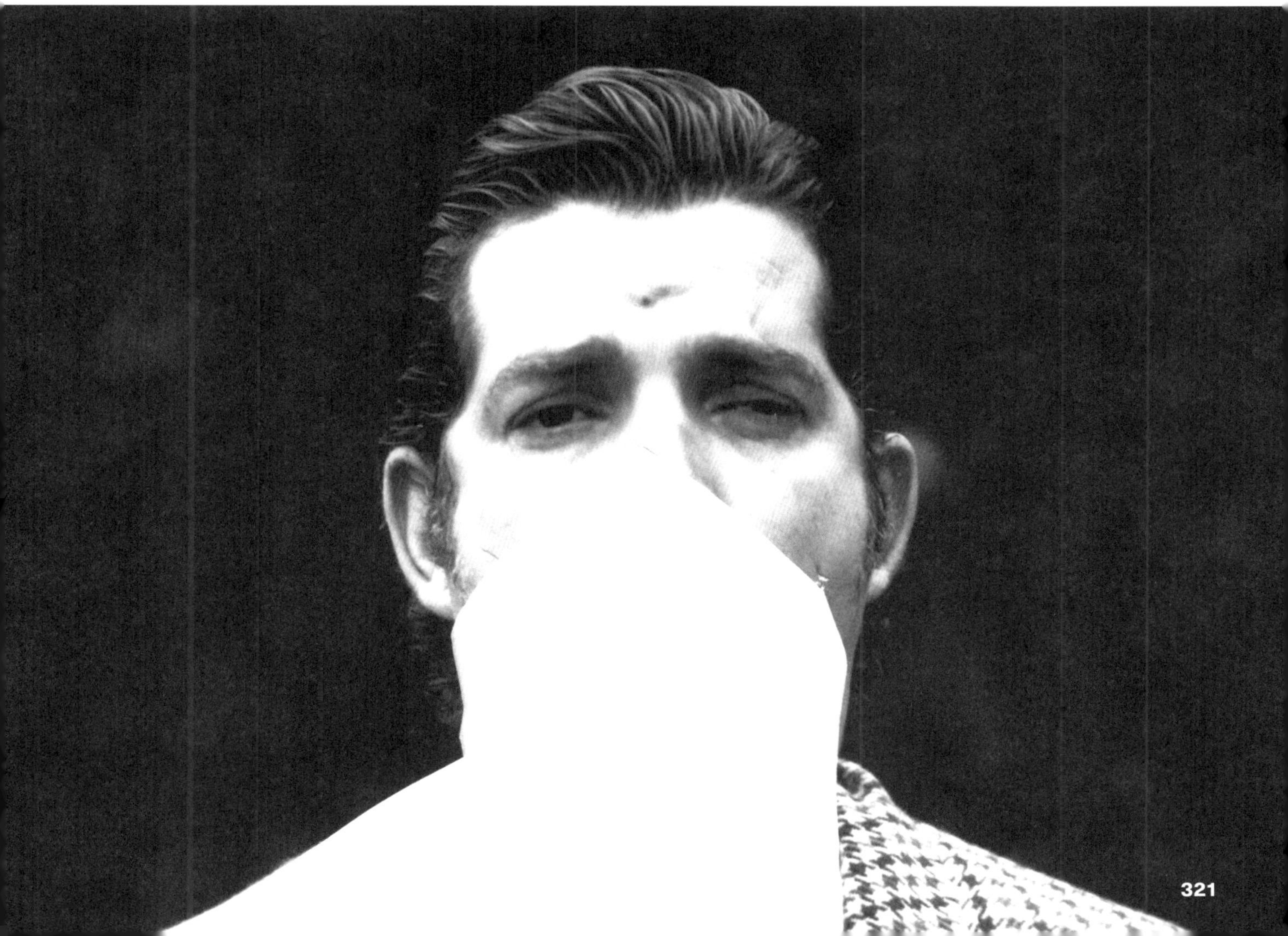

HOW HOW file: text50.wps
12" remix version YELLO 5:53, June 22, 1994

Man, woman, love, I'm bad
How How
How How

Man, woman, love, I'm bad

My life is in a serious mess
My baby's gone
A sentimental stress
I never knew love
But I know it now
I wanna give you my heart
But how how
How how

Man, woman, love, I'm mad
How How
How How
How How
How How

I'm in dry mental desert some miles behind
You're driving my heart, you're in command of my mind
I never knew love
But I know it now
I wanna give you my heart
But how how

Man, woman, love, I'm bad
Man, woman, love, I'm mad

Man, woman, love
Man, woman, love

I'm in a dry mental desert some miles behind
You're driving my heart, you're in command of my mind
I never knew love
But I know it now
I wanna give you my heart
But how how
How How

Man, woman, love, I'm bad
Man, woman, love, I'm mad

Man, woman, love
Man, woman, love

Songtext zu «How How».

Lyrics for 'How How'.

323–325

Video-Animationen für *How How* von Herbert Gupper.

Herbert Gupper's animations for the How How *music video.*

2 002
02 003
02 004
02 005
02 012
02 013
02 014
2 006
02 007
02 008
02 009
02 016
02 017
02 018
2 010
02 011
02 012
02 013
02 020
02 021
02 022
2 023
02 024
02 025
02 026
02 033
02 034
02 035
2 027
02 028
02 029
02 030
02 037
02 038
02 039
2 031
02 032
02 033
02 034
02 041
02 042
02 043

Comedy-Sketch für MTV London,
«Dr. Van Steiner: I Met Tarzan».
Video-Stills von MTV, «Most Wanted», 1994.

Comedy sketch for MTV London,
'Dr Van Steiner: I Met Tarzan'.
Stills from MTV, 'Most Wanted', 1994.

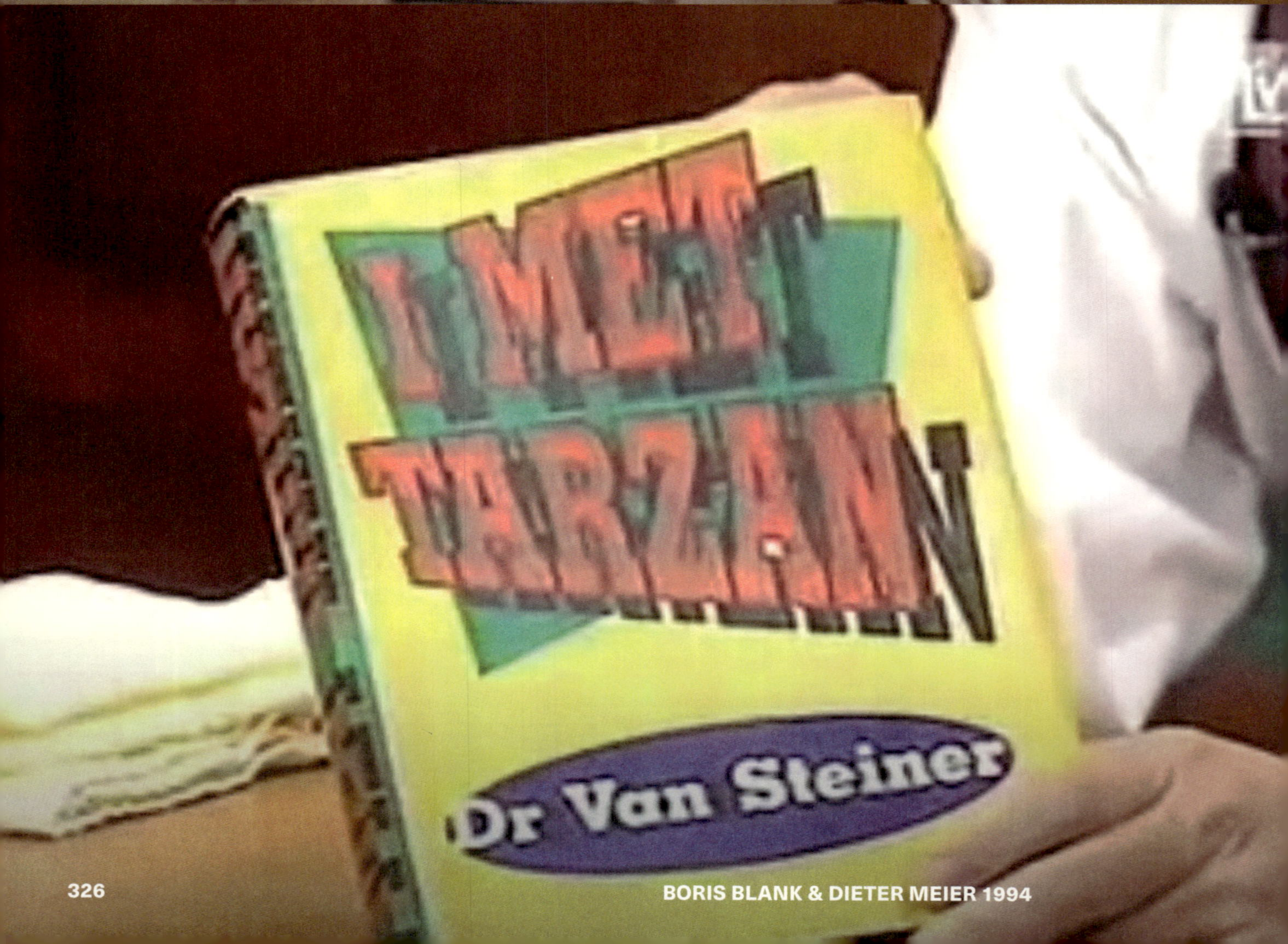

Dieter Meier Text für HANDS ON YELLO (Einleitung)

„Als Boris Blank in der Küche seiner Mutter den „Bumms“ des Faustschlags auf den Kühlschrank zur Tonbandschleife zusammenklebte, die seine erste Bass Drum wurde, wollte er keinen neuen Tanz erfinden, er hatte keine andere Wahl. Wenn dies der Urknall unserer Musik war und Yello heute zu den „godfathers“ zählen, dann war das nie so gedacht und freut uns aber umso mehr, dass die Grossmeister des Tanzkults ihre *Hands on Yello* legen.“

Dieter Meier, Yello

Engl. Version:

„The young Boris Blank recorded and edited a tape loop with the sound of a fist banging on a fridge in his mother`s kitchen. This was his first bass drum. He didn`t get out to create a new dance music but he had no other choice. If this was the Big Bang of our music and if Yello is now counted among ist Godfathers, it was never intended. However, we are even more pleased that the Grandmasters of the dance cults lay their *hands on Yello.*“

Dieter Meier, Yello

Album-Grafik *Hands on Yello* von K7.

K7's sleeve design for Hands on Yello.

Text von Dieter Meier für den Flyer zu *Hands on Yello.*

Dieter Meier's text for the Hands on Yello *flier.*

Yello live am Mayday, Dortmund, 1995.
Foto: Michael Herman.

Yello live at Mayday, Dortmund, 1995.
Photo: Michael Herman.

11.1.95

Neue Zürcher Zeitung

Techno-Gruss aus Berlin

Westbams «Bostich» als Vorgeschmack auf ein Remix-Album mit Yello-Stücken

ch. h. Man kann den Grad der Verehrung, den Pop- und Dance-Musiker(innen) geniessen, auch daran messen, wie oft deren Stücke «remixt» oder Schnipsel daraus als Samples zitiert werden: Remixes sind Interpretationen bestehender Vorlagen, und das Geflecht der gegenseitigen Bearbeitung von Songs und Tracks hat durchaus Ähnlichkeit mit einem disziplinären Diskurs. Dem Zürcher Duo Yello wird von vielen Techno-Produzenten nicht nur im Gespräch, sondern gerade auch mittels neuer Abmischungen seiner Stücke Reverenz erwiesen, was Yellos Pionierstatus in der Geschichte der elektronischen Musik belegt. *Derrick May* zum Beispiel, einer der Miterfinder des Detroit-Techno, hat um 1990 «The Race» gemixt, und auch *Andrew Weatherall,* ein gefragter Remixer, hat sich schon an Yello versucht. – Und nächstens erscheint unter dem Titel *«Hands on Yello»* ein Album, welches ausschliesslich aus Neuversionen «klassischer» Yello-Songs besteht, geliefert von so illustren Techno-Produzenten wie *The Orb, Cosmic Baby, Carl Craig.*

Ein Stück aus diesem Album ist bereits heute greifbar. Der Berliner Techno-König *Westbam* hat tief in seiner Plattensammlung gegraben und Hand an «Bostich» (1980) gelegt, also an die zweite Single Yellos überhaupt und den ersten echten Hit. «Bostich» ist ein aus heutiger Sicht gemächliches Disco-Rap-Stück, dessen Struktur und Charakter schon diejenigen Elemente enthält, die sich im Verlauf der achtziger Jahre in weiten Bereichen der populären Musik dann auch durchgesetzt haben: Es ist rhythmusbetont, es ersetzt den Gesang durch Rap und die Melodie durch Synthesizer-Klänge.

Was macht nun Westbam – wie Yello ein alter Hase im Dance-Geschäft – mit dieser 15 Jahre alten Vorlage? Er übernimmt vom Original den Anfang mit dem schleifenden Snare-Wirbel und Teilen der Synthi-Klänge, blendet dann die Bassspur ein und unterlegt eine tiefe und satte Bassdrum, um dem Stück die heute übliche Härte zu geben. Darüber streicht er ein gurgelndes Synthesizer-Thema, das sich aus der Basslinie herauslöst und immer höher über die Unterlage erhebt und so das Stück über zehn Jahre Musikgeschichte mitnimmt in die Ära des Acid House und des Techno, wie er sich zu Beginn der neunziger Jahre angehört hat, spannt den Bogen dann wieder zurück in die Achtziger, indem er das zentrale Rap-Thema von «Bostich» einblendet, welches nun als menschliche Stimme mit dem Synthesizer-Thema in einen Dialog tritt und um die Wette spuckt und speit (denn um einiges schneller als das Original ist der Techno-Mix des Westbam natürlich allemal). Zur konstruktiven Auseinandersetzung zwischen diesen frühen Versuchen elektronischer Dance-Musik und dem Techno-Pop von heute kommt es aber nicht. Westbams Remix ist sein Baustein zum Yello-Denkmal, mehr nicht.

Westbam's hands on Yello: Bostich. Urban/Polygram.

Notizen

Westbam präsentiert seinen Remix von «Bostich», *Neue Zürcher Zeitung*, 11. Januar 1995.

Westbam presents his remix of 'Bostich', Neue Zürcher Zeitung, *11 January 1995.*

Carl Craig im Yello-Studio, 1995.
Foto: Serge Höltschi.

*Carl Craig at the Yello Studio, 1995.
Photo: Serge Höltschi.*

Patrizia und Boris Blank treffen den Dalai Lama in Savoyen, Frankreich.

Boris Blank: «Freunde von uns kannten Loten, ein grosser Yello-Fan und früherer Bodyguard des Dalai Lama. Loten war sehr darauf bedacht, dass wir den Dalai Lama kennenlernen und ihm ein paar CDs überreichen sollten. Tatsächlich wurden wir dann ins Savoyische eingeladen, wo der Dalai Lama eine Art Auftritt hatte. Man hat uns in ein kleines Vorzelt geführt, wo wir auf ihn warten sollten. 5000 Menschen sassen im Publikum. Ihre Aufregung haben wir durch die Zeltplachen hindurch gespürt. Dann sind die Bodyguards eingetroffen und endlich auch der Dalai Lama selber. Ich konnte mich des Gefühls nicht erwehren, dass dieser Mensch eine ganz besondere Ausstrahlungskraft hatte. ‹Your Holiness, I have some music for you›, sagte ich. Er hat uns angelacht und sich sehr herzlich bedankt und uns diese Schals umgelegt. Es war wirklich ein wunderbares Erlebnis.»

Fotos: Loten.

Patrizia and Boris Blank meet the Dalai Lama in Savoy, France.

Boris Blank: 'We had friends who knew Loten, a former bodyguard of the Dalai Lama and a big Yello fan. Loten was very keen for us to meet the Dalai Lama personally and present him with some CDs. An invitation duly arrived for a public appearance of the Dalai Lama in Savoy. We were taken to this small tent to wait for him. In the main tent, 5,000 people were also waiting. We could feel their excitement through the canvas.
In due course, the bodyguards arrived and finally the Dalai Lama himself. I could not help feeling that this person had a very special aura. "Your Holiness, I have some music for you," I said. He smiled at us, thanked us very warmly and carefully placed these shawls around our shoulders. It was a really wonderful experience.'

Photos: Loten.

339

Der Stadtpräsident von Zürich teilt mit, dass Yello den Kunstpreis der Stadt Zürich im Jahr 1997 erhalten wird.

The mayor of Zürich announces that Yello will be awarded the Kunstpreis der Stadt Zürich for the year 1997 (the most important award for the arts handed out by the City of Zürich).

DER STADTPRÄSIDENT VON ZÜRICH
Stadthaus
Stadthausquai 17, 8022 Zürich
Telefon 01/216 31 20
Telefax 01/212 08 58

<Yello>
Herrn Boris Blank
Herrn Dieter Meier
Zürich

Zürich, 22. November 1996

Kunstpreis der Stadt Zürich an <Yello>

Sehr geehrter Herr Blank
Sehr geehrter Herr Meier

Ich freue mich, Ihnen mitzuteilen, dass der Stadtrat von Zürich auf Antrag der Popkredit-Kommission beschlossen hat, <Yello> den Kunstpreis der Stadt Zürich zu verleihen.

Mit diesem Preis, der mit Fr. 40'000.-- dotiert ist, möchten wir Ihr bisheriges musikalisches Gesamtwerk auszeichnen. Der kometenhafte Aufstieg von <Yello> zur Kultband, die den wichtigsten Schweizer Beitrag zur Popmusik liefert, hat bereits vor vielen Jahren begonnen. Überzeugen und begeistern konnte diese Musik von Anfang an, weil sie nicht kopflastig ist, sondern auch in die Beine fährt und das Publikum tanzen lässt.

Die Übergabe des Preises soll im Rahmen einer Feier stattfinden, deren Zeitpunkt wir mit Ihnen noch abstimmen möchten. Um die Einzelheiten dieses Anlasses zu besprechen, wird sich meine Mitarbeiterin Susanna Tanner demnächst mit Ihnen in Verbindung setzen.

Inzwischen möchte ich Ihnen herzlich zu dieser Auszeichnung gratulieren und hoffe, dass sie Ihnen Ansporn sei zu vielen weiteren attraktiven Kompositionen.

Mit freundlichen Grüssen

Josef Estermann

Der Kunstpreis ist im pulsierenden Leben gelandet: Dieter Meier und Boris Blank. BILD BEAT MART

Alchimisten im Olymp

Mit dem Kunstpreis will das Popduo Yello Musikschüler unterstützen

Nach Millionen verkauften Schallplatten haben Yello den Kunstpreis der Stadt Zürich erhalten – und geben die Preissumme gleich weiter.

VON BERNHARD SUTTER

Mittwochabend, 20.30 Uhr, der grosse Moment: Im Theaterhaus Gessnerallee übergibt Stadtpräsident Josef Estermann den Preis – in Form zweier unscheinbarer Umschläge – an Dieter Meier (52) und Boris Blank (44).

430 Freunde und Gäste auf der Tribüne werden sich bewusst, was sie eben beiwohnten: der endgültigen Aufnahme eines einstigen Enfant terrible der Kunstszene und eines eigenwilligen Klangtüftlers in den Zürcher Kunstolymp.

Applaus. Yello-Klänge. Videobeam. Die Verleihung Zürichs höchster kultureller Auszeichnung ist eine Performance. So schön wie einer der seltenen Yello-Auftritte. Und sie ist ein Brückenschlag.

Bis 1990 ehrte Zürich nur die «schönen Künste». Dann folgte ein Sinneswandel. Nun geht der Preis erstmals in die Popmusik. Wie formuliert der Stadtpräsident? Yello hätten eine Brücke von Avantgarde zu Pop geschlagen, nun benutze der Kunstpreis die Brücke, um Vorurteile abzubauen und Lust am anderen zu wecken.

Dann kommt, was Yello letzten Dezember im TA angekündigt haben: Sie spenden die 40 000-Franken-Preissumme hälftig an Schulkinder, die sich sonst keinen Musikunterricht leisten könnten, und an eine Stiftung für Behinderte. Dieter Meier erklärt, dies stehe einer Gruppe mit so hohen Plattenverkäufen wohl an.

Das Publikum quittiert die Geste mit kräftigem Beifall. Am Buffet oder bei Yello-Videoclips ist Gelegenheit, Claude Nobs' Laudatio Revue passieren zu lassen. Zum Auftakt der Feier hat der Vater des Montreux-Jazz-Festivals die Väter des Techno als Klangalchimisten geehrt. Meier und Blank zupften sich dabei gerührt am Schnauz.

Eines wird an diesem Abend deutlich: Mit ihrem Sound haben die beiden Zürcher der modernen Tanzmusik den Weg bereitet. Nun hat diese Kultur auch in Zürich offiziell Eingang in die Kunst gefunden. Oder ist es umgekehrt? Ist der Kunstpreis, wie der Stadtpräsident sagt, im pulsierenden Leben gelandet?

Der *Tages-Anzeiger* berichtet über die Preisverleihung, 19. Juli 1997.

The Tages-Anzeiger *newspaper's report from the award ceremony, 19 July 1997.*

Dieter und Boris gemorphed. Foto: Andrew EN.

Dieter and Boris morphed. Photo: Andrew EN.

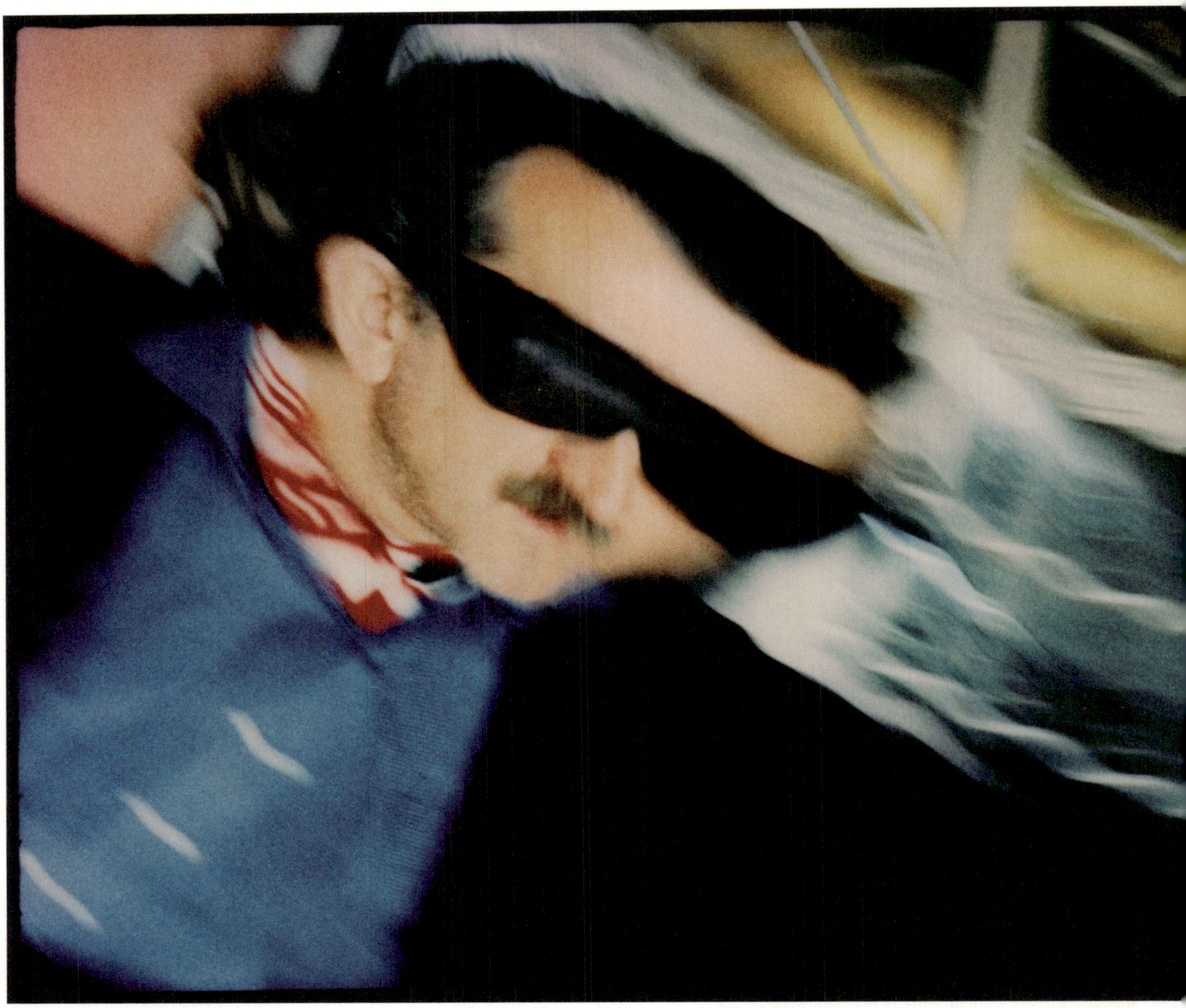

Dieter und Boris als Wellenreiter.
Foto: Andrew EN, 1997.

Dieter and Boris riding the wave.
Photo: Andrew EN, 1997.

Foto: Philip Lethen.

Photo: Philip Lethen.

Yello-Logo: Design von LWS Kaarst.

Yello logo: design by LWS Kaarst.

RHP 220
FUJI RHP

Foto: Philip Lethen. / *Photo: Philip Lethen.*

Yello-Signet von Weissraum, 1996.

Yello icon: design by Weissraum, 1996.

Foto: Peter Gallina.

Photo: Peter Gallina.

352–355

Video-Stills von *On Track*, Premiere Multimediaschau im Planetarium München, 1997.

Stills from the On Track *music video, premiered at a multimedia show at the Munich Planetarium, 1997.*

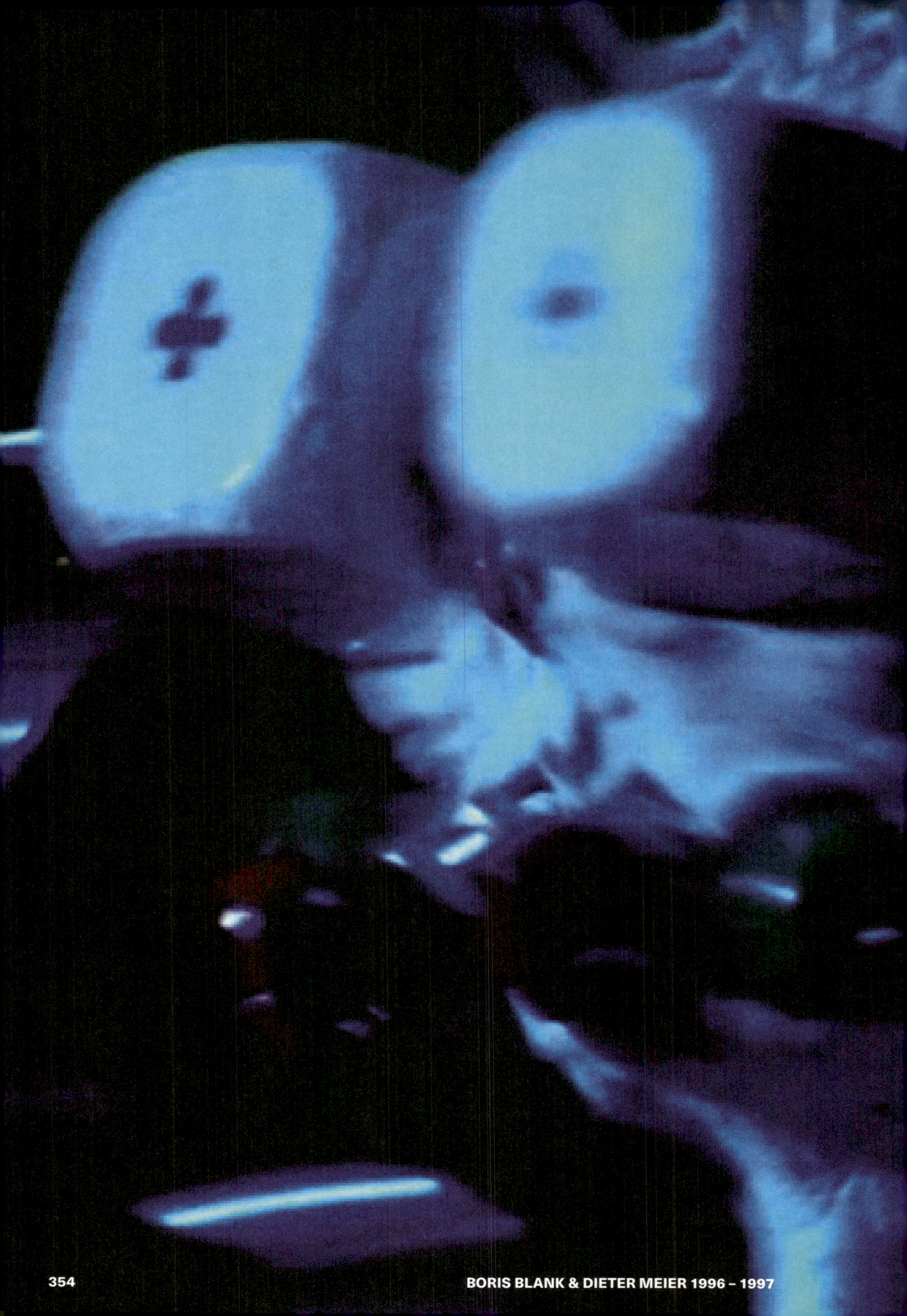

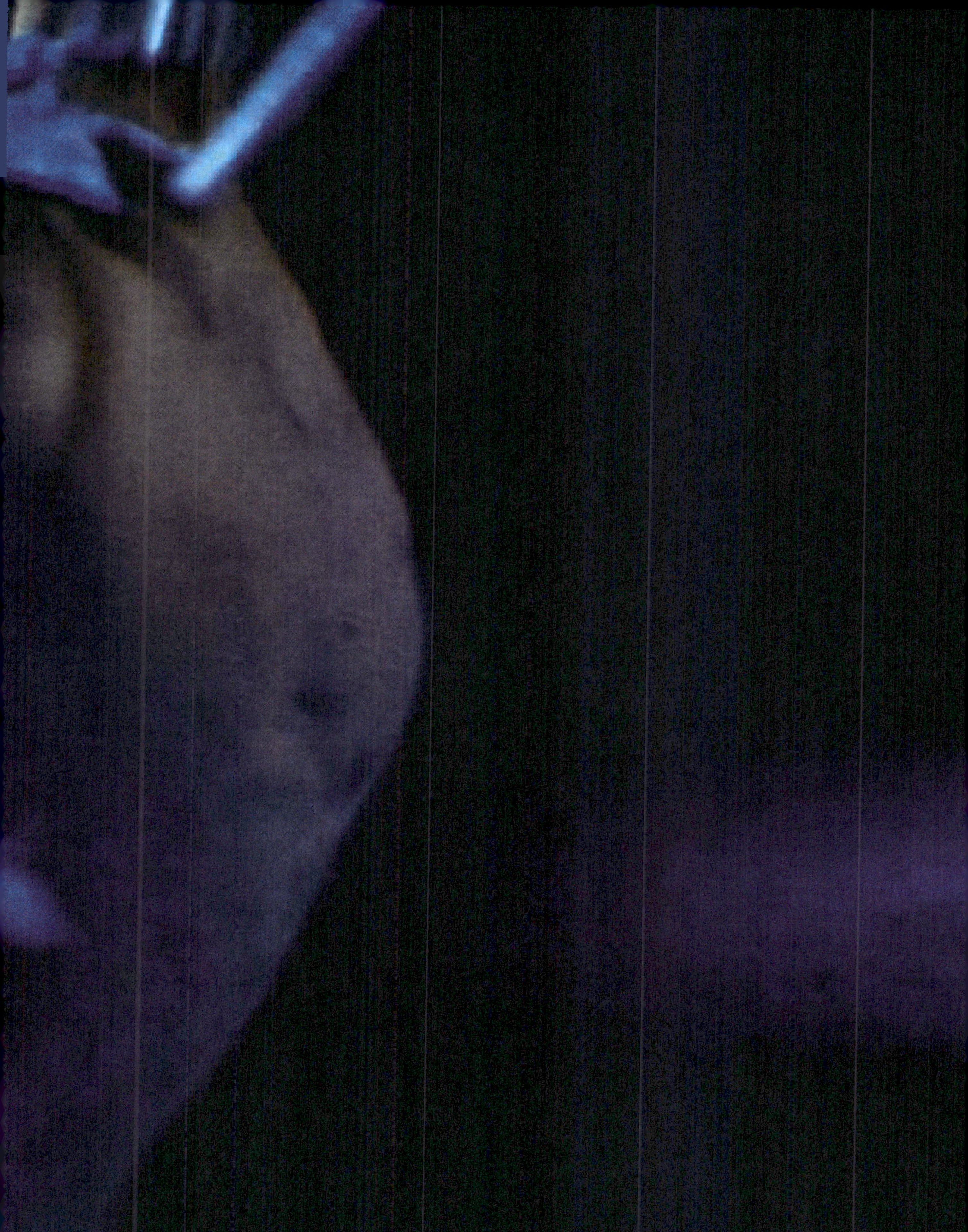

Video *Gizmo* von Martin Wanner,
der auch alle Yello-Cover seit 1997 gestaltet hat.

Gizmo *music video by Martin Wanner – also since 1997 the designer of all Yello's sleeves.*

Carl Cox mit Boris Blank.
Foto: Serge Höltschi.

Carl Cox and Boris Blank.
Photo: Serge Höltschi.

Handgeschriebener Text zu
«To The Sea» von Stina Nordenstam.

Stina Nordenstam's handwritten
lyrics for 'To The Sea'.

(PROPHET)

Take me to the sea

You may have many problems
but I was never one
all I ask is take me to the sea

It had to take me somewhere
I realize that now
Listen now, you take me to the sea

Away from flickering eyes and crowded streets
away from blinding lights and shining needs
away from loosing height and breathing hard
away from always being on your guard

VOW This will be my way out
and you will be my guide
Don't argue, take me to the sea

I'll only ask you this once
Just take me for a ride
All I ask is Take me to the sea

Then leave me with the seagulls
Smile your sweetest smile
I'll kiss you like the salty northern breeze

Drop silver on your forhead
and wave my last goodbye
All you do is take me to the sea

To the sea
to the sea

(cm)

FINE

358–361

Video-Stills aus *To The Sea*.
Regie: Paul Morgans, 1997.

Boris Blank: «Dieses Shooting war faszinierend. Die Idee – Turmspringer, die sich von den Wolkenkratzern herunter in die Häuserschluchten von New York stürzen – kam vom Regisseur. An einem Abend sind wir in London in ein riesiges Hallenbad gegangen. Dort gab es einen Zehn-Meter-Sprungturm, und an den Wänden rundum hing wie ein Vorhang eine Blue Screen. Die Taucher gehörten alle zum britischen Olympia-Team. Die hatten unglaublich Spass an der Sache. Haben sich richtig gefreut, für einmal einfach springen zu dürfen, ohne an die technische Perfektion denken zu müssen. Es ist einem halb schlecht geworden beim Zusehen, so verwegen gingen sie ans Werk. Dieter und ich mussten dann auch noch ins Wasser. In den Kleidern. Bald merkte ich, dass es nicht mal so ohne ist, mit Anzug, Hemd und Schuhen in einen Pool zu springen und sich zu bewegen zu versuchen. Ich bin ein guter Schwimmer, habe 35 Jahre lang jeden Tag einen Kilometer gemacht. Aber in den Kleidern, das zieht dich ganz schön hinunter!»

Stills from the To The Sea *music video, directed by Paul Morgans, 1997.*

Boris Blank: 'This was a truly fascinating video shoot. The idea – divers plunging from New York skyscrapers into the urban canyons below – came from the director, Paul Morgans. One evening we were taken to a huge indoor swimming pool in London. There was a 10-metre platform and a blue screen on the walls around it like a curtain. The divers were all members of the British Olympic team. Happy to be able to dive without thinking about technical perfection, they had a lot of fun doing it. Their stunts were hair-raising. It made you feel sick just watching. Dieter and I were required to go in the water, too – fully clothed. I realised very quickly that it's not so easy to jump into a pool wearing a suit, shirt and shoes, and then try to swim. I'm a good swimmer – I did a kilometre every day for thirty-five years. But your clothes, they really drag you down!'

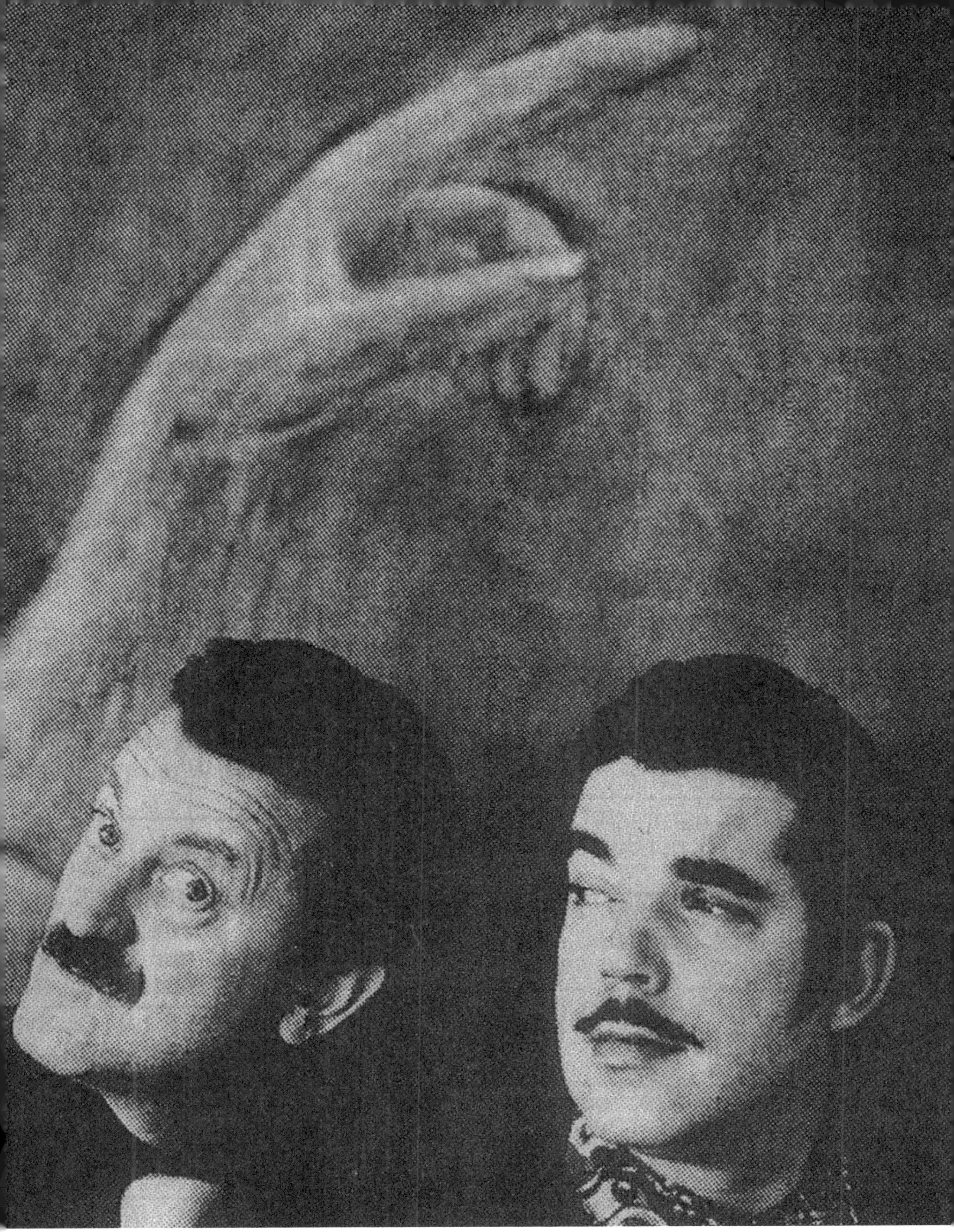

El Loco, ein Bild von Gregoire Muller.
Foto: Serge Höltschi.

In front of El Loco, *a painting by Gregoire Muller.*
Photo: Serge Höltschi.

BORIS BLANK & DIETER MEIER 1999

Aufzeichnung für die internationale Millenium-Show «2000 Today» auf dem 3466 m ü. M. gelegenen Jungfraujoch. Fotos: Herbert Steiner.

Recording for the international Millennium show '2000 Today', at 3,466 metres above sea level on the Jungfraujoch in the Alps. Photos: Herbert Steiner.

Cover der CD *Construction Sonor, eine Klangreise unter die Alpen*, mit dem Instrumentalstück «Lithosphere» von Boris Blank, 2004.

CD cover of Construction Sonor, eine Klangreise unter die Alpen*, with an instrumental track, 'Lithosphere', by Boris Blank, 2004.*

Fotosession in Wien für *Rondo*
(Beilage von *Der Standard*), 2003.
Fotos: Bernd Preiml, Miloš Kopták.

Photo shoot in Vienna for Rondo
(a supplement of a daily paper, Der Standard*), 2003.*
Photos: Bernd Preiml, Miloš Kopták.

370–371

Electronic Beats Classics präsentiert *Touch Yello – The Virtual Concert*, Premiere im Kino International, Berlin, 1. Oktober 2009.

Dieter Meier: «Ich mache mich oft über mich selber lustig in unseren Videos. Ich lache gern über meinen Dilettantismus. Niemand würde mich als einen professionellen Sänger bezeichnen. Was ich mit meiner Stimme anstelle, liegt näher bei der Perkussion als beim Gesang. Wie ein Schauspieler übernehme ich je nach Stimmung eines Liedes eine andere Rolle. ‹Oh Yeah›, ‹Heavy Whispers› oder sogar so etwas wie ‹Solar Driftwood›, das sind lauter verschiedene Rollen. Mit dem *Touch Yello*-Film näherten wir uns langsam, langsam wieder dem Konzept einer Live-Show. Wie zieht man eine Live-Show im Stil von Yello auf?»

Electronic Beats Classics presents Touch Yello – The Virtual Concert. *Premiere at the Kino International, Berlin, 1 October 2009.*

Dieter Meier: 'I often make fun of myself in our music videos. I enjoy laughing at my own dilettantism. You could never describe me as a professional singer. What I do with my voice is closer to percussion, really, than singing. Depending on the mood of the song I take on a different role, like an actor. "Oh Yeah", "Heavy Whispers", even something like "Solar Driftwood" – it's all different roles. With the Touch Yello *film we were slowly, slowly re-approaching the concept of a live show. How do you put on a live show, Yello-style?'*

 BORIS BLANK & DIETER MEIER 2009

Foto: Lars Borges.

Photo: Lars Borges.

372–375

Video-Stills von *Tiger Dust* und *The Race* für *Touch Yello – The Virtual Concert*; Tochter Olivia Blank lässt einen Mini-Boris in der Luft zappeln. Video-Stills: Kevin Blanc.

Video stills from Tiger Dust *and* The Race *for* Touch Yello – The Virtual Concert*; daughter Olivia Blank holds Mini-Boris aloft. Video stills: Kevin Blanc.*

Bei Proben im Kino International in Berlin.
Foto: Leon Kahane.

Rehearsals at the Kino International, Berlin.
Photo: Leon Kahane.

Wiedersehen mit Rap-Legende Afrika Bambaataa anlässlich eines Panels am Montreux Jazz Festival, 2011.

Reunion with the hip-hop legend Afrika Bambaataa for a panel talk at the Montreux Jazz Festival, 2011.

UNIVERSAL ZULU NATION
BAMBAATAA

Fototermin mit Quincy Jones und Claude Nobs, dem Gründer des Montreux Jazz Festivals, vor dessen Villa hoch über Montreux. Fotos: Oliver Rosa.

Photo shoot with Quincy Jones and Claude Nobs, founder of the Montreux Jazz Festival, near Nobs's villa high above Montreux. Photos: Oliver Rosa.

382–387

Yellofier-App; das allererste «Yellofier»-Diagramm von Jonatan Liljedahl, Stockholm, 2011.

Der schwedische Produzent und DJ Håkan Lidbo hatte sich bei Boris Blank gemeldet, weil er diesen für eine Sendung interviewen wollte, die er für das schwedische Radio produzierte. Die beiden Elektronica-Fans verstanden sich blendend und blieben in Kontakt. Es entstand sogar ein gemeinsamer Song: «Planet Dada» für das Yello-Album *The Eye*. Als Lidbo wieder einmal in Zürich weilte, liess Blank die Bemerkung fallen, wie toll es wäre, wenn es eine Musik-App gäbe, die nicht mit Pre-Sets daherkäme, die einem schon nach zehn Minuten verleidet seien. Eine, wo man individuell mit Samples arbeitete, die dann auch noch in einer endlosen Kombination von Effekten behandelt werden könnten. Lidbo war von der Idee hell begeistert und zeichnete noch im Restaurant die erste Skizze. Zurück in Stockholm mobilisierte er den befreundeten Programmierer Jonatan Liljedahl, welcher einer solchen Herausforderung nicht widerstehen konnte. Boris Blank: «Die Programmierung war sehr schwierig. Über zwei Jahre kam schliesslich eine Beta-Version zustande. Optisch sieht die App einfach aus, fast schon wie ein Kinderspielzeug. Aber es hat sehr viele Layers, die im Hintergrund wirken. Ich brauche sie noch heute sehr häufig und bin damit auch an Panels aufgetreten. Soeben haben wir eine neue Version veröffentlicht.»

The Yellofier app: Jonatan Liljedahl's very first 'Yellofier' diagram, Stockholm, 2011.

The Swedish producer and DJ Håkan Lidbo had contacted Boris Blank for an interview for the program he was producing for national radio in Sweden. Big electronic music fans both, the pair hit it off and stayed in touch. Their first creative effort together was the track 'Planet Dada' for the Yello album The Eye. *On one of Lidbo's subsequent visits to Zürich, Blank made a casual remark: How great would it be if there were a music app that came with pre-sets that didn't bore you to death after ten minutes; an app that would allow you to make samples and treat them individually with an endless combination of effects. Lidbo was instantly smitten with the idea, and drew the first sketch there and then at the restaurant table. Back in Stockholm, he mobilised his programmer friend Jonatan Liljedahl, who was similarly enthusiastic about the concept. Boris Blank: 'The programming was very difficult. After two years, we finally had a beta version. Visually, the Yellofier looks simple, almost like a child's toy. But it has a lot of layers that work in the background. I still use it a lot today and I have performed with it on panel discussions and other stage performances. We released an updated version only a few months ago.*

YELLOFIER

NOTE: this is only a functional diagram, the look and shapes of the various symbols and elements are decided by the designer.

The arrows represent navigation between the screens.

J. Liljedahl 2011-06

RECORD AND SLICE

EDIT SONG

SAVE AND SHARE

EDIT SAMPLE CUTS

START SCREEN
- record a new sound
- go to SONG VIEW
- share/save/load song
- edit recording split-points
- tempo and start/stop

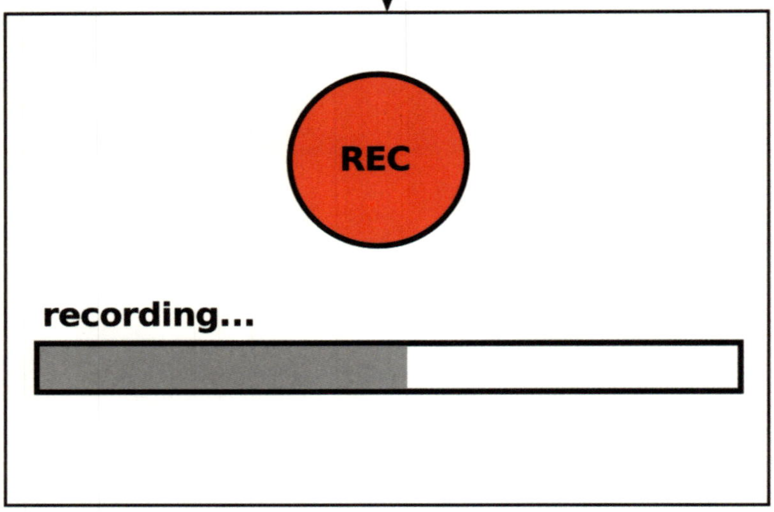

RECORD CUSTOM SOUND
When pressing REC button, it starts recording up to 15 seconds.

Transients are detected and the recording is cut up into 8 parts, each part is assigned to a sound and color. The cut points can be edited afterwards if needed.

When done, the SONG VIEW is shown, with a pattern choosen randomly from a set of pre-programmed patterns. The other tracks could be filled with pre-programmed patterns based on yello sounds?

The recorded and sliced sound is part of the current song.

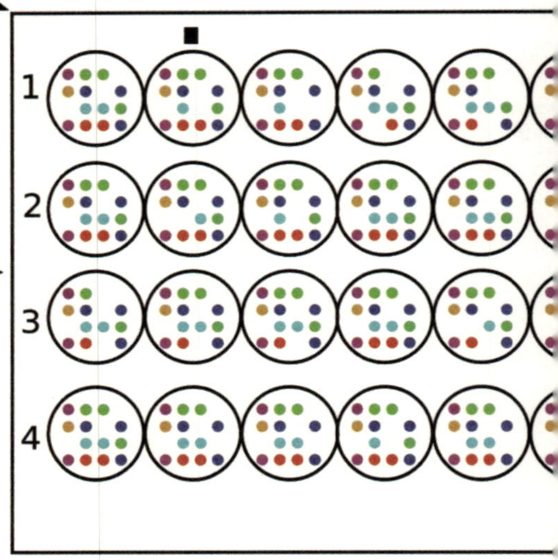

SONG VIEW
- Grid of patterns
- Four tracks for multi-timbrality
- Touch a pattern to zoom in and
- Swipe to scroll (or divide into pa
- Drag pattern to copy
- Hold pattern to show library of patterns
- A cursor shows current position

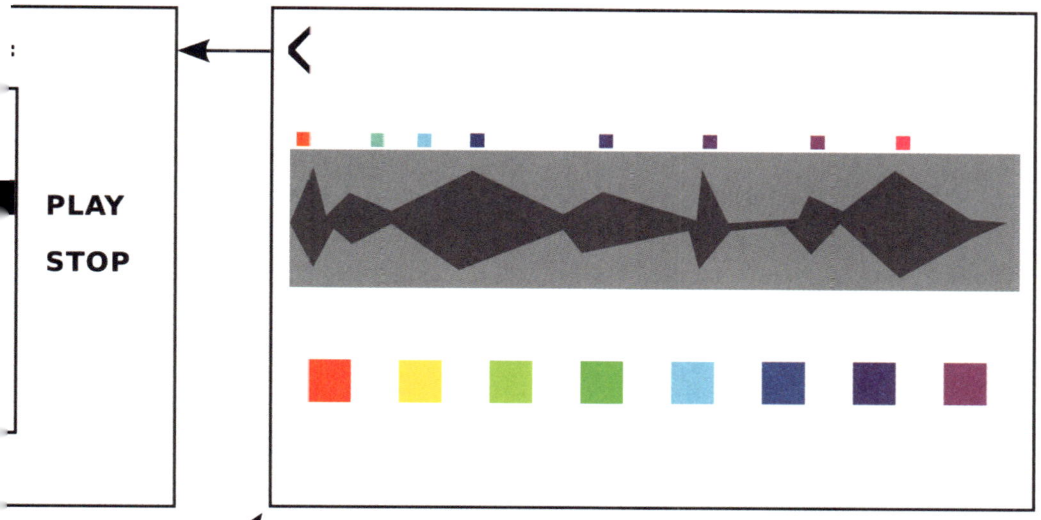

SAMPLE CUT EDIT
- The recording split-points can be edited by dragging the cut marks
- the pads can be pressed to listen to that specific slice

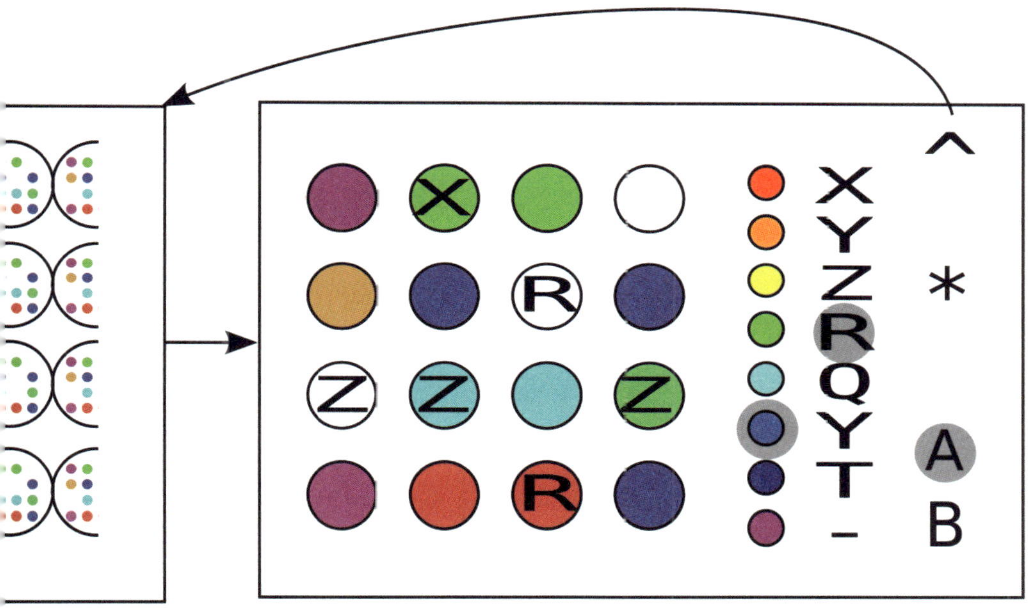

PATTERN VIEW
- 16 steps, one bar.
- Each step has a pause or a sound, represented by colors.
- Each step also has an optional effect combination, represented by symbols.
- Each effect combo consists of one or more of the following effects: beatrepeat, reverse, transpose (pitch), vocal filter, delay
- Touch a step to set it to the currently selected sound and effect. Touch again to unset it (pause).
- Touch and drag a step to adjust volume (up/down) and effect parameter (left/right)
- Symbols A and B to select sound bank: custom recording or pre-produced yello sounds
- * symbol randomizes pattern
- Swipe up/down to go to pattern on other track

grammed

Video-Dreh für den Yellofier-Trailer, Berlin, 2014.
Fotos: Darius Ramazani.

*Video shoot for the trailer for the Yellofier app. Berlin, 2014.
Photos: Darius Ramazani.*

Yellofier-Banner von Håkan Ullberg
für die Apple IOS Applikation.

*Yellofier banner designed by Håkan Ullberg
for the Apple iOS app.*

Zürich by night. Foto: Boris Blank.

Zürich by night. Photo: Boris Blank.

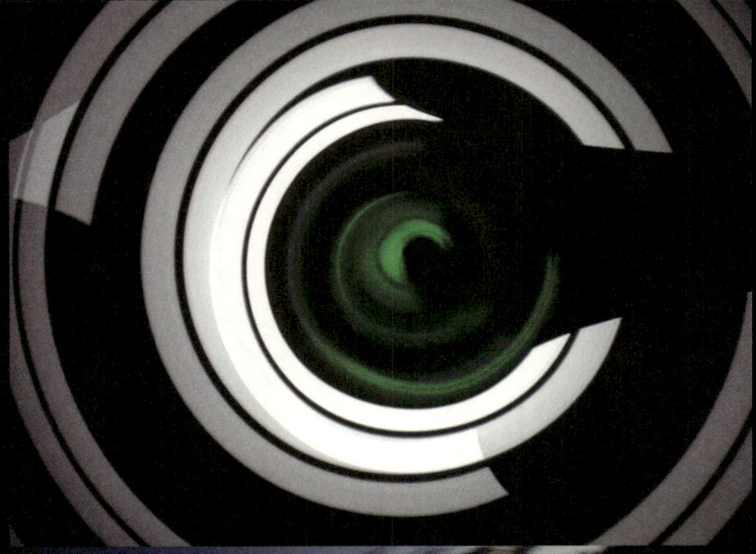

Video-Stills aus *The Time Tunnel* von Dirk Koy.

Stills from The Time Tunnel *music video, with animation by Dirk Koy.*

HERO3

Kaufleuten, Zürich, 2016.

Die Kameraposition im Zentrum des Rades von seinem Auto ergibt die geniale Bildperspektive des *Time Tunnel*-Videos. Foto: D rk Koy.

The amazing perspective of The Time Tunnel *music video was achieved by placing the camera at the centre of a wheel on the director's own car. Photo: Dirk Koy.*

Yello live im Kraftwerk Berlin, 2016
und auf Tournee, 2017.

Am 26. Oktober 2016 in einem stillgelegten Kraftwerk im ehemaligen Ostberlin trat Dieter Meier ans Mikrofon und machte eine Ansage, die viele – Meier inbegriffen und erst recht Boris Blank – lang für unmöglich gehalten hätten. «Hier kommt das erste Stück, es heisst ‹Do It›.» Endlich hatte sich Yello in eine ausgewachsene Live-Band verwandelt.

Die Idee stammte von Ian Tregoning und wurde von Meier herzhaft unterstützt. Tregoning hatte gemeint, die Songs vom neuen Album *Toy* würden sich ausgezeichnet für eine Bühnenshow eignen. Blank, durch den Erfolg der *Touch-Yello*-Tournee schon ein bisschen lockerer eingestellt, liess sich darauf ein: «Ich dachte, okay, lass es uns einmal probieren. Vielleicht ist es ja doch eine Erfahrung wert.»

Ein Grund dafür, dass Blank sich so lang gesträubt hatte, live aufzutreten, bestand darin, dass er glaubte, ein Live-Kontext könne der Wirkung einer Musik nur schaden, die fast ausschliesslich aus dem Computer kam. Um diese Befürchtungen endgültig zu zerstreuen, entschied man sich, eine Band zusammenzustellen, zu der neben dem Schlagzeuger Beat Ash und dem Gitarristen Jeremy Baer auch ein Perkussionist, eine Bläsergruppe und die Gastsängerinnen Malia und Fifi Rong gehörten.

Am ersten Abend beim Gang auf die Bühne habe er sich gefühlt wie ein Anfänger auf der Zehn-Meter-Plattform, sagt Blank. «Aber man will nicht zaudern wie Mr. Bean, und so springt man halt.» Am zweiten Abend war schon alles ganz anders. Blank war bereit, sich zu amüsieren. «Ich dachte immer, es sei abgedroschen, wenn Künstler behaupten, das Publikum trage einen mit seiner Energie. Aber die Euphorie, die ich nach diesen Shows erlebte, sagte mir, dass es stimmt.»

Auch Dieter Meier freute sich. «Es gibt keine bessere Medizin gegen die Verdummung, als zwei Stunden lang auf der Bühne zu stehen und Lieder zu singen.»

Die Yellofier-App in Aktion beim Konzert im Kraftwerk Berlin, 2016. Fotos: Michael Wilfling.

The Yellofier app in action at the concert at Kraftwerk Berlin, 2016. Photos: Michael Wilfling.

Yello live at Kraftwerk Berlin, 2016 and on tour, 2017.

On 26 October 2016, in a disused power station in the former East Berlin, Dieter Meier stepped up to the microphone and made an announcement that many, including Meier himself, not to mention Boris Blank, would never have thought possible. 'This first song is called "Do It",' he said. 'After thirty years of not doing it, we decided to DO IT!' At last, Yello had become a live band.

The idea had been suggested by Ian Tregoning and heartily supported by Dieter Meier. Having heard the new album, Toy, *Tregoning felt that this particular collection of songs would be ideally suited for a stage show. Blank, softened up by the virtual* Touch Yello *tour, found himself relenting: 'I thought, "OK, let's try it just this once. It might be an experience worth having after all."' One of the reasons Blank had been so reluctant to take to the stage was his feeling that a live show would only serve to dull the impact of music that came almost entirely from a computer. To allay his fears, it was decided to put together a live band that included their frequent collaborators, drummer Beat Ash and guitarist Jeremy Baer, as well as a percussionist, a brass section, and guest singers Malia and Fifi Rong.*

'Walking up to my instruments on that first night felt like looking down from the 10-metre diving platform and realising how big a drop it is,' recalls Blank. 'But you don't want to dither and look like Mr Bean, and so you jump.' By the second night, everything was already much easier. Blank was ready to enjoy himself: 'I always thought it was a bit hackneyed when artists talked about feeding off audiences' energy. The euphoria I felt after those shows told me it wasn't a cliché – it was true.'

Dieter Meier, too, had a good time: 'There's no better medicine against going doolally,' he says, 'than standing on stage for two hours, singing songs.'

396–398

Fotos: Michael Wilfling.

Photos: Michael Wilfling.

Malia und Fifi Rong treten als Gastsängerinnen auf.
Foto: Thomas Entzeroth.

Malia and Fifi Rong, Yello guest vocalists.
Photo: Thomas Entzeroth.

Video-Still *RTS*, Montreux Jazz Festival, 12. Juli 2017.

RTS *Montreux Jazz Festival, 12 July 2017.*

Hubertus von Hohenlohe dreht eine Reportage über Montreux und Yello. Der Regisseur wünschte sich, dass Yello auf dem Pedalo mittels Yellofier spontan ein Lied komponierten, das dann auch in der Sendung gezeigt wurde. Die Kamera war auf einem zweiten Boot platziert.
Foto: Hubertus von Hohenlohe.

Hubertus von Hohenlone shooting a documentary about Montreux and Yello. The director asked Yello to sit in a pedalo and compose a song on the spot for his program, using the Yellofier. The cameraman was filming from a second boat.
Photo: Hubertus von Hohenlohe

Hallenstadion, Zürich, 30. November 2017.
Foto: Heinz Saurer.

Hallenstadion, Zürich, 30 November 2017.
Photo: Heinz Saurer.

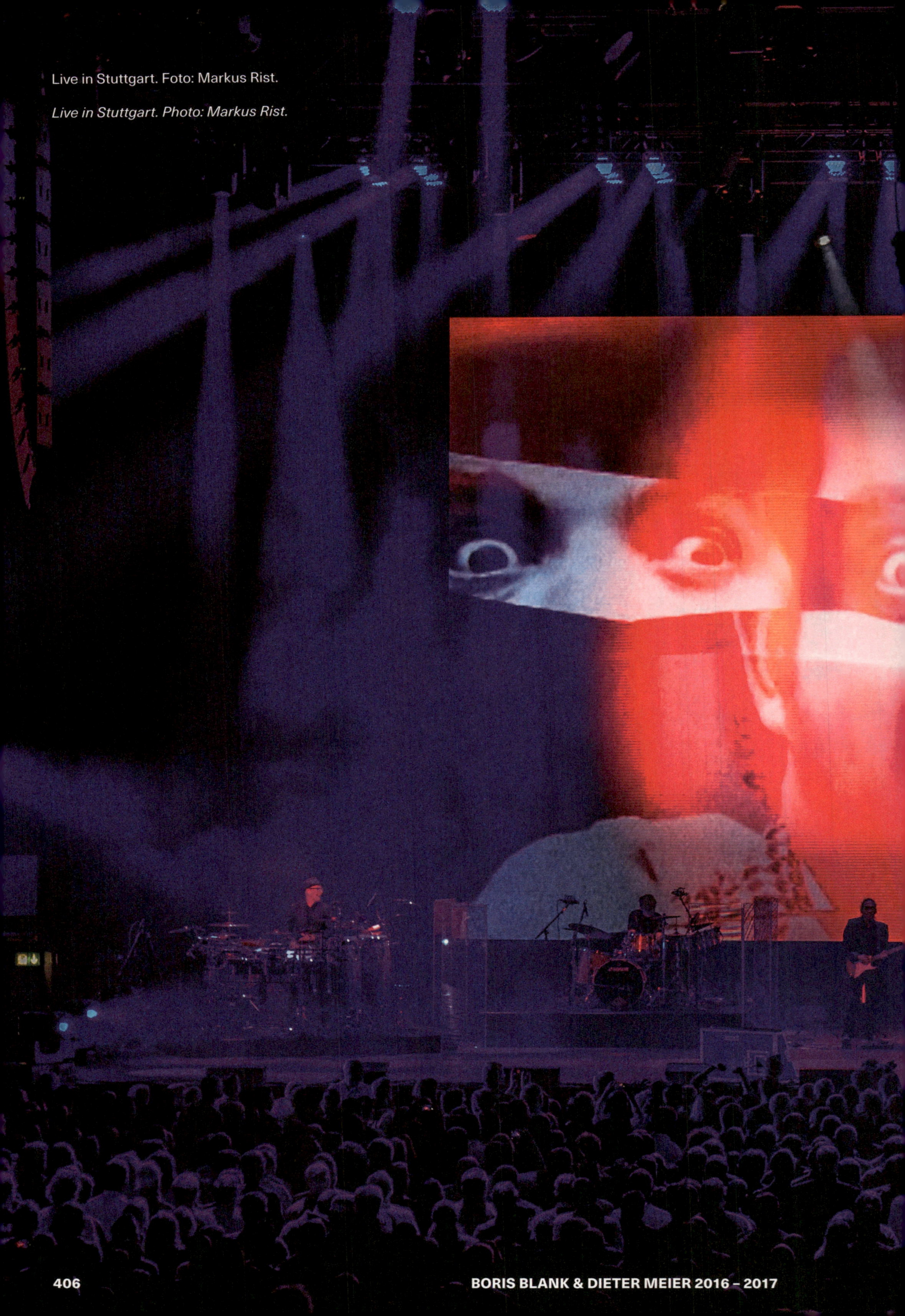

Live in Stuttgart. Foto: Markus Rist.

Live in Stuttgart. Photo: Markus Rist.

«Jack in the Box»-Fotosession bei Helen Sobiralski, Berlin, 2016.

'Jack in the Box' photo shoot in Helen Sobiralski's studio, Berlin, 2016.

Ursli Weber, Sound Engineer, kümmert sich seit dem Anfang um das Mastering der meisten Yello-Alben. Foto: Boris Blank.

Sound engineer Ursli Weber has mastered most Yello albums since the very beginning. Photo: Boris Blank.

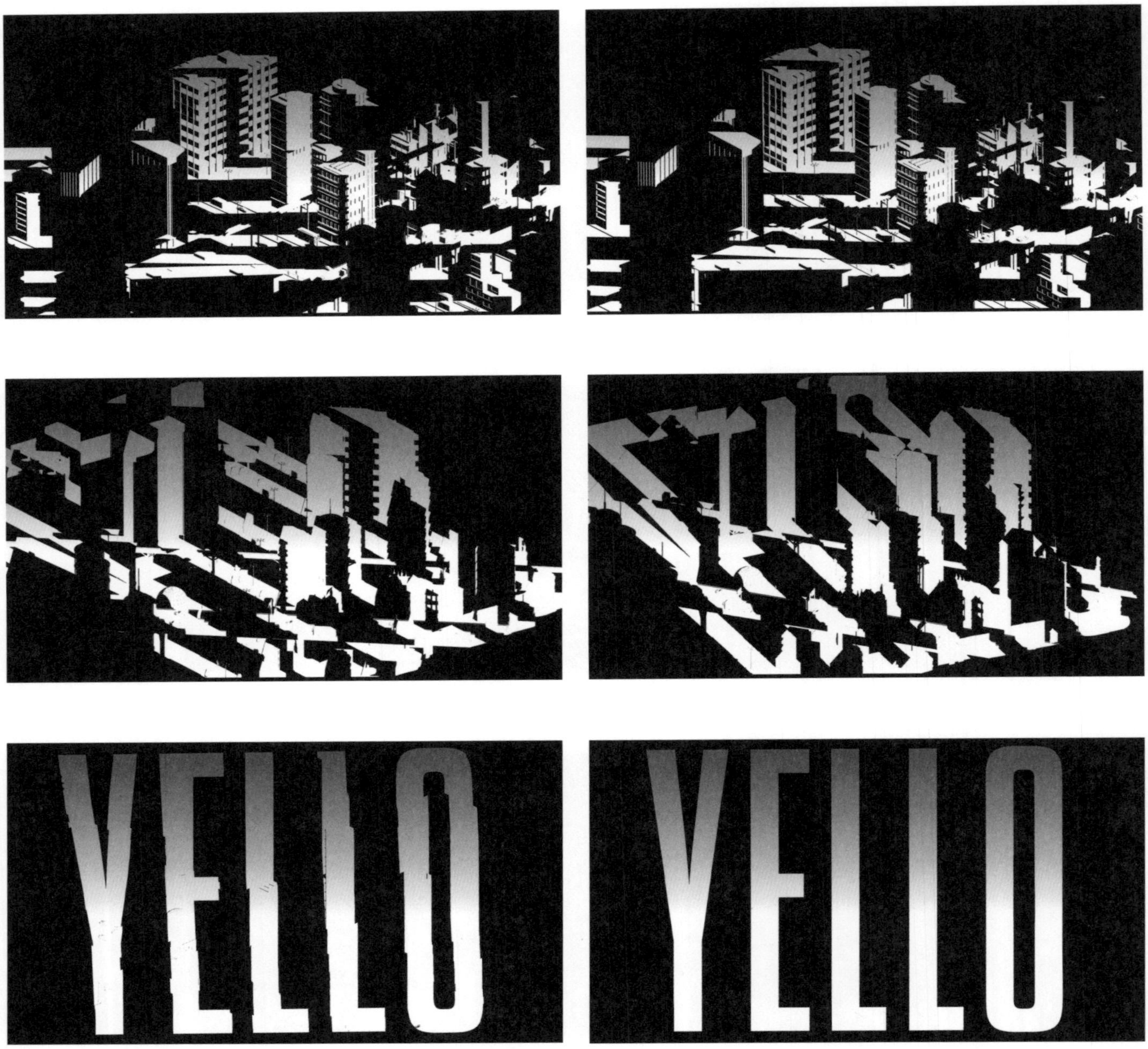
YELLO
YELLO

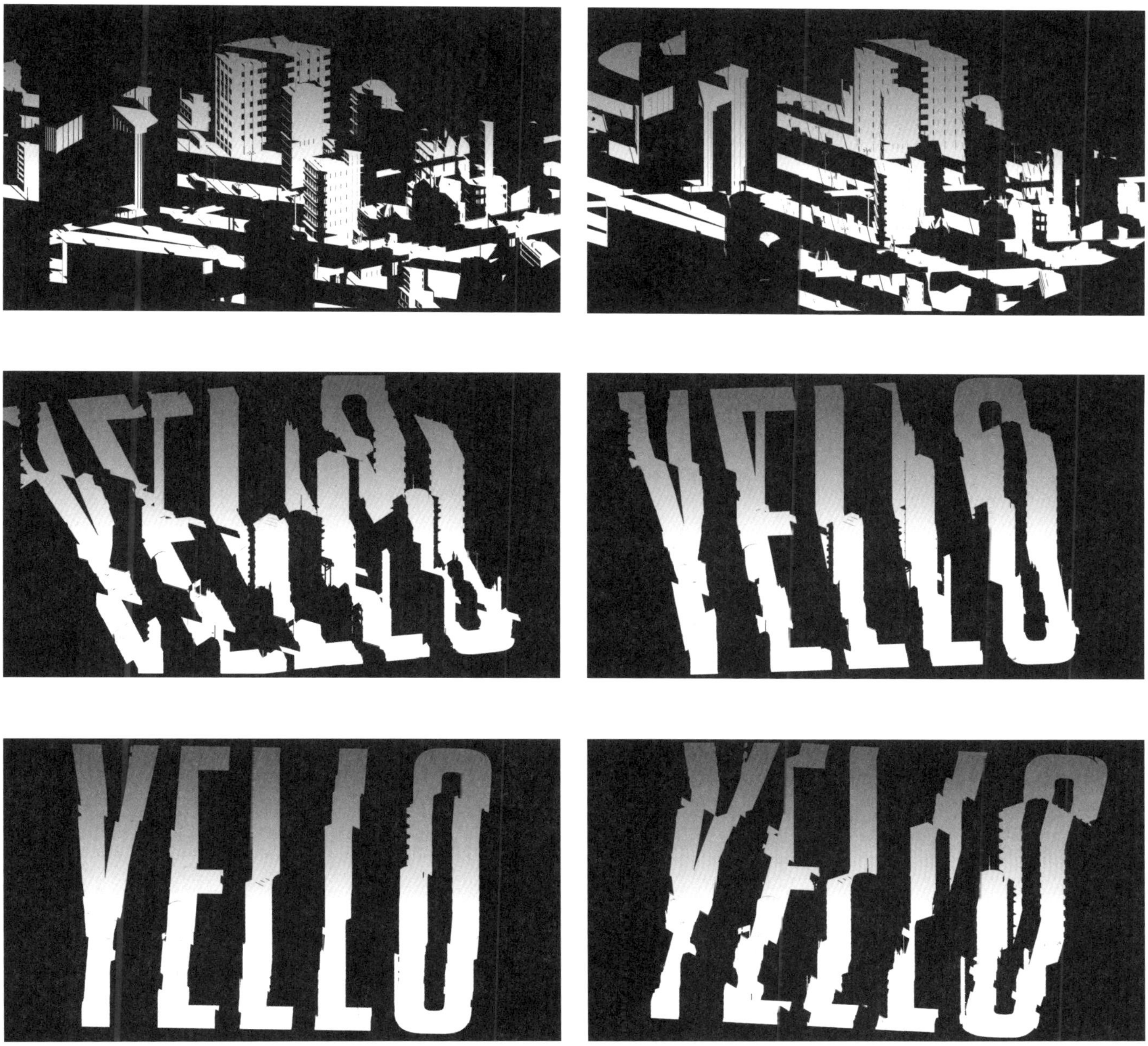

Eine Stadt verwandelt sich in einen Yello-Schriftzug.
Animation: Dirk Koy.

A city morphs into the name Yello.
Animation: Dirk Koy.

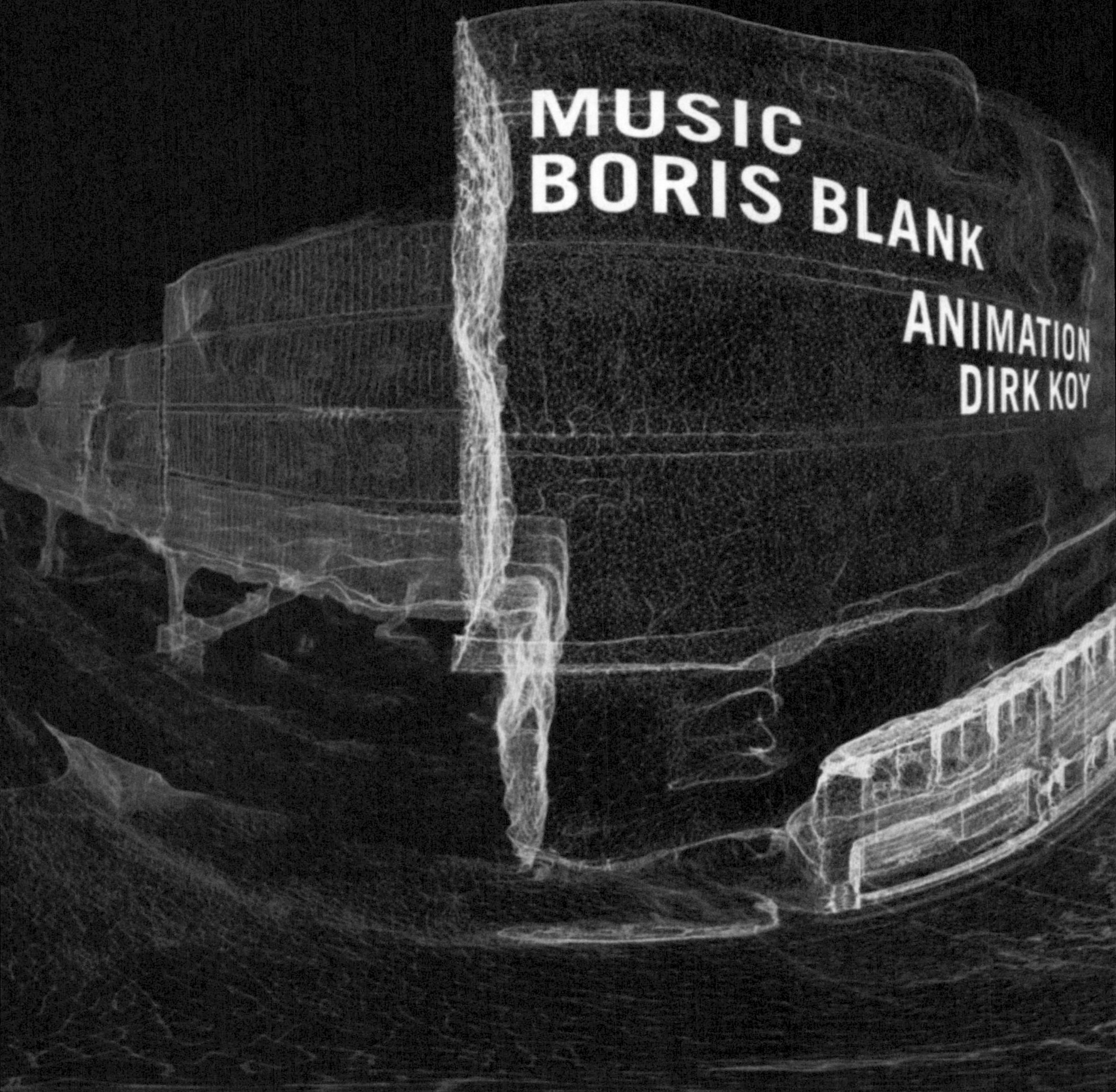
MUSIC
BORIS BLANK
ANIMATION
DIRK KOY

Still aus dem preisgekrönten Video *Escape Route*. Regie: Dirk Koy.

Still from the award-winning Dirk Koy-directed Escape Route *music video.*

418–421

Video-Stills aus *Waba Duba*, 2020.

Stills from the Waba Duba *music video, 2020.*

422–425

Video-Stills aus *Out of Sight*.
Regie: Dirk Koy, 2020.

Stills from the Out of Sight *music video, directed by Dirk Koy, 2020.*

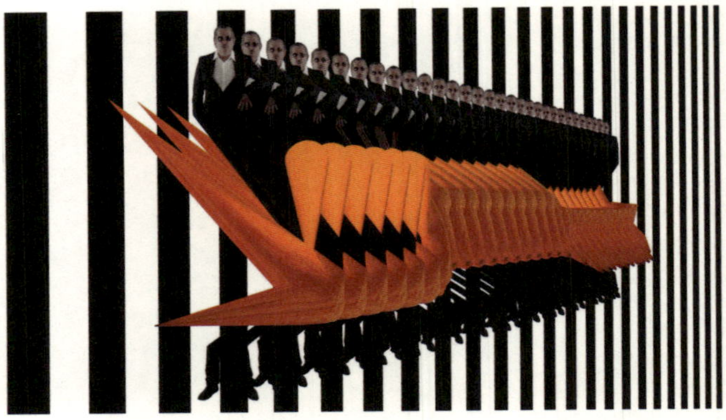

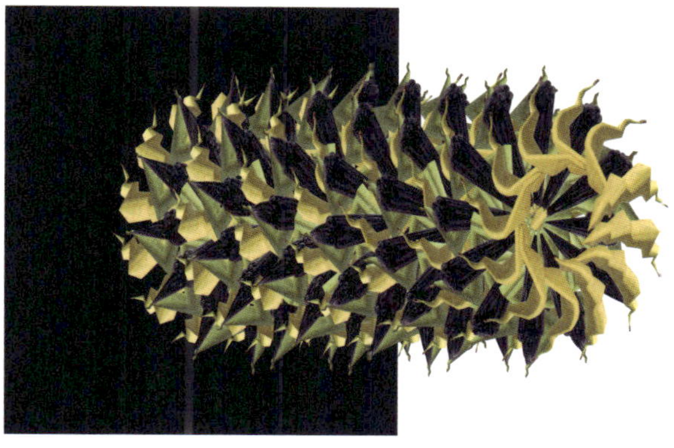

I am gona loose
my mind

Spinning around

You'r gonna give me
your love

I am on a shaky ground

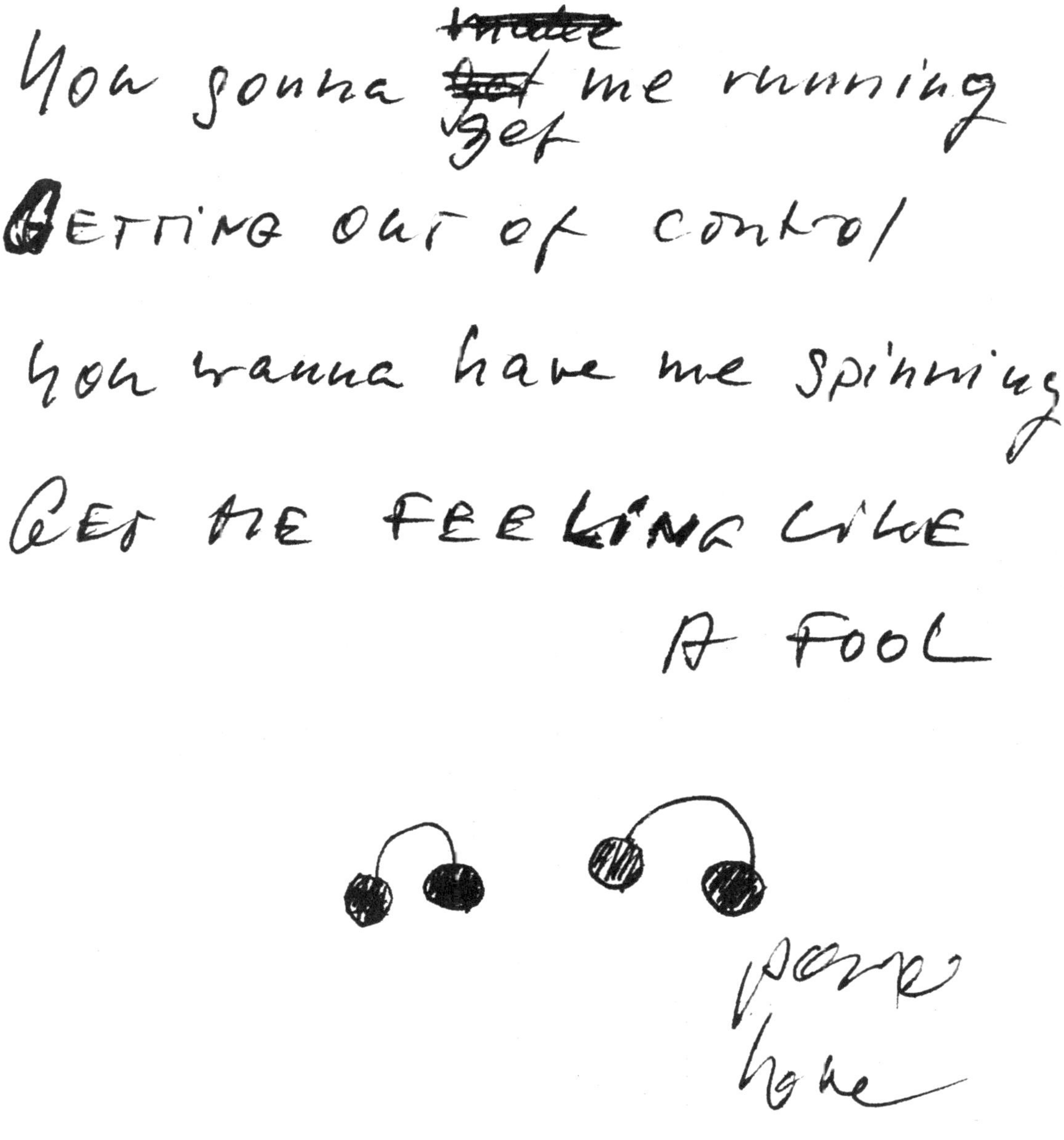

You gonna ~~make~~ ~~let~~ get me running
Getting out of control
You wanna have me spinning
Get me feeling like
a fool

Textentwurf von Dieter Meier für «Spinning My Mind».

Draft lyrics by Dieter Meier for 'Spinning My Mind'.

«The Long Goodbye» nach dem Konzert in der Porsche-Arena, Stuttgart, 8. Dezember 2017. Foto: Markus Rist.

'The Long Goodbye' after the concert at the Porsche Arena, Stuttgart, 8 December 2017. Photo: Markus Rist.

VIDEOGRAPHY

Regie: Dieter Meier / Director: Dieter Meier

The Evening's Young, 1981 / 3:33

Pinball Cha Cha, 1982 / 3:34

I Love You, 1983 / 3:16

Lost Again, 1983 / 3:20

Bostich, 1984 / 3:16

Vicious Games, 1985 / 3:34

Desire, 1985 / 4:17 (Long Vers. 7:45)

Goldrush, 1986 / 3:51 (Long Vers. 6:14)

Oh Yeah, 1987 / 3:05

Call It Love, 1987 / 3:40

The Rhythm Divine, 1987 / 3:30

The Race, 1988 / 3:20

Tied Up, 1988 / 3:30 (Long Vers. 8:13)

Of Course I'm Lying, 1989 / 4:06

Blazing Saddles, 1989 / 3:52

Rubberbandman, 1991 / 3:28

Who's Gone, 1991 / 3:54 (Long Vers. 6:20)

Jungle Bill, 1992 / 4:05

Drive Driven, 1993 / 3:37

Do It, 1994 / 3:12 (Long Vers. 7:48)

How How (2 Variations), 1994 / 2:40

Tremendous Pain, 1995 / 3:58

Tremendous Pain - Suite 904, 1995 / 4:05

To The Sea, 1997 / 3:51 (directed by Paul Morgans)

Planetarium Versions, 1996

Celsius / 5:59
On Track (Album Vers.) / 5:33
Pan Blue / 5:31
Resistor / 7:13

On Track (Single Vers.), 1997 / 3:11

Squeeze Please, 1999 / 3:12
(directed by Jason Glenister)

Planet Dada (Original Vers.), 2003 / 3:06
(co-directed by Daniel Cherbuin)
+ Remix Vers. Northern Lite **Visting The Planet** / 3:12

Non-musical comedy sketch
Boris Blank Live From New York, 2003 / 3:19

Touch Yello – The Virtual Concert, 2009

01 Intro / 1:47
02 Till Tomorrow / 3:28
03 The Expert / 2:53
(Bridge) / 0:55
04 You Better Hide / 4:21
05 Out Of Dawn / 3:10
06 Bostich (Reflected) / 3:57
07 Kiss In Blue / 3:43
08 Vertical Vision / 4:18
09 Tiger Dust / 3:03
10 Tangier Blue / 2:38
11 Oh Yeah 2009 / 2:24
12 The Race 2008 / 2:07
13 Credits / 1:32

Mean Monday, 2010 / 3:30

Limbo, 2016 / 3:22

Live In Berlin, 2016 / 2:00
(20 Tracks, 2 CD, DVD, Blu-ray)

Waba Duba, 2020 / 3:05 (directed by Boris Blank)

Out Of Sight, 2020 / 2:40 (directed by Dirk Koy)

Spinning My Mind, 2020 / 2:35

Live at Montreux Jazz Festival 2017 / 2:00
(20 Tracks, DVD, Blu-ray in Point Collector's Box)

Point / Edition of short videos, 2020
(directed by Boris Blank)

01 Arthur Spark / 1:27
02 Hot Pan / 1:39
03 Way Down / 1:30
04 Siren Singing / 1:45
05 Basic Avenue / 0 58
06 Rush For Joe / 1:30
07 Core Shift / 1:15
08 Meet My Angel / 1:48
10 Zephyr Calling Part 1 / 2:00 and 2 / 1:20

DISCOGRAPHY

Music composed, arranged and engineered by Boris Blank. Lyrics and vocals by Dieter Meier.
Special thanks for compiling this discography to André P. Tschan and Lurker Grand.

Abbreviations:
+ designates specific contributions by additional musicians.
v vocals, g guitar, d drums, a accordion, cl clarinet, fl flute, h flugelhorn, ha harmonica, k keyboard, p percussion, pia piano, t trumpet, trom trombone, + guests guest musicians, liner liner notes, (A) artwork, (P) photos, (D) film director.

I.T.Splash
I.T.Splash // Glue Head
12" 1979
Periphery Perfume (CH)
PP 0179
+g Chico Hablas
+d Felix Haug
(A) Boris Blank

Glue Head
Glue Head // I.T. Splash
7" 1979
Celluloid (FR) CEL 6221
+g Chico Hablas
+d Felix Haug

Bimbo
Bimbo // I.T.Splash
7" 1980
Ralph Records (US)
/ Do It Records (UK)
YL-8058-S / DUN 11 (1981)
+ guests

Solid Pleasure
Bimbo / Night Flanger / Reverse Lion / Downtown Samba / Magneto / Massage / Assistant's Cry / Bostich // Rock Stop / Coast To Polka / Blue Green / Eternal Legs / Stanztrigger / Bananas To The Beat
LP & CD & MC 1980
Ralph Records (US) / Vertigo (CAN) / Vertigo (DE) / Do It Records (UK) / Celluloid (FR) / Mercury (US) LP YL 8059-L / LP 818 339-1 / MC 818 339-4 / LP 6435 094 (1981) / CD 818 339-2 (1984) / MC 7106 094 (1981) / LP RIDE 4 (1981) / LP 529808 (1981) / LP CEL-6580 (1981) / CD 818 339-2 (1985) LP Hit Thing HT LP011 (2005)
Remaster Series 1 (2005)
Bonus Tracks: Thrill Wave / I.T. Splash / Glue Head / Smirak's Train / Bostich (N'est-Ce Pas)
CD Vertigo 9830904
YELLO 960015 (2014)
+g Chico Hablas
+d Felix Haug
+d Walt Kaiser
(A) Nick Urbaniak

Night Flanger
Night Flanger // Bostich
7" 1981
Celluloid (FR) 106403
+ guests

YELLO for Thierry Mugler
Night Flanger //
She's Got A Gun
Promo 7" 1981
Celluloid (FR) CEL-6223
+ guests

Ralph (US),
Cover Variations 1–3

Claro Que Si
Daily Disco / No More Roger / Take It All / The Evening's Young / She's Got A Gun // Ballet Mecanique / Ouad El Habib / The Lorry / Homer Hossa / Pinball Cha Cha
LP & MC 1981
Ralph Records (US) / Vertigo (DE) / Do It Records (UK) / Vertigo (CAN) / Mercury (US)
LP YL-8159 / LP 6435 123 / CD 818 340-2 (1984) / LP RIDE 8 / MC 818 340-4 / CD 818 340-2 (1985)
LP Hit Thing HT LP012
Remaster Series 2 (2005)
Bonus Tracks:
Tub Dub / She's Got A Gun (Live At The Palladium, NY, Sept. 1985) / Daily Disco (1985 Version) / The Evening's Young (1985 Version) / Pinball Cha Cha (12" Mix) / Desire for Desire
CD Vertigo 9830756,
YELLO 960039 (2014)
+g Chico Hablas
+d Beat Ash
+v Zine el Abidine
(A) Jim Cherry

Jetzt und Alles Soundtrack
1982 Film *Take It All / Jetzt und Alles*
directed by Dieter Meier.
Various Artists
Richy Müller & YELLO:
Jetzt und Alles /
There Is No Reason
YELLO: Smirak's Train /
Thrill Wave
+v Richy Müller
Mercury LP 6435 126

Bostich
Bostich //
She's Got A Gun
7" 1981
Do It Records (UK)
DUN 13
(A) Paul Ridout

Bostich
Bostich (Full Length Mix) //
Downtown Samba /
Daily Disco
12" 1981
Do It Records (UK)
DUN IT 13
+ guests
(A) Paul Ridout

Bostich
Bostich / She's Got A Gun // Downtown Samba / Daily Disco
12" 1981
Stiff America (US)
TEES 12-10
+ guests
(A) Paul Ridout

Bimbo
Bimbo // Smile On You
12" 1982
Ralph Records (US)
YL-8209
+ guests

She's Got A Gun
She's Got A Gun //
Bluehead
7" 1982
Do It Records (UK)
DUN 18
+ guests
(A) Jim Cherry

She's Got A Gun
She's Got A Gun //
The Evening Is Young /
There Is No Reason
12" 1982
Do It Records (UK)
DUN IT 18
(A) Jim Cherry

She's Got A Gun
She's Got A Gun //
Daily Disco
12" 1982
Phonogram (FR)
6400 542
+ guests
(A) Jim Cherry

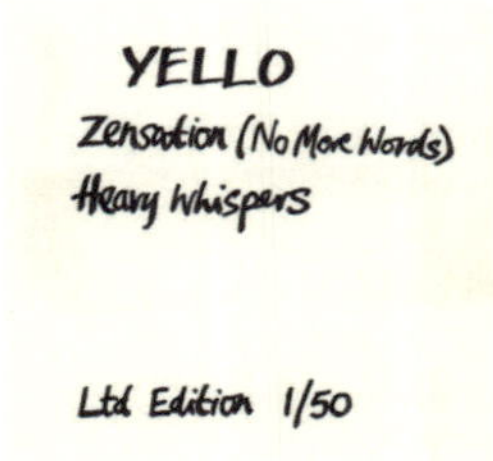

Zensation (Promo)
Zensation (No More Words) / Heavy Whispers // Salut Mayoumba (Extended Version)
12" 1982
Do It Records (UK)
DUN IT 25
+ guests

Pinball Cha Cha
Pinball Cha Cha // Bostich (N'est-Ce Pas)
7" & 12" 1982
Vertigo (DE) 6005 205 /
6400 571
+ guests
(A) Ernst Gamper

Pinball Cha Cha
Pinball Cha Cha //
Homer Hossa
12" 1982
Vertigo (DE) 812 311-1
+ guests
(A) Ernst Gamper

Pinball Cha Cha
Pinball Cha Cha //
Smile On You
7" 1982
Do It Records (UK)
DUN 23
+ guests
(A) Ernst Gamper, Martyn Atkins, Town And Country Planning

Pinball Cha Cha
Pinball Cha Cha (Extended) //
Smile On You
12" 1982
Do It Records (UK)
DUN IT 23
+ guests
(A) Ernst Gamper, Martyn Atkins, Town And Country Planning

You Gotta Say Yes To Another Excess
You Gotta Say Yes To Another Excess //
Heavy Whispers
12" 1982
Stiff America (US)
TEES 12-12
+ guests
(A) Ernst Gamper

You Gotta Say Yes To Another Excess
You Gotta Say Yes To Another Excess //
Desire For Desire
12" 1983
Vertigo (DE) 811 137-1
+ guests
(A) Ernst Gamper

You Gotta Say Yes To Another Excess
I Love You / Lost Again / No More Words / Crash Dance / Great Mission / You Gotta Say Yes To Another Excess // Swing / Heavy Whispers / Smile On You / Pumping Velvet / Salut Mayoumba
LP & MC 1983
Vertigo (DE) / Stiff Records (UK) / Elektra (US) LP 812 166-1 / CD 812 166-2 (1984) / MC 812 166-4 / LP SEEZ 48 / MC Z SEEZ 48 / LP 9 60271-1 / MC 60271-4
Remaster Series 3 (2005)
Bonus Tracks: Base for Alec / Rubber West / You Gotta Say Yes To Another Excess (UK Promo 12" Version) / Live At The Roxy, NY, Dec. 1983 / Pumping Velvet (12" Mix) / I Love You (12" Mix)
CD Vertigo 9830760, YELLO 960053 (2014)
+g Chico Hablas
+d Beat Ash
(A) Ernst Gamper
(P) Ray Photography

Es Positive Lo Excesivo
Te Amo (I Love You) / Perdido Otra Vez (Lost Again) / Sin Mas Palabras (No More Words) / Invitarse Al Baile (Crash Dance) / Una Gran Mision (Great Mission) / Es Positive Lo Excesivo (You Gotta Say Yes To Another Excess) // Swing / Susurros Pesados (Heavy Whisper) / Sonriete (Smile On You) / Violeta Oscuro (Pumping Velvet) / Salud Mayoumba (Salut Mayoumba)
LP 1983
Vertigo (ARG) 27022
+g Chico Hablas
+d Beat Ash
(A) Ernst Gamper
(P) Ray Photography

Vertigo (DE)

I Love You
I Love You // Rubber West
7" 1983
Vertigo (DE) /
Stiff Records (UK) /
Stiff Records (FR) /
Elektra (US) 812 150-7 / BUY 176 / 105 550 / 7-69824
+ guests
(A) Ernst Gamper
(P) Ray Photography

7" Picture Disc A-Side

7" Picture Disc B-Side

I Love You
7" Picture Disc 1983
Stiff Records (UK)
P-BUY-176
+ guests
(A) Ernst Gamper
(P) Ray Photography

Stiff (UK/FR)

Victoria (ES)

I Love You
I Love You (Extended Dance Version) // Swing / Bostich
12" 1983
Stiff Records (UK) /
Stiff Records (FR) /
Victoria (ES) BUY IT 176 / 600 909 / VIC-086
+d Beat Ash
(A) Ernst Gamper
(P) Ray Photography

I Love You
I Love You //
No More Words
12" 1983
Vertigo (NL) 814 247-1
+ guests
(A) Ernst Gamper
(P) Ray Photography

I Love You
I Love You (Extended Dance Version) //
Heavy Whispers
12" 1983
Elektra (US) 0-67917
+ guests
(A) Ernst Gamper
(P) Ray Photography

Let Me Cry
Let Me Cry //
Haunted House
12" 1983
Vertigo (DE) 814 101-1 /
872 413-1
+g Chico Hablas
(A) Ernst Gamper

Lost Again (Promo)
Lost Again // I Love You
7" 1983
Polydor (FR) 821 195-7
+ guests

Lost Again
Lost Again //
I Love You / Bostich
12" 1983
Vertigo (DE) / Polydor
(FR) 814 611-1 / 817 765-1
+ guests
(A) Ernst Gamper

Lost Again
(also as DJ Copy)
Lost Again //
Base For Alec
7" 1983
Vertigo (DE) 814 611-7
Stiff Records (UK) BUY
191 / BUY DJ 191
+ guests
(A) Ernst Gamper

Lost Again
1: Lost Again // Base
For Alec
2: Let Me Cry // She's
Got A Gun
Double 7" 1983
Stiff Records (UK)
D BUY 191
+ guests
(A) Ernst Gamper

Lost Again
Lost Again // Pumping
Velvet
7" 1984 Vertigo
(DE) 814 611-7

Lost Again
Lost Again / Base For
Alec // No More Words /
Pumping Velvet
12" 1983
Stiff Records (UK) /
Ariston Music (IT) BUY IT
191 / STX 6002
(A) Ernst Gamper

Pumping Velvet
Pumping Velvet (Extended Dance Version) / No
More Words (Extended
Dance Version) //
Lost Again (Extended
Dance Version) /
Bostich (Extended Dance
Version)
12" 1983
Elektra (US) 0-66979
+g Chico Hablas
+d Beat Ash
(A) Ernst Gamper
(P) Ray Photography

Bostich
Bostich // Base For Alec
7" 1984
Vertigo (DE) 822 160-7
+ guests
(A) Ernst Gamper

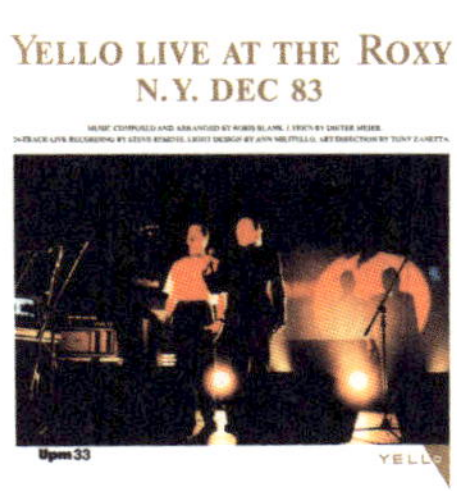

Yello Live At The Roxy N.Y. Dec 83
12" & CD Single
1984/1989
Vertigo (DE) 822 262-1 /
822 262-2 (1989)
+ guests
(A) Tony Zanetta
(F) Ray Photography

Stella
Desire / Vicious Games
/ Oh Yeah / Desert Inn /
Stalakdrama / Koladi-Ola
/ Domingo // Sometimes
(Dr. Hirsch) / Let Me Cry
/ Ciel Ouvert / Angel No
LP & CD & MC 1985
Vertigo (DE) / Elektra
(UK) / Polydor (FR) LP
822 820-1 / CD 822 820-2
/ MC 822 820-4 /
LP EKT 1 / MC EKT 1C /
LP 825 461-1
Remaster Series 4 (2005)
Bonus Tracks: Blue
Nabou / Oh Yeah (Indian
Summer Version) /
Desire (12" Mix) Vicious
Games (12" Mix)
CD Vertigo 960077
YELLO 9830759 (2014)
2014 Reissue Music on
Vinyl LP MOVLP276
Bonus Tracks: Oh Yeah
(Indian Summer Version)
/ Vicious Games
(12" Mix)
+g Chico Hablas
+d Beat Ash
+pia Annie Hogan
+v Rush Winters
(A) Ernst Gamper

Desire
Desire // Oh Yeah
7" & 12" 1985
Vertigo (DE) / Polydor
(FR) / Vertigo (EU) 880
895-7 / 880 895-1 / 883
346-7 / 883 346-7 /
880 895-1
+g Chico Hablas
+d Beat Ash
(A) Ernst Gamper
(P) Alexandre Cottet

Desire
Desire // Oh Yeah
7" & 12" 1985
Elektra (UK) EKR 17 /
EKR 17T
+g Chico Hablas
+d Beat Ash
(A/P) Ze Famouz

Desire
1: Desire // Oh Yeah
(Indian Summer –
The Stella Suite Pt. 2)
2: The Stella Suite Pt.1
(Oh Yeah Dance Mix) //
XS – The First Ever
Version
Double 12" 1985
Elektra (UK) EKR 17TF
+g Chico Hablas
+d Beat Ash
(A/P) Ze Famouz

Vertigo (DE)

Vertigo (ES)

Vicious Games
Vicious Games //
Blue Nabou
7" 1985
Vertigo (DE) / Elektra
(UK) / Polydor (FR) /
Vertigo (ES) 880 574-7 /
EKR1 / 881 749-7 /
880 574-7
(A) Ernst Gamper

Vicious Games
Vicious Games (Vocal) //
Vicious Games
(Instrumental)
12" 1985
Vertigo (DE) / Polydor
(FR) 880 574-1 /
881 746-1
(A) Ernst Gamper

Vicious Games
Vicious Games //
Vicious Games (Instrumental) / Blue Nabou
12" 1985
Elektra (UK) EKR 1T
+ guests
(A) Ernst Gamper

1980–1985
The New Mix In One Go
1: Daily Disco / Swing /
The Evening's Young /
Pinball Cha Cha // I Love
You / Vicious Games /
Sometimes (Dr. Hirsch) /
Base For Alec / Oh Yeah
2: Lost Again / Tub Dub
/ Angel No / Desire /
Bananas To The Beat /
Koladi-Ola // Domingo /
Bostich / Live At
The Roxy
Double LP & CD & MC
1986
Vertigo (DE) / Mercury
(UK) LP 826 773-1 / CD
826 773-2 / MC 826
773-4 / LP MERD 95 /
MERDC 95
+g Chico Hablas
+d Beat Ash
+v Rush Winters
(A) Ernst Gamper
(P) Anton Corbijn

1980–1985
The New Mix In One Go (Promo)
1: I Love You // Swing
2: Vicious Games //
Oh Yeah
Double 7" 1986
Barclay (FR) 6837 881
+g Chico Hablas
+d Beat Ash
+v Rush Winters
(A) Ernst Gamper

Vicious Games
Vicious Games (Remix) //
Live At The Roxy
7" 1986
Mercury (UK) MER 235
+g Chico Hablas
+g J. McL.
+v Rush Winters
(P) Anton Corbijn

Vicious Games
Vicious Games
(Vicious Remix) //
Live At The Roxy
(Highlights)
12" 1986
Mercury (UK) MERX 235
+g Chico Hablas
+g J. McL.
+v Rush Winters
(P) Anton Corbijn

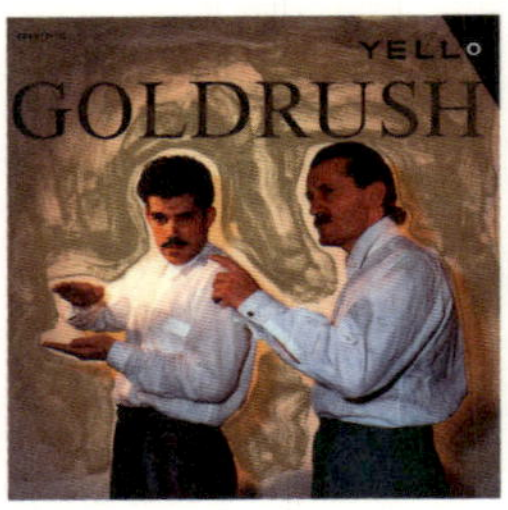

Goldrush
Goldrush I // She's Got A Gun (Live At The Palladium N.Y.)
7" 1986
Vertigo (DE) / Mercury
(UK) 884 877-7 / MER 218
+g Chico Hablas
+c Billy Mackenzie
(A) Ernst Gamper

Goldrush
Goldrush I / Goldrush II //
She's Got A Gun (Live At
The Palladium N.Y.)
12" & CD Single 1986
Vertigo (DE) / Mercury
(UK) 884 877-1 /
884 877-2 / MERX 218
+g Chico Hablas
+c Billy Mackenzie
(A) Ernst Gamper

Goldrush
1: Goldrush I // Goldrush
II / She's Got A Gun (Live
At The Palladium N.Y.)
2: Pinball Cha Cha //
Vicious Games
Double 12" 1986
Mercury (UK) MERXD 218
+ guests
(A) Ernst Gamper

Cover Variation 1

Cover Variation 2

Oh Yeah
Oh Yeah // Oh Yeah
(Indian Summer Music)
7" 1986
Mercury (US) 884 930-7
(A) Janet Perr

Cover Variation 1

Cover Variation 2

Oh Yeah
Oh Yeah (Dance Mix) //
Oh Yeah / Oh Yeah
(Indian Summer Music)
12" 1986
Mercury (US) 884 930-1

One Second
La Habanera / Moon On
Ice / Call It Love /
Le Secret Farida /
Hawaiian Chance //
The Rhythm Divine /
Santiago / Goldrush /
Dr Van Steiner / Si Señor
The Hairy Grill
LP & CD & MC 1987
Mercury (DE) / Mercury
(UK) / Mercury (US) LP
830 956-1 / CD 830 956-
2 / MC 830 956-4 / LP
MERH 100 / MC MERHC
100 / LP 832 675-1 /
CD 832 675-2 /
MC 832 675-4
Remaster Series 5 (2005)
Bonus Tracks: Goldrush
II (12" Mix) / The Rhythm
Divine (1992 Version) /
Call it Love (12" Mix) /
Life Is A Snowball /
Tool in Rose
CD Vertigo 9830758,
YELLO 960091 (2014)

2014 Music on Vinyl LP
MOVLP277
Bonus Track: L'Hôtel
+v Shirley Bassey
+v Billy Mackenzie
+v Farida
+v Santiago Alfonso
+v Rush Winters
+g Chico Hablas
+d Felix Haug
+pia/a Philip Kienholz
+trom Steve Trop
+trom Don Randolph
(A) Ernst Gamper

Snowball And The Sound Of Yello (Promo)
Life Is A Snowball / Life
For Sale / Hommage
A Méliès / Desire /
Vicious Games / Swing /
I Love You / Lost Again /
Goldrush / Ciel Ouvert
CD 1987
Vertigo (DE) 0647 205
+ guests
(A) Ernst Gamper

YELLO in the movies
Oh Yeah // La Habanera
7" 1987
Mercury (DE) 888 908-7
(A) Ernst Gamper
(P) Christian Jungwirth

Oh Yeah
Oh Yeah // Oh Yeah
(Indian Summer Music)
7" 1987
Vertigo (CAN) SOV 2398

Oh Yeah
Oh Yeah (Dance Mix) //
La Habanera / Oh Yeah
(Indian Summer Version)
12" & CD Single 1987
Mercury (DE) 888 908-1 /
872 399-1 / 888 908-2
(A) Ernst Gamper
(P) Christian Jungwirth

Oh Yeah
Oh Yeah //
Vicious Games
7" 1987
Mercury (AUS) 888 860-1

Call It Love
Call It Love // L'Hôtel
7" 1987
Vertigo (DE) / Mercury
(UK) 888 311-7 / MER 248
+g Chico Hablas
+d Beat Ash
+c Billy Mackenzie
(A) Ernst Gamper

Call It Love
Call It Love // L'Hôtel /
Call It Love (Trego Snare
Version)
12" & CD Single 1987
Vertigo (DE) / Mercury
(UK) 888 311-1 / 888 311-2
/ MERX 248
+g Chico Hablas
+d Beat Ash
+c Billy Mackenzie
(A) Ernst Gamper

Call It Love
Call It Love (Remix) /
Call It Love (Dub) //
Call It Love (Extended
Mix) / Call It Love (Trego
Snare Version) / L'Hôtel
12" 1987
Mercury (US) 888 994-1
+g Chico Hablas
+d Beat Ash
+c Billy Mackenzie
(A) Ernst Gamper

Call It Love
Call It Love (Trego Snare
Version 2) // Santiago
(Live At The Palladium
New York)
12" 1987
Mercury (UK) YELLO 12
+g Chico Hablas
+d Beat Ash
+c Billy Mackenzie
(A) Ernst Gamper

Mercury (DE)

Mercury (UK)

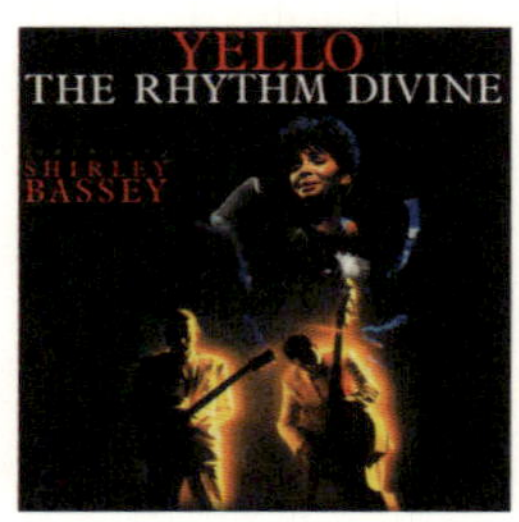

Mercury (FR)

The Rhythm Divine
The Rhythm Divine // Dr. Van Steiner (Instrumental)
7" 1987
Mercury (DE) / Mercury (UK) / Barclay (FR) 888 746-7 / MER 253
+v Shirley Bassey
+v Hubertus von Hohenlohe
+ guests
(A) Ines Boesch
(P) Kristian Wagner

The Rhythm Divine
The Rhythm Divine // Dr. Van Steiner (Instrumental) / Tool In Rose
12" & CD Single 1987
Mercury (DE) / Mercury (UK) / Barclay (FR) 888 746-1 / 888 746-2 / MERX 253
+v Shirley Bassey
+v Hubertus von Hohenlohe
+ guests
(A) Ines Boesch
(P) Kristian Wagner

The Rhythm Divine
Feat. Shirley Bassey
1: The Rhythm Divine (The Twelve Inch Version) // Dr. Van Steiner (Instrumental) / Tool In Rose
2: La Habanera // Live At The Roxy (The Original Live Mix New York Dec. 1983)
Double 12" & MC Single 1987 Vertigo (CAN) 870 318-1 / 870 318-4
+v Shirley Bassey
+v Hubertus von Hohenlohe
+ guests
(A) Me Company, Yello
(P) Christian Jungwirth

The Rhythm Divine
Feat. Billy Mackenzie
The Rhythm Divine (Version Two) // Dr. Van Steiner (Instrumental) / The Rhythm Divine (Original 7" Version)
12" 1987
Mercury (UK)
MERXR 253
+v Billy Mackenzie
+v Shirley Bassey
+ guests
(A) Me Company, Yello
(P) Christian Jungwirth

The 12" Collection
1: Let Me Cry // Haunted House
2: Lost Again // I Love You / Bostich (N'est-Ce Pas)
3: Yello Live At The Roxy N.Y. Dec. 83
4: The Rhythm Divine // Dr. Van Steiner (Instrumental) / Tool In Rose
5: Goldrush I // Goldrush II / She's Got A Gun (Live At The Palladium N.Y.)
6: Call It Love // L'Hôtel / Call It Love (Trego Snare Version)
12" Yellow Vinyl
Box Set 1988
Mercury (EU) 872 401-1
+ guests
(A) Tony Zanetta, Ann Militello, Ernst Gamper

Goldrush
Vicious Games / Desire / Angel No / Goldrush / Goldrush (Video PAL)
CDV 1988
Fontana (UK & EU)
080 306-2
+ guests
(A) Ernst Gamper

Oh Yeah
La Habanera / Call It Love / Si Señor The Hairy Grill / Oh Yeah / Oh Yeah (Video PAL)
CDV 1988
Fontana (UK & EU)
080 308-2
– guests
(A) Ernst Gamper

Flag
Tied Up / Of Course I'm Lying / 3rd Of June / Blazing Saddles // The Race / Alhambra / Otto Di Catania / Tied Up In Gear
LP & CD & MC 1988
Fontana (DE) / Mercury (UK) LP 836 426-1 / CD 836 426-2 / MC 836 426-4 / LP 836 778-1 / CD 836 778-2 / MC 836 778-4
Remaster Series 6 (2005)
Bonus Tracks: The Race (Break Light Mix) / Wall Street Bongo / The Race (12" Mix)
CD Vertigo 9830757
YELLO 960114 (2014)

2012 Music on Vinyl LP MOVLP535
+g Chico Hablas
+d Beat Ash
+v Billy Mackenzie
+cl Leos Gerteis
(A) Ernst Gamper

The Race
The Race // Another Race (Magician's Version For Tempest & Cottet)
7" & 12" & CD Single 1988
Fontana (EU) 870 330-7 / 870 330-1 / 870 330-2
+ guests
(A) Ernst Gamper

The Race
The Race (Video Mix) // The Race (Sporting Mix) / Another Race (Magician's Version For Tempest & Cottet)
7" 1988
Mercury (UK) YELLO 1 / 870 622-7
+ guests
(A) Ernst Gamper

The Race
The Race (The Pits Mix) // Oh Yeah (Dance Mix)
12" 1988
Mercury (UK & EU) YELLR 112 / 870 676-1
+ guests

12"

CD Single

The Race
The Race // La Habanera
12" & CD Single 1988
Mercury (UK & EU)
YELLO 112 / 870 622-1 / YEL CD 1
(A) Ernst Gamper

The Race (Promo)
The Race // Another Race
12" 1988
Mercury (UK) YDJ 1

The Race (Promo)
The Race // La Habanera
12" 1988
Mercury (DE) YDJ2

The Race (Promo)
The Race (The Pits Mix) / Oh Yeah (Dance Mix) / The Race (The Sporting Mix)
12" 1988
Mercury (UK) YDJ 3

The Race
The Race // Another Race
7" 1988
Vertigo (CAN) 870 615-7

The Race
The Race (Extended Version) // The Race (The Pits Mix) / Another Race
12" 1988
Vertigo (CAN) 870 676-1

The Race
The Race / Oh Yeah // The Race (7" Version) / Oh Yeah (Dance Mix) / Another Race (Magician's Version For Tempest & Cottet)
12" & CD Single & MC Single 1988
Vertigo (CAN) 870 615-1 / 870 615-2 / 870 615-4
(A) Ernst Gamper

The Race
The Race (Extended Version) / Another Race (Magician's Version For Tempest & Cottet) / The Race (Video PAL)
CDV 1988
Fontana (UK & EU)
080 528-2
+ guests

Tied Up
Tied Up In Red //
Wall Street Bongo
7" 1988
Mercury (DE) / Mercury (UK & EU) 872 366-7 /
YELLO 2
+g Chico Hablas
+p Beat Ash

Tied Up
Tied Up In Red //
Wall Street Bongo /
Tied Up
12" & CD Single 1988
Mercury (EU) / Mercury (DE)872 367-1 /
872 367-2
+g Chico Hablas
+p Beat Ash

Tied Up
Tied Up In Life //
Tied Up In Red /
Wall Street Bongo
12" 1988
Mercury (UK) YELLO 212
+g Chico Hablas
+p Beat Ash

Tied Up
Tied Up In Life / Oh Yeah (Indian Summer Version) / Wall Street Bongo /
Tied Up (7" Version)
CD Single 1988
Mercury (UK & EU)
YELCD2 / 872 397-2
+g Chico Hablas
+p Beat Ash

Tied Up (Promo)
Tied Up In Life //
Tied Up In Gear
12" 1988
Mercury (UK) FLAGDJ1
+g Chico Hablas
+p Beat Ash

Tied Up (Remix)
Tied Up In Mind / I Love You // Tied Up In Fantasia / Wall Street Bongo
12" 1988
Mercury (UK) YELLR 212 / 872 481-1
+g Chico Hablas
+p Beat Ash

Tied Up (Promo)
Tied Up In Gear / Tied Up In Fantasia / Tied Up In Africa (Edit) / Tied Up In Africa (Part 2)
12" 1988
Mercury (US) PRO 768-1
+g Chico Hablas
+p Beat Ash

Tied Up (Remix)
Tied Up In Fantasia //
Tied Up In Mind / Tied Up In Africa (Part 1)
12" & MC Single 1988
Vertigo (CAN) 872 481-1 / 872 481-4
+g Chico Hablas
+p Beat Ash

Tied Up
Tied Up In Life / Tied Up In Mind // Tied Up In Africa (Part 1) / Tied Up (African Beats) / Oh Yeah
CDV 1988
12" 1989
Mercury (US) 872 761-1
+g Chico Hablas
+p Beat Ash

Tied Up
Tied Up In Red /
Wall Street Bongo /
Third Of June / Tied Up (Video PAL)
CDV 1988
Mercury (UK & EU)
080 644-2
+g Chico Hablas
+p Beat Ash

The Race
The Race // Another Race (Magician's Version For Tempest & Cottet)
12" Picture Disc 1989
Fontana (EU) 870 331-1
+ guests
(A) Ernst Gamper

The Race
The Race (High Octane Mix) / The Race (Formula One Mix) // Blazing Saddles (Latinohouse Mix) / Blazing Saddles (Latinohouse Dub) /
The Race (Spare Parts Mix)
12" 1989
Mercury (US) 874 939-1
+ guests
(A) Ernst Gamper

The Race (Promo)
The Race (Rockamerica Radio Mix) / The Race (Swiss Mix) / The Race (Rockamerica Radio Instrumental)
CD Single 1989
Mercury (US) CDP 113
+ guests

The CD Single Collection
1: Goldrush I / Goldrush II / She's Got A Gun (Live At The Palladium N.Y.)
2: The Race / Another Race (Magician's Version For Tempest & Cottet) -
3: Oh Yeah (Dance Mix) / La Habanera / Oh Yeah (Indian Summer Version)
4: Tied Up In Red / Wall Street Bongo / Tied Up
5: Let Me Cry /
Haunted House
CD Single Box Set 1989
Windsong International (DE) 874 477-2
+ guests

Interview Picture Disc
(Interview)
12" 1989
Baktabak (UK) BAK 2132
(P) Tabak Marketing Ltd.

Of Course I'm Lying
Of Course I'm Lying //
Oh Yeah
7" 1989
Mercury (DE) / Mercury (UK & EU) 872 748-7 /
CD Single 1989
YELLO 3 / 872 944-7
+v Billy Mackenzie
+p Beat Ash
(A) Ernst Gamper

Of Course I'm Lying
The Yello Metropolitan Mix Down 1989 Part I /
Of Course I'm Lying (The Truth Is) // The Yello Metropolitan Mix Down 1989 Part II
12" 1989
Mercury (EU) 872 749-1
+v Billy Mackenzie
+p Beat Ash
(A) Ernst Gamper

Of Course I'm Lying
1: Of Course I'm Lying /
Oh Yeah (Dance Mix) //
The Yello Metropolitan Mixdown 1989 Part I
2: Of Course I'm Lying / Bostich // The Yello Metropolitan Mixdown 1989 Part II
Double 12" 1989
Mercury (UK & EU)
YELLO 312 / 872 945-1 / 872 947-1
+v Billy Mackenzie
+p Beat Ash
(A) Ernst Gamper

Of Course I'm Lying
Of Course I'm Lying / Oh Yeah (Dance Mix) // The Yello Metropolitan Mix Down 1989 Part I
12" & CD Single 1989
Mercury (UK & EU)
YELLO 312 / 872 945-1 / YELLCD 3 / 872 945-2
+v Billy Mackenzie
+p Beat Ash
(A) Ernst Gamper

Of Course I'm Lying
Of Course I'm Lying / Bostich // The Yello Metropolitan Mix Down 1989 Part II
12" & CD Single 1989
Mercury (UK & EU)
YELLO 322 / 872 947-1 / YELLCD 32 / 872 947-2
+v Billy Mackenzie
+p Beat Ash
(A) Ernst Gamper

Of Course I'm Lying
The Yello Metropolitan Mix Down 1989 Part I / The Yello Metropolitan Mix Down 1989 Part II / Of Course I'm Lying
CD Maxi 1989
Mercury (EU) 872 749-2
+v Billy Mackenzie
+p Beat Ash
(A) Ernst Gamper

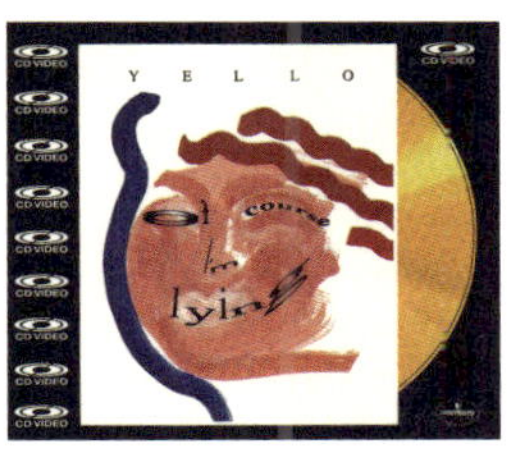

Of Course I'm Lying
Of Course I'm Lying / Third Of June / Alhambra / Otto Di Cantania / Of Course I'm Lying / Of Course I'm Lying (Video PAL)
CDV 1989
Mercury (UK & EU)
080 832-2
+v Billy Mackenzie
+p Beat Ash
(A) Ernst Gamper

Blazing Saddles
Blazing Saddles // I Love You
7" & MC Single 1989
Mercury (DE) / Mercury (UK & EU) 874 928-7 / YELLO 4 / 874 718-7 / YELLMC 4 / 874 718-4
+ guests

Blazing Saddles
Blazing Saddles (Latinohouse Remix) / Blazing Saddles (Latinohouse Dub) // I Love You (The Emilio Pasquez Rubber Band Mix) / I Love You
12" 1989
Mercury (UK & EU)
YELLO 412 / 874 719-1 / 874 929-1
+ guests

Mercury (UK & EU)

Blazing Saddles
Blazing Saddles (Latinohouse Remix) / I Love You (The Emilio Paquez Rubber Band Mix) / The Rhythm Divine (Feat. Shirley Bassey) / Blue Nabou
CD Single 1989
Mercury (EU) / Mercury (UK & EU) 874 929-2 / YELCD 4 / 874 719-2 / YELLCD 44 / 874 751-2
+ guests

A Trip Around The World In 1800 Seconds (Promo)
Blazing Saddles / The Race / Oh Yeah / Of Course I'm Lying / Tied Up / The Rhythm Divine (Feat. Shirley Bassey) / Vicious Games / I Love You
CD 1989
Mercury (UK & EU)
YELLO 1989
+ guests

Unbelievable
(Theme From *Ford Fairlane*)
Ford's 12" Mix / Ford's Edit) / X-Rated Mix // Morales Mix / Dub Me Mix / Techno Mix
12" 1990
Elektra (US) 0-66611
+k Eric Kupper
+k Satoshi Tomite
+p David Morales

The Adventures Of Ford Fairlane Soundtrack
Including Yello: Unbelievable (Theme From *Ford Fairlane*)
1990 LP & CD & MC
Elektra (EU) / Elektra (US) LP 7559-60952-1 / EKT74 / CD 7559-60952-2 / MC 9 60952-2

Nuns On The Run Soundtrack
Including Yello: The Race / Hawaiian Chance / Tied Up / Moon On Ice / Dr. Van Steiner / Goldrush / On The Run
1990 LP & CD & MC
Mercury (EU & US) Mercury (DE) LP 846 043-1 / 846 435-1 CD 845 435-2 / 846 043-2 / MC 846 435-4 / 846 043-4

Rubberbandman
Rubberbandman (7" Version) // Sweet Thunder
7" & MC 1991
Mercury (EU) / Mercury (EU & UK) / 7" 868 340-7 / 7" YELLO 5 / MC 868 340-4 / MC YELMC 5
+c Billy Mackenzie
+g Marco Colombo
+p Beat Ash
(A) Ernst Gamper, En Soie Zürich
(P) Francesca Giovanelli

Rubberbandman
Rubberbandman (Extended Version) // Rubberbandman (Single Version) / Sweet Thunder
12" & CD Single & CD Single with Yellow Rubber Sleeve 1991
Mercury (EU) / Mercury (EU & UK) / 12" 868 341-1 / CD Single 868 341-2 / 12" YELLO 512 / CD Single YELCD 5

Rubberbandman
(Rubber Version) / The Race (The Pits Mix) / The Rhythm Divine (Feat. Shirley Bassey)
CD Single 1991
Mercury (EU) / Mercury (EU & UK) / 868 457-2 868 341-2 / YELCD 55

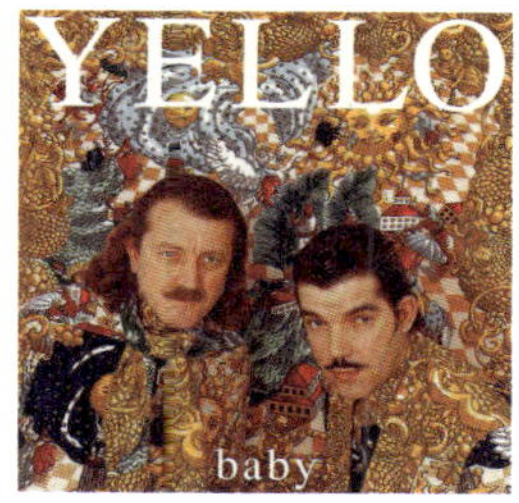

Baby
Homage To The Mountain / Rubberbandman / Jungle Bill / Ocean Club / Who's Gone? / Capri Calling // Drive/Driven / On The Run / Blender / Sweet Thunder
LP & CD & MC 1991
DCC 1992
Mercury (EU) / Mercury (UK) / LP 848 791-1 / CD 848 791-2 / MC 848 791-4 / DCC 848 791-5
+v/c Billy Mackenzie
+g Ernst Gamper
+g Marco Colombo
+a Rolf Aschwanden
+c Patrizia Fontana
+p Beat Ash
(A) Ines Boesch, En Soie Zürich
(P) Francesca Giovanelli

LP Reissue 2021
Universal (EU / Yello (CH) / Polydor (EU) / 0602435719429 / 7640161960992

Who's Gone?
Who's Gone? // Ocean Club
7" 1991
Mercury (EU) / 868 764-7
+p Beat Ash
(A) Ernst Gamper, Ines Boesch
(P) Francesca Giovanelli

Who's Gone?
(Extended Version) // Who's Gone? (Single Version) / Ocean Club
12" & CD Single
Mercury (EU)
12" 868 765-1
CD Single 868 765-2

Bostich
Bostich (Reese Uptempo Mix) / Bostich (Reese Break Beat Mix) / Bostich (Reese Respect Mix) // Bostich (New Life Mix) / Bostich (The Reese Savage Mix) / Bostich (Original Version)
12" Yellow Vinyl & MC Single 1992
FFRR (US) /
12" 162 350 005-1 /
MC 162 350 005-4

Jungle Bill
(Green Sleeve)
Jungle Bill (Single Version) // Blender (Album Version)
7" 1992 Mercury (EU) /
Mercury (UK) / 868 874-7 / 866 374-7 / MER 376
+g Marco Colombo
+p Beat Ash
(A) Z-Art
(P) Carolin Kewer

Jungle Bill
Jungle Bill (Big Pig Shuffle) // Jungle Bill (Space Shuffle)
12" 1992
Mercury (EU) / 868 875-1

Jungle Bill
Jungle Bill (Single Version) / Jungle Bill (Big Pig Shuffle) / Jungle Bill (Space Shuffle)
CD Single 1992
Mercury (EU) / 868 875-2

Jungle Bill
(Big Pig Shuffle) / Jungle Bill (Ian Tregoning Mix) // Jungle Bill (Chicken Dive Mix) / Jungle Bill (Space Shuffle)
12" & MC Single 1992
Smash Records (US) /
12" 162-880 003-1 /
MC 162-880 003-4
(A) Go! Big Active (London)

Jungle Bill
Jungle Bill / Jungle Bill (Big Pig Shuffle) / Jungle Bill (Space Shuffle) // Jungle Bill (Voodoo Fudge Mix) / Jungle Bill (Chicken Dive Mix)
CD Single 1992
Mercury (EU & UK) / 864 373-2 / MERCD 376

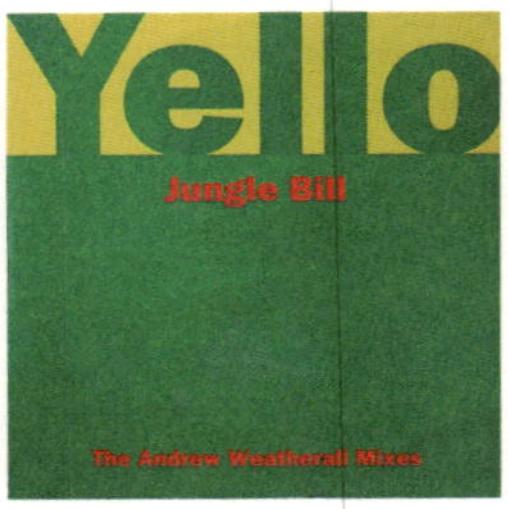

Jungle Bill
(The Andrew Weatherall Mixes)
Jungle Bill (Sabres Of Paradise Part 1) / Jungle Bill (Sabres Of Paradise Part 2) // Jungle Bill (Too Tough 4 Trego Part 1) / Jungle Bill (Too Tough 4 Trego Part 2)
12" 1992
Mercury (EU & UK) /
864 375-1 / MRXX 376

Jungle Bill
(Red Sleeve)
Jungle Bill (Single Version From The Album *Essential*) // On The Run (Long Version From The Album *Baby*)
7" 1992
Mercury (EU) / 864 438-7
+g Marco Colombo
+p Beat Ash
(A) Z-Art
(P) Carolin Kewer

Jungle Bill
Jungle Bill (Long Version From The Album *Baby*) // Jungle Bill (Chicken Dive Mix)
12" 1992
Mercury (EU) / 864 439-1

Jungle Bill
Jungle Bill (Single Version From The Album *Essential*) // Jungle Bill (Long Version From The Album *Baby*) / Jungle Bill (Chicken Dive Mix)
CD Single 1992
Mercury (EU) / 864 439-2

Essential
Oh Yeah / The Race / Rubberbandman / Vicious Games / Tied Up / Lost Again / I Love You // Of Course I'm Lying / Pinball Cha Cha / Bostich / Desire / Jungle Bill / Goldrush / The Rhythm Divine
LP 1992
Mercury (EU) / LP 512 390-1
+ guests
(A) Z-Art
(P) Carolin Kewer

Oh Yeah / The Race / Drive/Driven / Rubberbandman / Vicious Games / Tied Up / Lost Again / I Love You / Of Course I'm Lying / Pinball Cha Cha / Bostich / Desire / Jungle Bill / Call It Love / Goldrush / The Rhythm Divine
CD & MC & DCC 1992 & 1999
Mercury (EU) / Smash Records (US) / CD 512 390-2 / CD 162-888 002-2 / MC 512 390-4 / MC / 162-888 002-4 /
DCC 512 390-5

Essential Christmas
The Single Collection
Bonus Tracks:
Tremendous Pain / Jingle Bells
CD 1995 & 2005
Mercury (EU & US) /
528 944-2

CD Reissue 2014
Yello (EU) /
7640161960152

The Race / Bostich
The Race // Bostich
7" & MC 1992
Mercury (EU & UK) / 7" 864 634-7 / 7" MER 382/ MC 864 634-4 / MC MERMC 382
(A) Go! Big Active

The Race / Bostich
The Race // Bostich (Reese Uptempo Mix) / Bostich (Reese Break-beat)
12" 1992
Mercury (EU & UK) /
864 635-1 / MERX 382

The Race / Bostich
The Race / The Race / The Race / Bostich (Reese Respect Mix)
CD Single 1992
Mercury (EU & UK) /
864 635-2 / MERCD 382

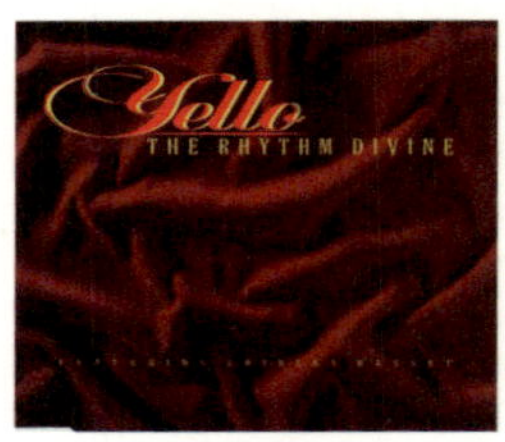

The Rhythm Divine
(Feat. Shirley Bassey)
The Rhythm Divine / The Rhythm Divine (1992 Version) / Ocean Club
CD Single 1993
Mercury (EU) / 864 963-2
+v Shirley Bassey
+ guests
(A) Z-Art

Drive/Driven
Drive/Driven (Edit) / Drive/Driven (Album Version)
CD Single Promo 1993
Smash Records (US) /
PRCD 010-2

Vicious Games
Vicious Games (Yello Belly Trippin' Trance Mix) / Vicious Games (Vicious Radio Mix) // Vicious Games (Mo's Dirty Ol' Dub #1) / Vicious Games (Vicious Vocal Club Mix)
12" 1993
Smash Records (US) /
1624-440 812-1

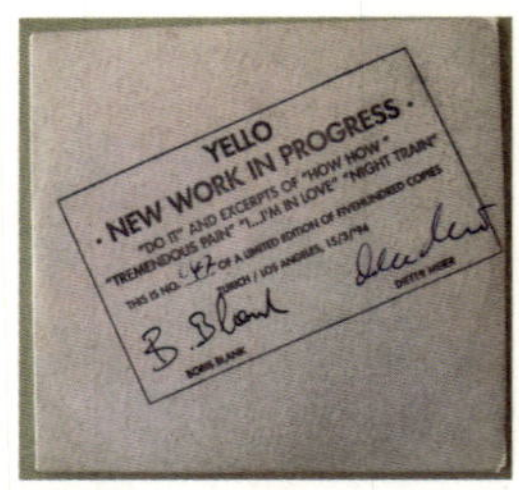

New Work In Progress
Do It / and excerpts of How How / Tremendous Pain / I... I'm In Love / Night Train
CD Promo
(500 signed copies) 1994
Mercury (DE)

Do It
Do It (Marky P. & Teri B. Dub) / Do It (Single Version) // Vicious Games (Belly Trippin' Trance Mix)
12" 1994
Mercury (EU) / 858 695-1
+v Rush Winters
(A) LWS

Do It
Do It (Marky P. & Teri B. Dub) // Do It (Blessed & Beaten)
12" 1994
Mercury (EU) / 858 513-1

Do It
Do It (Single Version) / Do It (Marky P. & Teri B. Dub) / Do It (Instrumental Version) / Vicious Games (Belly Trippin' Trance Mix)
CD Single 1994
Mercury (EU) / 858 695-2

Do It
1: Do It (Blessed & Beaten) / Do It (Boris 7") // Do It (Buddah-Pic Mix) / Do It (Marky P. & Teri B. Dub)
2: Do It (Flow Dub) / Do It (Boris 7" Instrumental) // Do It (Flow Mix) / Do It (Spinout & Mellow Mix)
Double 12" 1994
Smash Records (US) / 162-445 815-1

Do It
Do It (Boris 7") / Do It (Radio) / Do It (Boris 7" Instrumental) / Do It (Spinout & Mellow Mix) / Do It (Buddah-Pic Mix) / Do It (Flow Mix)
CD Single 1994
Smash Records (US) / 162-445 815-2

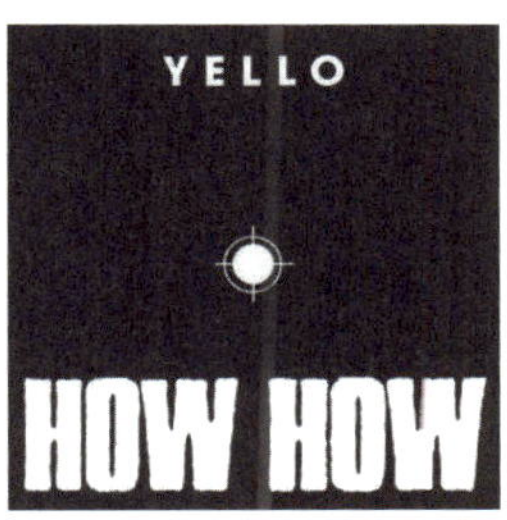

How How
How How (The PreMix by Yello) / How How (Dee Doo Dee Mix) // How How (Dee Doo Dee Dub Mix) / How How (In Silence Mix) /How How (Saxophone Mix)
12" 1994
Mercury (EU & UK)
856 249-1 / MERX 414
(A) LWS

How How
How How (Papa-Who-Ma-Mix) / How How (Dee Doo Dee Mix) / How How (Dee Doo Dee Dub) // How How (The PreMix by Yello) / How How (In Silence Mix) / How How (Drummer's Mix)
12" 1994
4th & Broadway (US) / 162-440 604-1

How How
The Fluke Mixes
How How (Papa-Who-Ma-Mix) / How How (Brown Cow Mix) // How How (Dee Doo Dee Mix) / How How (The PreMix by Yello)
12" 1994
Mercury (EU) / 856 137-1

How How
The Plutone Mixes
How How (Drummer's Mix) / How How (In Silence Mix) // How How (Saxophone Mix) / How How (The PreMix by Yello) / How How (A Capella)
12" 1994
Mercury (EU) / 856 139-1

How How
How How (Single Version) / How How (The PreMix by Yello) / How How (Papa-Who-Ma-Mix) / How How (Dee Doo Dee Mix) / How How (Brown Cow) / How How (Drummer's Mix) / How How (In Silence Mix)
CD Single 1994
Mercury (EU & UK)
856 249-2 / MERDD 414

How How
How How (Single Version) / Vicious Games (Belly Trippin Trance Mix) / Do It (Marky P & Teri B Dub) / Do It (Blessed & Beaten Mix)
CD Single 1994
Mercury (EU & UK) /856 251-2 / MERCD 414

How How - 1
- The Originals
How How (Single Version) / The PreMix (How How) / Moon Dog
CD Single 1994
Mercury (EU) / 856 143-2
(A) LWS / Kaarst

How How - 2
- The Plutone Mixes
How How (Drummer's Mix) / How How (In Silence Mix) / How How (Saxophone Mix) / How How (Acapella)
CD Single 1994
Mercury (EU) / 856 139-2

How How - 3
- The Fluke Mixes
How How (Papa-Who-Ma-Mix) / How How (Dee Doo Dee Mix) / How How (Dee Doo Dee Dub Mix) / How How (Brown Cow Mix)
CD Single 1994
Mercury (EU) / 856 137-2

How How - 4
- Breaks, Beats & Loops
- The D.J. / Musician Edition
How How (Single Version / The Premix (How How) / Breaks, Beats & Loops (The How How Samples)
CD Single 1994
Mercury (EU) / 856 141-2

How How
How How (Single Mix) / How How (Dee Doo Dee Mix)
MC 1994
Mercury (EU & UK) / 856 248-4 / MERMC 414

Zebra
Suite 909 / How How / Night Train / Do It / I... I'm In Love / S.A.X. / Fat Cry // Tremendous Pain / Move Dance Be Born / The Premix (How How) / Poom Sharka
LP & CD & MC & Limited CD Tin Box + Watch 1994
Mercury (EU) / 4th & Broadway (US)
LP 522 496-1 / CD 522 496-2 / CD Tin Box 522 496-0 / MC 522 496-4 / CD 162-444 065-2 / MC 162-444 065-4
+g Marco Colombo
+g Chico Hablas
+c Ian Shaw, Eleonore Meier-Leuthold, Boris Blank
(A) Best Of..., LWS
(P) Carolin Kewer

CD Reissue 2007
Mercury (EU) / 522 496-2

CD Reissue 2014
Yello (EU) / 7640161960176

LP Reissue 2021
Universal (EU) / Yello (EU) / Polydor (EU) / 0602435719443 / 7640161961005

Blame On Yello (Steve Blame (MTV) Talks To Dieter Meier And Boris Blank)
CD Promo 1994
Mercury (EU) / Phonogram (EU) / Barclay (EU) / 4th & Broadway (US)

Tremendous Pain (Suite 904)
Tremendous Pain (Suite 904) / Tremendous Pain (Palace Mix) // Tremendous Pain (Bible Mix) / Tremendous Pain (Hell Mix)
12" 1995
Mercury (EU) / 856 749-1

Tremendous Pain
Tremendous Pain (D's House Mix) / Tremendous Pain (D's Deep Dub Mix) // Tremendous Pain (Extended Version) / Tremendous Pain (Tremendhouse Instrumental)
12" 1995
Mercury (DE) / 856 751-1

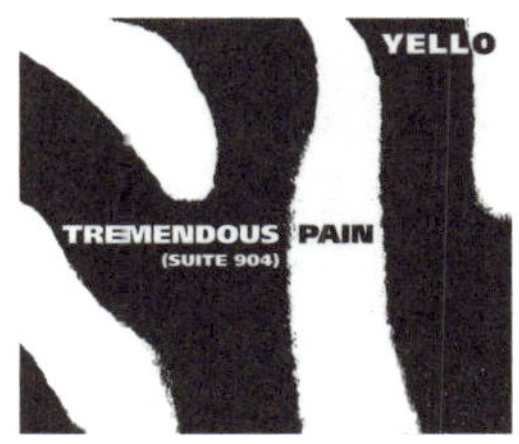

Tremendous Pain (Suite 904)
Tremendous Pain (Suite 904 – Single Version) / Tremendous Pain (Suite 904) / Tremendous Pain (Bible Mix) / Tremendous Pain (Bobby D'Ambrosio's House Mix) / Tremendous Pain (Steve Mac's Extended Mix) / Tremendous Paim (Album Version)
CD Single 1995
Mercury (EU) / 856 749-2
(A) Best Of..., LWS

Tremendous Pain
Tremendous Pain (D's Club Remix) / Tremendous Pain (D's House Mix) / Tremendous Pain (Album Version) // Tremendous Pain (Tremendhouse Vocal Mix) / Tremendous Pain (Suite 904 Alternative Vocal)
12' & CD Single 1995
4th & Broadway (US) / 162-440 608-1 / 162-440 608-2

Westbam's Hands On Yello - Bostich
Bostich (Machine Mix) // Bostich (Rush Push Mix)
12" 1995
Urban (DE) / 851 357-1
(A) KM7
(P) Serge Hölschi

Westbam's Hands On Yello - Bostich
Bostich (Machine Mix) / Bostich (Rush Push Mix) / Bostich (Video Cut)
CD Single 1995
Urban (DE) / 851 357-2

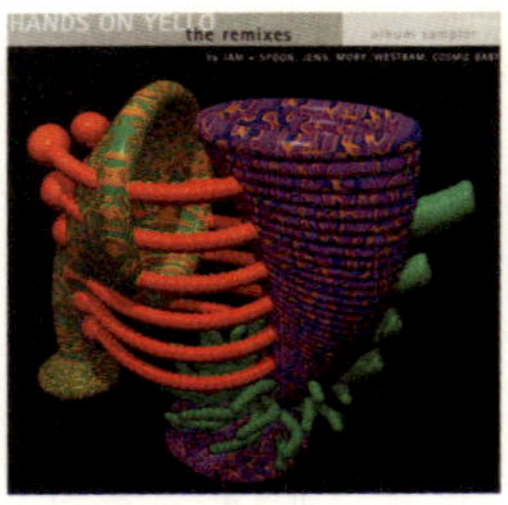

Hands On Yello (Album Sampler)
1: Jam & Spoon's Hands On Yello - You Gotta Say Yes To Another Excess // Jens' Hands On Yello - Ciel Ouvert
2: Moby's Hands On Yello - Lost Again // Westbam's Hands On Yello - Bostich / Cosmic Baby's Hands On Yello - Doctor Van Steiner
Double 12" Promo 1995
Urban (UK) / YELLODJ
(A) Creative Mission

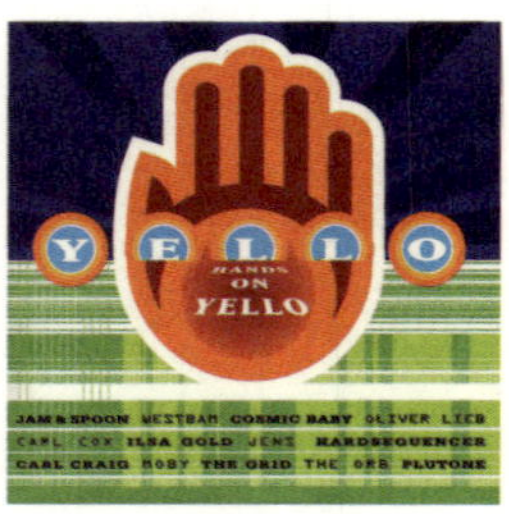

Hands On Yello
Cosmic Baby's Hands On Yello - Dr. Van Steiner / Westbam's Hands On Yello - Bostich / Jens' Hands On Yello - Ciel Ouvert / Jam & Spoon's Hands On Yello - You Gotta Say Yes To Another Excess - Great Mission // Oliver Lieb's Hands On Yello - Crash Dance / The Grid's Hands On Yello - Vicious Games (12" Edit) / Plutone's Hands On Yello - Oh Yeah // Ilsa Gold's Hands On Yello - Live At The Roxy / Hardsequencer's Hands On Yello - I Love You / Carl Cox's Hands On Yello - L'Hôtel // Carl Craig's Hands On Yello - La Habanera / The Orb's Hands On Yello - Excess / Moby's Hands On Yello - Lost Again
Double LP & CD & MC 1995
Urban (EU) / Double LP 527 603-1 / CD 527 383-2 / MC 527 383-4
(A) KM7
(P) Serge Höltschi

Jam & Spoon's Hands On Yello - You Gotta Say Yes To Another Excess
You Gotta Say Yes To Another Excess - Great Mission (Uff Die 12-Mix) // You Gotta Say Yes To Another Excess- Great Mission (Haus Mix)
12" 1995
Urban (EU & UK) / 851 811-1 / PZ 343 / 579093-1
(A) KM7
(P) Serge Hötschi

You Gotta Say Yes To Another Excess
- Great Mission (Uff Die 12-Mix) / You Gotta Say Yes To Another Excess- Great Mission (Haus Mix) / You Gotta Say Yes To Another Excess- Great Mission
CD Single 1995
Urban (EU) / 851 811-2

You Gotta Say Yes To Another Excess
- Great Mission (Radio Edit) / You Gotta Say Yes To Another Excess - Great Mission (Uff Die 12-Mix) / You Gotta Say Yes To Another Excess- Great Mission (Haus Mix)
CD Single 1995
Urban & Polydor (EU & UK) / 579093-2 / PZCD 343

Hands On Yello
1: Cosmic Baby's Hands On Yello - Dr. Van Steiner // The Orb's Hands On Yello - You Gotta Say Yes To Another Excess
2: Westbam's Hands On Yello - Bostich (Machine Mix) // Westbam's Hands On Yello - Bostich (Rush Push Mix)
3: Jam & Spoon's Hands On Yello - You Gotta Say Yes To Another Excess - Great Mission (Uff Die 12-Mix) // Jam & Spoon's Hands On Yello - You Gotta Say Yes To Another Excess - Great Mission (Haus Mix)
4: Jens' Hands On Yello - Ciel Ouvert / Moby's Hands On Yello - Lost Again // Ilsa Gold's Hands On Yello - Live At The Roxy / Hardsequencer's Hands On Yello - I Love You
5: Carl Cox's Hands On Yello - L'Hôtel // Plutone's Hands On Yello - Oh Yeah / Carl Craig's Hands On Yello - La Habanera
6: Oliver Lieb's Hands On Yello - Crash Dance // Oliver Lieb's Hands On Yello - Desire / The Grid's Hands On Yello - Vicious Games (Instrumental Acid)
12" Box Set 1995
Urban (EU) / 527 383-1
(A) KM7
(P) Serge Höltschi

Hands On Yello (The Updates)
Ilsa Gold's Hands On Yello - Live At The Roxy / Westbam's Hands On Yello - Bostich (Machine Mix) / Carl Cox's Hands On Yello - L'Hôtel (Long Version) / Jam & Spoon's Hands On Yello - You Gotta Say Yes To Another Excess - Great Mission (Uff Die 12-Mix) / Oliver Lieb's Hands On Yello - Crash Dance / Hardsequencer's Hands On Yello - I Love You / Oliver Lieb's Hands On Yello - Desire V2 / Plutone's Hands On Yello - Oh Yeah / Cosmic Baby's Hands On Yello - Dr. Van Steiner / Jens' Hands On Yello - Ciel Ouvert / Carl Craig's Hands On Yello - La Habanera / The Grid's Hands On Yello - Vicious Games (Ambient Mix) / Moby's Hands On Yello - Lost Again / The Orb's Hands On Yello - Excess (Long Version)
Double CD 1995
Urban (EU) / 527 728-2
(A) KM7
(P) Serge Höltschi

Plutone's Hands On Yello - Oh Yeah
Oh Yeah (Video Edit) / Oh Yeah (Experimental Mix) / Oh Yeah (Plutone Remix) / Oh Yeah (Sun + Moon Mix
CD Single 1995
Urban (EU) / 577 089-2
(A) KM7
(P) Serge Höltschi

Jingle Bells
(From Disney's *The Santa Clause* Soundtrack)
Jingle Bells (Santa Club Mix) // Jingle Bells (Movie Version)
12" 1995
Mercury (EU) / 852 487-1

Jingle Bells
(From Disney's *The Santa Clause* Soundtrack)
Jingle Bells (Single Version) / Jingle Bells (Movie Version) / Jingle Bells (Santa Club Mix)
12" & CD Single 1995
4th & Broadway (US) / 12" 162-448 018-1 / CD Single 162-448 018-2

Jingle Bells
(From Disney's *The Santa Clause* Soundtrack)
Jingle Bells (Single Version) // Jingle Bells (Movie Version)
12" 1995
Mercury (EU) / 852 486-2

Jingle Bells
(From Disney's *The Santa Clause* Soundtrack)
Jingle Bells (Single Version) / Jingle Bells (Movie Version) / Jingle Bells (Santa Club Mix)
CD Single 1995
Mercury (EU) / 852-487-2

On Track (The Mixes)
1: On Track (Original Version) // On Track (Tokapi's On Track Mix)
2: On Track (By Awex) / On Track (Doug Laurent's First Journey) // On Track (Doug Laurent's Second Journey) / On Track (By Timewriter)
3: On Track (Hard Express Rhythm Masters) // On Track (Doug Laurent's First Journey Dub)
Triple 12" 1996
Mercury (EU) / 587 627-1
(A) Weissraum

To The Sea
(Feat. Stina Nordenstam)
The Sea (Bangin' Mix) / To The Sea (Planet Trax 'Yello Dubmarine' Mix) // To The Sea (Original Mix) / To The Sea (Tswl Mix)
12" 1997
Mercury & Barclay (EU) / 574 477-1
+v Stina Nordenstam
(A) Martin Wanner

To The Sea - The Mixes
(Feat. Stina Nordenstam)
To The Sea (Northern Mix) / To The Sea (Planet Trax 'Yello Dubmarine' Mix) //
To The Sea (Aqualite Mix) / To The Sea (Original Version)
12" 1997
Mercury (EU) / 574 125-1

To The Sea
(Feat. Stina Nordenstam)
To The Sea (Radio Version Northern Mix) / To The Sea (Original Version) / To The Sea (Southern Mix)
CD Single 1997
Mercury (EU) / 574 121-2

Pocket Universe
1: Solar Driftwood / Celsius / More // On Track / Monolith / To The Sea /
2: Magnetic / Liquid Mountain / Pan Blue // Resistor / Beyond Mirrors
CD Bonus Track: To The Sea (Remix by Steve B-Zet)
Double LP & CD & MC 1997 & 1999
Mercury (EU & UK)
Double LP 534 353-1 /
CD 534 353-2 /
MC 534 353-2
+v Stina Nordenstam
(A) Martin Wanner

CD Reissue 2014
Yello (EU) /
7640161960190

Double LP Reissue 2021
Universal (EU) & Polydor (EU) / Yello (EU) / 0602435719450 /
7640161961012

On Track
CD: On Track (Doug Laurent's First Journey - Single Version) /
On Track (Original Version - Edit) / On Track (Doug Laurent's First Journey)
CD-Rom: Video - On Track / Video -
To The Sea
CD Single 1997
Mercury 044 115-2
(A) Martin Wanner

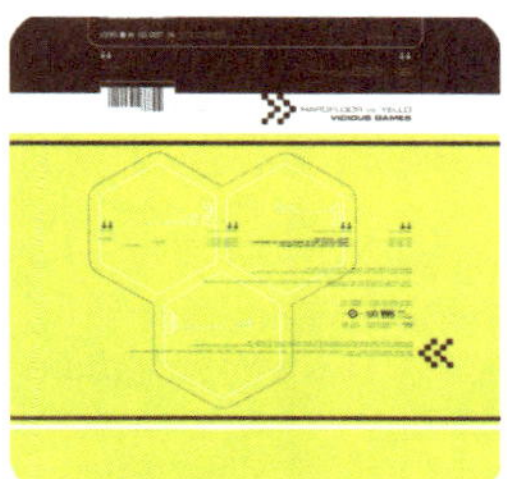

Hardfloor Vs. Yello
Vicious Games
Vicious Games (Hardfloor Remix) // Vicious Games (Boris Blank & Olaf Wollschläger Remix) / Vicious Games (Vorsprung Durch Technik Remix)
12" (Part 1/5) 1998
Gang Go Music (EU) & Orbit Records (EU) /
GG007
+v Diana Böge
(A) Hartwerk

Yello Vs. Hardfloor
Vicious Games
1: Hardfloor Edition
2: The Dance Mixes
Double 12" (Part 2/5)
Promo 1998

Yello Vs. Hardfloor
Vicious Games
(Hardfloor Edition)
Vicious Games (Vocal Club Version) / Vicious Games (Slow Vocal Mix) // Vicious Games (Hardfloor Dub Mix) / Vicious Games (Slow Dub Mix)
12" (Part 3/5) 1998
Gang Go Music (EU) & Orbit Records (EU) /
GG007R1

Yello Vs. Hardfloor
Vicious Games
(The Dance Mixes)
Vicious Games (Da Bomb Mix) / Vicious Games (Blank & Jones Mix) // Vicious Games (Boris Blank & Olaf Wollschläger Mix) / Vicious Games (Headroom Mix) / Vicious Games (Gorgeous Mix)
12" (Part 4/5) 1998
Gang Go Music (EU) & Orbit Records (EU) /
GG07R2

Yello Vs. Hardfloor
Vicious Games
Vicious Games (Radio / Video Edit) / Vicious Games (Club Mix) / Vicious Games (Boris Blank & Olaf Wollschläger Mix) / Vicious Games (Slow Vocal Mix) / Vicious Games (Da Bomb Remix) / Vicious Games (Headroom Remix)
CD Single (Part 5/5) 1998
Gang Go Music (EU) & Orbit Records (EU) & Virgin (EU) / 895 562

Vicious Games
Vicious Games (Art Of Trance Remix) // / Vicious Games (Club Mix)
12" (Part 1/2) 1998
Platipus (UK) / PLAT52
(A) Mark Neal

Vicious Games
Vicious Games (Headroom Mix) // Vicious Games (Da Bomb Remix) / Vicious Games (Boris Blank & Olaf Wollschläger Remix)
12" (Part 2/2) 1998
Platipus (UK) / PLAT52X

Yello Vs. Hardfloor
Vicious Games
Vicious Games (Radio/ Video Edit) / Vicious Games (Art Of Trance Remix) / Vicious Games (Da Bomb Remix)
CD Single 1998
Platipus (UK) /
PLAT52CD

Eccentrix Remixes
The Race (Brake Light Mix) / How How (Papa-Who-Ma-Mix) / More (Rockabilly Mix) / Do It (Marky P. & Teri B. Dub) / Topaz (Insect Mix) / How How (In Silence) / On Track (Doug Laurent's First Journey) / Vicious Games (B. Blank & Olaf Wollschläger Mix) / Rubberbandman (Rubber Mix) / She's Got A Gun (Live At The Palladium NY) / To The Sea (TSWL Mix)
CD & MC 1999 & 2005
Mercury (EU) / 538 584-2
(A) Martin Wanner, Raphael Schenker

CD Reissue 2014
Yello (EU) /
7640161960213

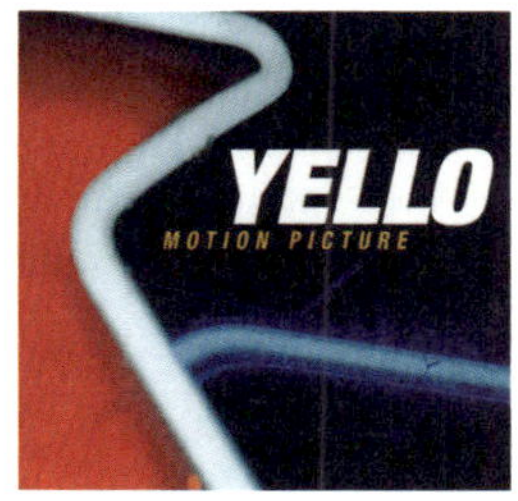

Motion Picture
Get On / Houdini / Prisoner Of His Mind / Distant Mirror / Time Freeze / Croissant Bleu / Liquid Lies / Squeeze Please / Shake And Shiver / Bubbling Under / Point Blank / Cyclops
CD & MC 1999
Mercury (EU) / CD
546 706-2 /
MC 546 706-4
+k/pia Gino Todesco
(A) Martin Wanner
(P) Martin Wanner

Double LP Reissue 2021
Universal (EU) / Polydor (EU) / 0602435719474
Yello (EU) /
07640161961029

Squeeze Please
Squeeze Please (Sounds Of Life Radio Mix) / Squeeze Please (Sounds Of Dub Radio Mix) // Squeeze Please (Original Radio Mix) / Squeeze Please (Goldkind's Different Class Of Brass Mix)
12" 1999
Mercury (EU) / 562 421-1
+g Malte Hagemeister
+b Martin Gotarski
+k Sven Kaiser
(A & P) Martin Wanner

Squeeze Please
Squeeze Please (Original Radio Mix) / Squeeze Please (Sounds Of Life Radio Mix) / Squeeze Please (Sounds Of Life Dub Mix) / Squeeze Please (Sounds Of Life Club Mix) / Squeeze Please (Goldkind's Different Class Of Brass Mix)
CD Single 1999
Mercury (EU) / 562 421-2

Squeeze Please (Remixes)
1: Squeeze Please (Wackside Tweaker Mix) / Squeeze Please (Wackside Dub Mix) // Squeeze Please (Oliver Moldan Vocal Remix) / Squeeze Please (Oliver Moldan 'Dub-Dance' Remix)
2: Squeeze Please (De-Phazz Mix) / Squeeze Please (Original Radio Mix) // Squeeze Please (Sounds Of Life Club Mix)
Double 12" 2000
Mercury (EU) / Yello 2000

Squeeze Please
Squeeze Please (Wackside Radio Mix) / Squeeze Please (De-Phazz Radio Mix) / Squeeze Please (Original Radio Mix) / Squeeze Please (Wackside Tweaker Mix) / Squeeze Please (Oliver Moldan 'Dub-Dance' Mix) / Squeeze Please (Wackside Dub Mix) / Squeeze Please (Oliver Moldan Vocal Remix)
CD Single 2000
Mercury 562 639-2
(A) Martin Wanner

The Race 2003
The Race 2003 (Tomcraft On Yello) // Planet Dada (Northern Lite Remix) / Planet Dada (Futuristic Funk)
12" 2003
Motor (EU) / 981 102 1
(A) Martin Wanner

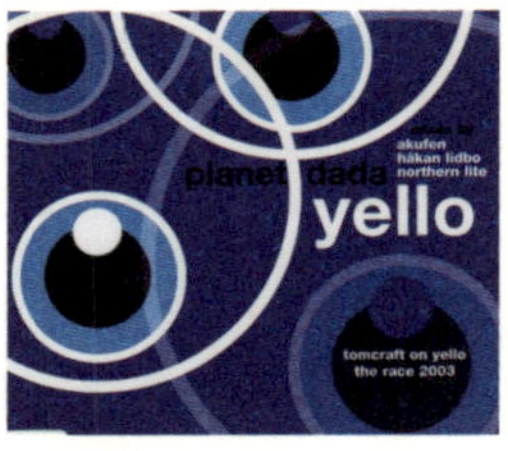

Planet Dada
Planet Dada (Original Version) / The Race 2003 (Tomcraft On Yello) / Planet Dada (Visiting The Planet) / Planet Dada (Akufen's Delta Panda Mix) / The Race 2003 (Tomcraft On Yello Extended) / Planet Dada (Northern Lite Mix) / Planet Dada (Futuristic Funk)
CD Single 2003
Motor (EU) / 06024 9813515 (0)
(A) Martin Wanner

The Eye
Planet Dada / Nervous / Don Turbulento / Soul On Ice / Junior B / Tiger Dust / Distant Solution / Hipster's Delay / Time Palace / Indigo Bay / Unreal / Bougainville / Star Breath / Planet Dada (Flamboyant)
Enhanced CD: Planet Dada (Visit The Planet Mix) / Planet Dada (Akufen's Delta Panda Mix) / Planet Dada (Northern Light Mix) / Planet Dada (Futuristic Funk Mix) / The Race 2003 (Tomcraft On Yello Remix) / The Race 2003 (Tomcraft On Yello) / Video: Planet Dada
CD 2003
Universal (EU) / Motor (EU & UK) / CD 0602498658635
+v Jade Davies
+b Pogo
+c Monks from the Gyuto Monastry, Bombila
(A) Martin Wanner
(P) Beat Pfändler

CD 5-Track Promo Sampler 2003
Motor (EU)

Enhanced CD + CD 2005
Radikal Records (US) / Motor (US) / RAD90083-2

CD Reissue 2014
Yello (EU) / 7640161960237

Double LP Reissue 2021
Universal (EU) / Polydor (EU) / Yello (EU) / 7640161960237

Base For Alec
Base For Alec
12" (Single Sided) & Digital File (WAV) 2004
Output (UK) / OPR59
(A) Ernst Gamper

Remaster Series
1: **Solid Pleasure**
Bonus Tracks: Thrill Wave / I.T. Splash / Gluehead / Smirak's Train Bostich (N'est-Ce Pas)
2: **Claro Que Si**
Bonus Tracks: Tub Dub / She's Got A Gun (Live At The Palladium NY Sep. 1985) / Daily Disco (2005) Version / The Evening's Young (1985 Version) / Pinball Cha Cha (12" Mix) / Desire For Desire
3: **You Gotta Say Yes To Another Excess**
Bonus Tracks: Base For Alec / Rubber West / You Gotta Say Yes To Another Excess (UK Promo 12" Version) / Live At The Roxy NY Dec. 1983 / Pumping Velvet (12" Mix) / I Love You (12" Mix)
4: **Stella**
Bonus Tracks: Blue Nabou / Oh Yeah (Indian Summer Version) / Desire (12" Mix) / Vicious Games (12" Mix)
5: **One Second**
Bonus Tracks: Goldrush II (12" Mix) / The Rhythm Divine (1992 Version) / Call It Love (12" Mix) / Life Is A Snowball / Tool In Rose
6: **Flag**
Bonus Tracks: The Race (Break Light Mix) / Wall Street Bongo / The Race (12" Mix)
CD Box Set 2005
Vertigo (EU) & Universal Music (EU) / 0602498349182

Remaster Series - Twelve From Six
Solid Pleasure: Bostich / I.T. Splash
Claro Que Si: Pinball Cha Cha / The Evening's Young (1985 Version)
You Gotta Say Yes To Another Excess: Lost Again / You Gotta Say Yes To Another Excess (UK Promo 12" Version)
Stella: Oh Yeah / Vicious Games (12" Mix)
One Second: Goldrush / The Rhythm Divine (1992 Version)
Flag: Otto Di Catania / The Race (12" Mix)
CD Promo 2005
Vertigo (EU)

Oh Yeah 'Oh Six - The Remixes
Oh Yeah 'Oh Six (Big Room Vocal Mix) // Oh Yeah 'Oh Six (Big Room Dub) / Oh Yeah 'Oh Six (Big Room Radio Mix)
12" & CD Promo 2006
Not on Label (US)

Oh Yeah 'Oh Six The Remixes Part 1
Oh Yeah 'Oh Six (Booka Shade Remix) // (Bodzin & Huntemann Remix) / (Luetzenkirchen Remix)
12" 2006
Vertigo (EU) / Universal (EU) / 170 150-6 / 0602517015067

Oh Yeah 'Oh Six The Remixes Part 2
Oh Yeah 'Oh Six (Ralphi Rosario Big Room Vocal Mix) // Oh Yeah 'Oh Six (Sander Van Doorn Remix)
12" 2006
Vertigo (EU) / Universal (EU) / 170 150-8 / 0602517015081

Progress And Perfection
Countdown / Distant Light / Driving Force / Umbria / Kite Vision / Chasing The Horizon / Distant Light (Instrumental) / Topaz / Pacific Rim / Kite One
CD Promo Metal Box (For Audi A5 Campaign) 2007
Not on Label

Touch Yello
The Expert / You Better Hide / Out Of Dawn / Bostich (Reflected) / Till Tomorrow / Tangier Blue / Part Love / Friday Smile / Kiss In Blue / Vertical Vision / Trackless Deep / Stay / Electric Frame / Takla Makan
CD 2009 & 2016
Polydor (EU) / 0602527194851
+v Heidi Happy
+fl Dorothee Oberlinger
+k Gino Todesco
+p Beat Ash
+t/h Till Brönner
(A) Martin Wanner
(P) Dieter Meier, Johannes Ritter, Martin Wanner, Roman Lehmann

Double LP 2010
Polydor (EU) / 0602527206l9

CD Reissue 2014
Polydor (EU) / 7640161960251

Touch Yello + The Virtual Concert
The Expert / You Better Hide / Out Of Dawn / Bostich (Reflected) / Till Tomorrow / Tangier Blue / Part Love / Friday Smile / Kiss In Blue / Vertical Vision / Trackless Deep / Stay / Electric Frame / Takla Makan
CD Bonus Tracks: X-Race / Petro Oleum / Oh Yeah 2009 / Umbria / Bostich (Duck Mobile) / Scorpio Rising
DVD: Intro / Till Tomorrow / The Expert / You Better Hide / Out Of Dawn / Bostich (Reflected) / Kiss In Blue / Vertical Vision / Tiger Dust / Tangier Blue / Oh Yeah 2009 / The Race 2008
CD + DVD 2009 & 2010 & 2014
Universal (EU) & Polydor (EU) / 00602527276946 / 0602527365817 / 7640161960275
(D) Boris Blank, Dieter Meier, Kevin Blanc

Touch Yello Remixes
The Expert (Booka Shade Remix) / The Expert (Spencer & Hill Remix) / Part Love (Turntablerocker Remix) / Takla Makan (Martin Roth Remix)
Digital release

Yello By Yello The Singles Collection
Including The Videos 1980-2010
CD: Vicious Games 2010 (Feat. Heidi Happy) / Tremendous Pain / The Race / To The Sea (Feat. Stina Nordenstam) / Planet Dada / Oh Yeah / The Expert / Bimbo / Bostich (Reflected) / How How / She's Got A Gun (Live At The Palladium NY 1985) / Part Love / Drive/Driven / Rubberbandman / Goldrush / Lost Again / Who's Gone / Squeeze Please / Of Course I'm Lying / Desire / The Rhythm Divine (Feat. Shirley Bassey)
DVD: The Evening's Young / Pinball Cha Cha / I Love You / Lost Again / Bostich / Vicious Games / Desire / Goldrush / Oh Yeah / Call It Love / The Rhythm Divine / The Race / Tied Up / Who's Gone / Jungle Bill / Do It / To The Sea / On Track / Planet Dada / The Expert / Tiger Dust / Tangier Blue / Bostich (Reflected)
CD + DVD 2010
Polydor (EU) / 06025 2753156 4
(A) Martin Wanner
(D) Dieter Meier, Boris Blank, Kevin Blanc

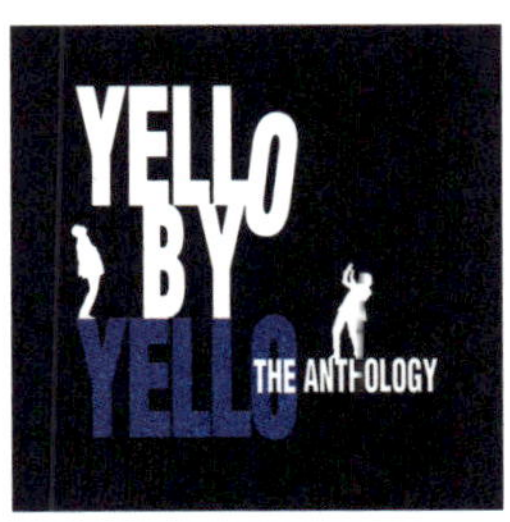

Yello By Yello The Anthology
Vol. 1: Dialectical Kid / Liquid Lies (2010) / Tears Run Dry (Feat. Malia) / Out Of Dawn / Distant Solution (Feat. Jade Davies) / Soul On Ice / Stay (Feat. Heidi Happy) / Junior B (Feat. Jade Davies) / S.A.X. / Tangier Blue / Fat Cry / Time Palace (Feat. Jade Davies) / Oh Yeah 2009 / Star Breath / Tiger Dust (The Virtual Concert) / Get On / Kiss In Blue / Move Dance Be Born / Poom Shanka / Planet Dada (Flamboyant)
Vol. 2: Solar Driftwood / Time Freeze / Moon On Ice (Feat. Billy Mackenzie) / The Evening's Young / Angel No (Feat. Rush Winters) / Base For Alec / Capri Calling (Feat. Billy Mackenzie) / Sometimes (Dr. Hirsch) / Otto Di Catania / Ciel Ouvert / Swing / You Gotta Say Yes To Another Excess / La Habanera / Koladi-Ola / Daily Disco / Crash Dance / Si Señor The Hairy Grill / Homer Hossa / Downtown Samba / I.T. Splash / Night Flanger
The Singles Collection: Vicious Games 2010 (Feat. Heidi Happy) / Tremendous Pain / The Race / To The Sea (Feat. Stina Nordenstam) / Planet Dada / Oh Yeah / The Expert / Bimbo / Bostich (Reflected) / How How / She's Got A Gun (Live NY 1985) / Part Love / Drive/Driven / Rubberbandman / Goldrush / Lost Again / Who's Gone / Squeeze Please / Of Course I'm Lying / Desire / The Rhythm Divine (Feat. Shirley Bassey)
DVD: The Evening's Young / Pinball Cha Cha / I Love You / Lost Again / Bostich / Vicious Games / Desire / Goldrush / Oh Yeah / Call It Love / The Rhythm Divine / The Race / Tied Up / Who's Gone / Jungle Bill / Do It / To The Sea / On Track / Planet Dada / The Expert / Tiger Dust / Tangier Blue / Bostich (Reflected)
CD + DVD Box 2010
Polydor (EU) / 0602527531595
(A) Martin Wanner
(D) Dieter Meier, Boris Blank, Kevin Blanc

Yello By Yello The Anthology (Promo)
Dialectical Kid / Vicious Games 2010 (Feat. Heidi Happy) / Liquid Lies (2010) / Tears Run Dry (Feat. Malia) / Distant Solution (Feat. Jade Davies) / The Evening's Young / Tremendous Pain
CD Promo 2010
Polydor (DE)

Yello Remixes
Vicious Games (Ahmet Sendil Summer In Bosphorus Remix) / Oh Yeah (Bodzin & Huntemann Remix) / Oh Yeah (Booka Shade Remix) / Oh Yeah (Sander Van Doorn Remix) / Oh Yeah (Lutzenkirchen Remix) / Oh Yeah (Simone Tavazzi Remix) / Bostich (The Cube Guys Re-Paint Mix) / Bostich (Red Cotton & Zidan Style Remix)
Digital Release (WAV)
2010 Tiger Records (DE) / Tiger25

Stereoplay – Die Besten Hörtest-Aufnahmen Aus 30 Jahren Yello-Geschichte
Oh Yeah (2009) / The Expert / Rubberbandman / Swing / The Race (2008) / The Expert (Stereoplay Version) CD Supplement for *Stereoplay* Magazine January 2010
Universal (DE) / Stereoplay (DE)

Mean Monday
Digital Single Download (AAC & MP3) for Book *Yello* by Daniel Ryser
2011 Yello (Self-Release DE & AT & CH)

The Key To Perfection
The Key - Der Song zum Golf / The Race / Oh Yeah / Goldrush / Vicious Games / Desire / Blue Horizon PM / Mean Monday
CD Box Set
Promo for Volkswagen Golf Campaign 2012
Not on Label

Oh Yeah (The Super Touchdown 2012)
Oh Yeah (Original Remastered) / Oh Yeah 'Oh Six (Ralphi Rosario's Big Room Radio Mix) / Mean Monday
Digital Single (AAC) on iTunes (US & CA) for Super Bowl 2012
Not on Label

Stranger (When Time Becomes Music)
Homage To The Mountain / Ocean Club / Mean Monday / La Habanera / Rubberbandman / Drive/ Driven / Tremendous Pain / Desire / Otto Di Catania
Video: Ulysse Nardin - Stranger - When Time Becomes Music
Memory Stick (WAV & MPEG-4) Promo 2013
Not on Label

Oh Yeah 'Oh Six
(The Remixes)
Oh Yeah 'Oh Six (Booka Shade Remix) / Oh Yeah 'Oh Six (Bodzin & Huntemann Remix) / Oh Yeah 'Oh Six (Luetzenkirchen Remix) / Oh Yeah 'Oh Six (Ralphi Rosario Big Room Vocal Mix) / Oh Yeah 'Oh Six (Sander Van Doorn Remix)
Digital Release (FLAC) 2014 Polydor (DE) & Universal (DE)

Limbo
Digital Single (FLAC) 2016
Polydor (EU)

Tool Of Love
Digital Single (FLAC) 2016
Polydor (EU)

Toy
Frautonium Intro / Limbo / 30'000 Days / Cold Flame (Feat. Malia) / Kiss The Cloud (Feat. Fifi Rong) / Pacific AM / Starlight Scene / Give You The World (Feat. Malia) / Tool Of Love / Dialectical Kid / Dark Side / Blue Biscuit / Magma / Frautonium
+v Malia
+v Fifi Rong
+v Heidi Happy
+g Jeremy Baer
CD 2016
Universal (EU) / Polydor (EU) / 00602547821607
(A) Martin Wanner
(P) Helen Sobiralski

1: Frautonium Intro / Limbo / 30'000 Days / Electrified II / Cold Flame (Feat. Malia) // Kiss The Cloud (Feat. Fifi Rong) / Starlight Scene / Tool Of Love / Give You The World (Feat. Malia) / Dialectical Kid
2: Dark Side / Pacific AM / Blue Biscuit / Lost In Motion (Feat. Fifi Rong) // Magma / Toy Square / Frautonium
Double LP & CD Deluxe Hardbook 2016
Universal (EU) / Polydor (EU) / 00602547602619

Limbo (The Remixes)
Limbo (Marcel Dettmann Remix) / Limbo (Mano LeTough Limbo On Down Baby Yeah Remix) / Limbo (Joe Goddard Remix) / Limbo (Circle Sky Remix) / Limbo (Boris Blank Remix)
Digital release (AAC) 2017
Universal Music (JP)

Frautonium (The Andrew Weatherall Remixes)
1: Frautoninum (Warehouse) // Frautonium (Half-Life)
2: Frautonium (Battery) // Frautonium (Reactor) / Frautonium (Lombok)
Double 12"
Blank Media (UK) / INKE3

Live In Berlin
Magma / Do It / The Evening's Young / Limbo / Bostich / Electrified II (Feat. Malia) / Cold Flame (Feat. Malia) / 30'000 Days / The Time Tunnel / Kiss The Cloud (Feat. Fifi Rong) / Lost In Motion (Feat. Fifi Rong) / Tied Up / Liquid Lies / Starlight Scene (Feat. Malia) / Tool Of Love / Oh Yeah / Blue Biscuit / Si Señor The Hairy Grill / The Yellofier Song / The Race
Double CD & DVD & Blu-ray 2017
Universal (EU) / Polydor (EU) / Double CD 0602567062271 / DVD 0602567062301 / Blu-ray 0602567062264
+ guests
(A) Martin Wanner
(P) Michael Wilfling, Martin Wanner

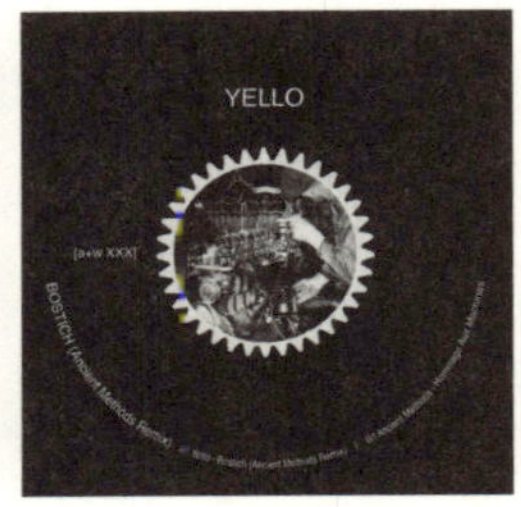

Bostich (Ancient Methods Remix)
Yello - Bostich (Ancient Methods Remix) // Ancient Methods - Hommage Aux Machines
12" 2019
Aufnahme + Wiedergabe (DE) / [a+w XXX]

Waba Duba
Digital Single (FLAC & MP3) 2020
Universal Music (EU) / Polydor (EU)

Spinning My Mind
Digital Single 2020
Universal Music (EU) / Polydor (EU)

Out Of Sight
Digital Single 2020
Universal Music (EU) / Polydor (EU)

Out Of Sight (Oliver Nelson Remix)
Digital Single 2020
Universal Music (EU) / Polydor (EU)

Point
Waba Duba / The Vanishing Of Peter Strong / Way Down / Out Of Sight / Arthur Spark / Big Boy's Blues // Basic Avenue / Core Shift / Spinning My Mind / Hot Pan / Rush For Joe / Siren Singing (Feat. Fifi Rong)
LP & CD 2020
Universal (EU) / Polydor (DE) / LP 08833779 / CD 0602508833748
+v Fifi Rong
+g Jeremy Baer
(A) Martin Wanner
(P) Helen Sobiralski

Collector's Box Point
LP: Picture Disc
CD + Bonus Tracks: Insane / Zephyr Calling / Meet My Angel (Feat. Fifi Rong)
DVD & Blu-ray: Yello Live At Montreux Jazz Festival Introduction by Mathieu Jaton / Magma / Do It / The Evening's Young / Limbo / Bostich / The Rhythm Divine (Feat. Malia) / 30'000 Days / Tool Of Love / The Time Tunnel / Kiss The Cloud (Feat. Fifi Rong) / Lost In Motion (Feat. Fifi Rong) / Tied Up / Liquid Lies / Starlight Scene / Oh Yeah / Blue Biscuit / Si Señor The Hairy Grill / The Yellofier Song / Vicious Games (Feat. Malia) / The Race
Picture Disc LP & CD & DVD & Blu-ray 2020
Polydor (DE, CH, AT)
0602508833755

Yell40 Years - Bostich Reborn In Vinyl
Bostich (N'est-Ce Pas) / Bimbo // Bananas To The Beat / Daily Disco
10" EP 2020
Universal Music (EU) / 04019589050319
+ guests
(A) Martin Wanner
(P) Helen Sobiralski

Yell40 Years - 2 LP
LP 1: Bimbo / Bostich (N'est-Ce Pas) / Vicious Games / Oh Yeah / Jungle Bill / Tremendous Pain / Mean Monday / The Expert / Waba Duba / The Race (Live In Berlin 2016)
LP 2: Desire / Drive/Driven / The Rhythm Divine (Feat. Shirley Bassey) / You Better Hide (Feat. Heidi Happy) / Till Tomorrow (Feat. Till Brönner) // 30'000 Days / Starlight Scene / Spinning My Mind / Liquid Lies / Meet My Angel (Feat. Fifi Rong) / Way Down
Double LP 2021
Polydor (EU) / 0602435738314
+ guests
+ liner Hanspeter Künzler
(A) Martin Wanner

Yell40 Years - 2 CD
CD 1 (The First 20 Years): Bimbo / Pinball Cha Cha / The Evenings Young / Bananas To The Beat / I Love You / Lost Again / Bostich (N'est-Ce Pas) / Daily Disco / Vicious Games / Oh Yeah / Blender / Goldrush / Tied Up / La Habanera / Rubberbandman / Jungle Bill / Night Train / Tremendous Pain / Houdini / Base For Alec / Liquid Lies
CD 2 (The Second 20 Years): Electrified II / Soul On Ice / Don Turbulente / Planet Dada / 30'000 Days / Arthur Spark / The Vanishing Of Peter Strong / Distant Solution / Mean Monday / Cold Flame / Dialectical Kid / The Expert / Basic Avenue / Waba Duba / Limbo / Spinning My Mind / Tiger Dust / Way Down / Hot Pan / The Race (Live In Berlin)
Double CD 2021
Polydor (EU) / 0602435602219

Yell40 Years - Earbook
CD 1 (The First 20 Years)
CD 2 (The Second 20 Years)
CD 3 (Mellow Yello) Solar Driftwood / Out Of Dawn / Stay (Feat. Heidi Happy) / Drive/Driven / Time Palace / Tangier Blue / Friday Smile / Till Tomorrow (Feat. Till Brönner) / Moon On Ice / Kiss The Cloud (Feat. Fifi Rong) / Capri Calling / Desire / You Better Hide (Feat. Heidi Happy) The Rhythm Divine (Feat. Shirley Bassey) / Starlight Scene / Otto Di Catania / Meet My Angel (Feat. Fifi Rong) / Pacific AM
CD 4 (Remixes) Do It (Marky P. & Teri B. Dub) / Limbo (Circle Sky Mix - Martin Dubka & Richard Norris) / Electrified II (Carl Craig Mix) / How How (Fluke - Papa-Who-Ma-Mix) / Bostich (DJ Hell - Brighter Mix) / Squeeze Please (Oliver Moldan - Vocal Remix) / Oh Yeah (Ralphi Rosario - Big Room Vocal Mix) / More (Boris Blank Rockabilly Mix) / Vicious Games (Mark Reeder's Wet & Hard Mix) / Takla Makan (Martin Roth Mix) / Planet Dada (Northern Light Mix) / Topaz (Boris Blank Insect Mix)
4 CD Compilation 2021
Polydor (EU) / 060043573260

Jungle Bill Reborn In Vinyl
Jungle Bill / Rubberbandman // Squeeze Please / How How
10" EP 2021
0602438609116
+ guests
(A) Martin Wanner

This discography focuses on YELLO releases from Europe and the USA.

It does not claim to be complete. However, it does provide a comprehensive overview of the rich and extensive body of work that YELLO has produced over the last 40 years.

Boris und Dieter sagen: Danke!

Boris and Dieter say: thank you!

Lang ist die Liste von Menschen, die geholfen haben, die Geschichte von Yello zu schreiben:

The list of people who have helped to shape the history of Yello is long:

Gastmusiker:innen / *Guest musicians*

Akufen, Santiago Alfonso, Rolf Aschwanden, Beat Ash, Jeremy Baer, Semjon Barlas, Shirley Bassey, Jotham Bleiberg, Booka Shade, Till Brönner, Marco Colombo, Carl Cox, Carl Craig, Vivien Cutiño Azahares, Jade Davies, Zine el Abidine, Farida, Noah Fischer, Chico Hablas, Heidi Happy, Felix Haug, Annie Hogan, Jam & Spoon, Petia Kaufmann, Walt Keiser, Philip Kienholz, Hakan Lidbo, Billy Mackenzie, Malia, Fabia Mantwill, Vanessa Mason, Eleonore Meier, Moby, Stina Nordenstam, Dorothee Oberlinger, Angela Paxi, Roland Peil, Carlos Peron, Mark Picchiotti, Ian Pooley, Don Randolph, Fifi Rong, Ralphi Rosario, Ulrich Röser, Kevin Saunderson, Louis Schuhmacher, Rebecca Schwietzke, Ian Shaw, Gino Todesco, Steve Trop, Alex Vesper, Andrew Weatherall, WestBam, Rush Winters.

Freund:innen und Mitwirkende / *Friends and collaborators*

Azzedine Alaïa, Curzio Bai, Kevin Blanc, Yves Blanc, Olivia Blank, Stefan Bock, Tom Bohne, Glenn Breda, Frank Briegmann, Dianne Brill, Alain Cap, Daniel Cherbuin, Jay Clem, Tobi Dammit, Max Dax, Michael Degkwitz, Ossi Drechsler, Adrian Flück, Patrizia Fontana, Ernst Gamper, Leos Gerteis, Tarquin Gotch, Jean-Paul Goude, Wolf-Dieter Gramatke, Paul Grau, Stephan Grühsem, Ed Heine, Wendelin Hess, Hubertus von Hohenlohe, Inga Humpe, Claudia Jonas, Jonathan Kamm, Lars Karlsson, Lutz Kleine-Herzbruch, Julian Kowalski, Dirk Koy, Hanspeter 'Düsi' Künzler, Brad LeBeau, Ralf Lülsdorf, Gabrielle Mazurczak, Balthasar Meier, Francis Meier, Monique Meier-Leuthold, Thierry Mugler, Edward Oleschak, Ulli Pallemanns, the Ralph Records team, Lea Rindlisbacher, Michael Roemer, Oliver Rosa, Martin Rutter, Daniel Ryser, Ivo Sacchi, Wolfgang Scherz, Rolli Schmid, Anka Schmid, Michael Schneider, Gerd F. Schultze, Hans-Christian Schwingen, Dieter Semmelmann, Louis Spillmann, Ed Steinberg, Edouard A. Stöckli, Lukas Strebel, Bettina Strehl, Thomas Thyssen, Tatiana Tokareva, Ian Tregoning, the Universal Music team, Paul Vajsabel, Martin Wanner, the Warner Chappell Music team, Ursli Weber, Peter Zumsteg.

... und viele mehr, die wir hier leider nicht nennen können. You know who you are!

... and too many more to mention. You know who you are!

Oh Yeah / Yello 40

Edited by Boris Blank & Dieter Meier,
Peter Vitzthum and Aaron Fabian

Texts
Boris Blank & Dieter Meier,
Hanspeter 'Düsi' Künzler

Editorial consulting
Patrick Frey and Andreas Koller

Proofreading
Jacob Blandy, Miriam Wiesel

Photo credits
Yello Archives, unless stated otherwise.

Art direction / book design
Aaron Fabian

Produced by Andreas Koller Studio

Printed and bound by Eberl & Koesel, Altusried-Krugzell
Paper: Salzer Eos Werkdruck 1.5 Vol., 115 g
Front endpaper: Sirio Color Nero, 140 g
Back endpaper: Pergraphica Natural Rough 1.3 Vol., 150 g
Cover: Buckram P., 135 g
Font: Neue Haas Unica

First edition: Edition Patrick Frey, 2021
Print run: 2100 copies
ISBN 978-3-907236-35-2

Printed in Germany

Despite best efforts, we have not been able
to identify or reach the holders of copyright
and printing rights for all the illustrations.
Copyright holders not mentioned in the credits
are asked to substantiate their claims, and
recompense will be made according to
standard practice.

© 2021 pictures: the authors
© 2021 texts: the authors
© 2021 for this edition: Edition Patrick Frey

Edition Patrick Frey, Limmatstrasse 268, 8005 Zürich, CH
www.editionpatrickfrey.com
mail@editionpatrickfrey.ch

All rights reserved. No part of this publication may be
reproduced, stored in a retrieval system or transmitted in
any form or by any means whatsoever (including electronic,
mechanical, microcopying, photocopying, recording or
otherwise) without the prior written permission of the publisher.

Distribution

Switzerland
AVA Verlagsauslieferung, Affoltern am Albis, CH
ava.ch

Germany, Austria
GVA Gemeinsame Verlagsauslieferung, Göttingen, DE
gva-verlage.de

France, Luxembourg, Belgium
Les presses du réel, Dijon, FR
lespressesdureel.com

United Kingdom
Antenne Books, London, GB
antennebooks.com

United States
ARTBOOK / D.A.P., New York, US
artbook.com

Japan
twelvebooks, Tokyo, JP
twelve-books.com

Australia, New Zealand
Perimeter Distribution, Melbourne, AU
perimeterdistribution.com

Other countries
Edition Patrick Frey, Zürich, CH
editionpatrickfrey.com